RED, WHITE & BLACKMORE

Best Wishes

Clayton Blackmore

CLAYTON BLACKMORE WITH WAYNE BARTON

EMPIRE
PUBLICATIONS

EMPIRE PUBLICATIONS
1 Newton Street, Manchester M1 1HW
© Clayton Blackmore and Wayne Barton 2017

ISBN: 978-1-909360-54-9

Cover image by Matt Wilkinson

Printed in Great Britain.

CONTENTS

FOREWORD

CLAYTON WAS A really intelligent footballer, very steady and consistent and one of the best strikers of a football I've seen – that's probably what makes him such a good golfer as well. The movement of his head is minimum and he strikes through really accurately. That was really my first impression of him, remembering how well he hit the ball and his passing was always really good.

If he'd had that touch more pace then I'm sure people would talk about him as one of the best full-backs ever but that's not to do him a disservice – he wasn't ever found wanting at the highest level because his reading of the game was exceptional. He was a very under-rated player and that was shown in how he was able to play well in a number of positions.

Because he understood the game so well, he could move into midfield easily – to be able to do that at a club like United is no mean feat and it is a testament to his knowledge and intelligence that whenever we played alongside each other in the middle I really enjoyed it.

It's no surprise to me that Clayton is most fondly remembered for his form in the 1990/91 season; his great goals from long distance and the clearance off the line against Barcelona stand out but in terms of his contribution and form, I'd have to say that was his best year for the club.

The longer you play with players the more friendly you become, so much so that they sometimes become more like family, and I remember a fair few summer barbecues with Clayton out in Portugal with great fondness. It helped cement that bond that we'd established on the pitch and I was as pleased for him as I was for myself when we both got our hands on that League title for Manchester United in 1993 – it meant that much more to do it with a friend like Clayton who'd been through so much with me.

When I became manager of Middlesbrough, just about the first thing I did was bring Clayton with me. Even though he'd had some rough luck with injuries, as soon I assessed the squad up at Boro I knew Clayton's understanding, awareness, versatility and quality would be a crucial asset so getting him in was a no-brainer. He was one of the first people I spoke to and thankfully he was keen to come along. It was a great signing and he had a huge hand in getting us promoted and helping Boro on the way to growing as a club.

We see quite a lot of each other, whether it be at the legends games or working at Old Trafford. We're close friends and I think really highly of Clayton - he's a real, genuine, hardworking lad.

Bryan Robson
October 2017

INTRODUCTION

I N FOOTBALL PEOPLE TEND to look at successes and failures and point to defining moments that changed the course of destiny or decisions which proved beneficial or costly. Looking back at the second half of the 1991/92 season for Manchester United, it's difficult to pinpoint what it was that caused the wheels to come off our challenge for the Division One championship. I have my opinions, which I will share in this book, about the external factors which contributed towards Leeds United winning the title that season. However, in football, those factors are sometimes given another name - excuses - and the career of a sportsperson is such that when you fail, you look for reasons closer to home.

I'll say it clearly; I firmly believe Manchester United were the best team in the country that season, although I do believe we could have done some things differently. After Christmas, we changed our shape slightly, to go 4-5-1, and looking back on it, it might be reasonable to suggest that with such a strong chance of success perhaps, subconsciously, we were over-cautious. There was a lot of pressure, the weight of history was on us and after such a flying start to the season, perhaps it was deemed sensible to not take risks. It's difficult to tell, because I can only speak for myself, but the results also do that, and from the time we changed our formation, we went from having scored forty-two times in twenty-one games to scoring twenty-one in the last twenty-one. My attitude rarely changed from game to game, I would just be out there to try and do my best, whatever the game and whatever the position.

It would be wrong, though, to say that any changes we made or any hesitation we felt cost us. If your players are good enough, they can play and adapt to the system. Mark Hughes was one of the very best players at holding the ball up and allowing players to get past him but the addition of Ryan Giggs and Andrei Kanchelskis to our team was a relatively new thing for us. Still, for as long as it was mathematically possible, we believed we could win the league and it's only with hindsight, after the season has ended, where you pinpoint the time when it was lost. But, then, hindsight works both ways, doesn't it? Most people look back on that Championship as one that Manchester United blew because we apparently had such a big lead and I have to admit that I had to go back and check the records because I wasn't entirely convinced that was the case. That's how these things can be changed in the memory over time. The truth is that we never held such a commanding lead over Leeds at any point in the season – we maintained a title fight with them despite having two or three games in hand.

Games in hand are perceived as an advantage but, as we were to discover, that isn't always the case. Anyone can take a look at how we were made to pay a hefty price for our success in domestic cup competitions by the farcical fixture scheduling which saw us play four games in six days and draw their own conclusions. It was outrageous. So many players picked up injuries because there simply wasn't enough time to recover from each game. If they still aren't convinced they can take a look at how the injury list increased during that period. Perhaps farcical is too lenient a word; it's not only damaging to a team, but it's too physically demanding of the players. The term 'flogging a dead horse' comes to mind. It wouldn't be allowed these days.

The summer of 1992 was a bit of a funny one, then; I was never one to be miserable about how things had gone, I'd always be looking for the next opportunity to win, though it's hard to deny that there was some frustration that we had come up short right at the end. And regardless of how confident we were that we were the better side, we were still looking for ways of how we could improve as we entered the new era of English football.

From Neath to Old Trafford

THE MAIN COACH AT our local boy's club in Neath was a scout for Chelsea, so a few of us ended up down in London for trials there. I went about six times when I was twelve and at comprehensive school which was coincidentally the same age I picked up a rugby ball for the first time, strange for a young boy from Wales, let alone an only child with parents who had a strong sporting background!

I lived in a small area that only had forty-nine homes; our street had its own football team, though the local lads would play whatever sport was on the television, and most of them were a little bit older than me but I joined in with them. I was keenest on football, probably because my Dad, Colin, was playing in the Welsh league against people like John Charles - in fact, I even ended up playing with him in a game when I was fourteen and he was forty-two. It was probably not the wisest move for a kid who'd just signed for the biggest club in the world to be mixing it with aggressive and uncompromising grown men but it was a fun experience and we won and I scored, so all was well. It's fair to say I idolised my dad, as most boys do - we would go running through the woods and up around the fields which had football, rugby and cricket pitches. Dad played semi-professionally and also worked as a foreman for BP chemicals for most of his career. He played up front and scored a lot of goals; he's only a little taller than me but he was an aggressive player, he'd use the old shoulder to get an advantage. He has a scrapbook with pictures of him scoring hat-tricks and playing for Llanelli, Pembroke & Briton Ferry... I remember Man United sending a team down to play Briton Ferry. The likes of Jimmy Nicholl and Sammy McIlroy played in a 2-1 win for United.

Dad was born in Surrey but Mum was Welsh; she was a netball coach for the Welsh national team. On Saturday mornings she'd teach badminton and netball at the local barn. They weren't pushy in the slightest but, being surrounded by that sort of activity, I naturally developed an aptitude for it. I quickly picked up rugby when I started to play it and on sports day I would win most races I entered. I was good at rugby and cricket but as football became more of a serious option, I started to cut those sports out before they got too serious. Whenever two of the sports were scheduled for the same day, football always won out, and that would tend to be the case.

Maybe being an only child helped me to fit in with the older kids and I would say it definitely helped my sporting education and progression, though I wouldn't say I necessarily felt 'above my years', as you might think. I also think that it helped being around older kids. It helps to make you stronger and quicker – you're going to get hurt along the way, that's for sure, and I think I came home in tears so often that my older friends invented a song to try and stop me from crying. One day we were out messing around on the hills and one of the local lads, Gary Bray (whose brother Ian went on to play for Huddersfield Town), pushed a huge JCB tyre and flattened me. He said he was laughing too much to shout to warn me and I got the full force of that one. It was that sort of good natured fun we'd tend to get up to – there was a local reservoir which we'd brave when it'd ice over, and it was a bit worrying when it sounded like it was going to break up. You'd end up with wet feet trying to get back to safety, but thankfully that was the worst of it because as far as I know there was never anything more serious than that which happened. As an impressionable youngster I would just follow the older boys, Wayne Edwards, Steven Edwards, Richard Williams and Gary and Ian Bray, and so if they weren't responsible enough, I would often find myself in precarious situations; though, as I say, fortunately never came to any real harm.

So, that team I played in... Manor Way Football Club, who between 1970 and 1980 suffered no defeats. There was Ian "Dobbson" Roberts in goal, Gareth "Mong" Stanton at right-back. Wearing number four was Wayne "Square" Edwards, a great cricketer and golfer who ended up in the RAF. Stephen "Eddie" Edwards was the other centre-half and Ian "Curly" Bray was at left-back. I wore number 6 in central midfield alongside Mark "Squeak" Wallace. Richard "Owly" Williams, a scratch golfer, who was on the right-wing and John "Ginger" Tallamy was on the left. Up front, Craig "Flung" Williams was partnered by Gary Bray.

I suppose I was like most footballers at school. That is to say, sport was the preference. Don't get me wrong, I tried, and I worked hard, but I also think at school we were only taught some of what we really needed. Okay, being taught history, for example, is useful, but there was so much that most of us felt unprepared for in the real world. I was lucky, because I had football, but it could easily have been a different story. As I've said, my parents weren't pushy about it but they were supportive and took me everywhere I needed to go. There was one time when I was fourteen I had a Welsh schoolboy's game up in Scotland and a Welsh boy's club game the next day, and they drove me to both without question. By that time, football was emerging as my best option, and playing the sport was my favourite thing to do. Growing up where I did Swansea were the local club, so it wasn't as straightforward as having that team you go and see as a kid in the traditional way. My version of doing that was watching Dad but again, that's not the same and, for some reason, though I hesitate to put it into print, the first team I can really remember following was Leeds United! It would be somewhat forgivable if you consider the John Charles connection but, really, it wasn't anything to do with him - I remember watching the 1974 World Cup as a boy of almost ten and seeing Peter Lorimer play for Scotland and hit shots so hard they were measuring how fast they went. I'm sure his were registered at 70 mph. It captured my imagination and he became a player I looked out for on a regular basis after the World Cup. I suppose it was more to do with him than the club; I also remember that my first ever football kit was an Inter Milan one. I don't know why Dad got me that, and not a Juventus one, thinking again of John Charles. Maybe I'd told him I liked the colour.

There's a difference between enjoying football and realising that you're actually good at it. I don't know what it was about our locality but there were a few good players in our area. Mark Bowen, who had such a good career with the likes of Spurs and Norwich City, was a year older than me and would normally be having trials at the same clubs as me. Obviously the Welsh clubs would be sniffing around. I had one training session down at Cardiff City, which I didn't really enjoy. I was sitting watching the cricket at Briton Ferry Town cricket ground and all of a sudden John Toshack came in through the door – everyone was confused about why he was there to watch a game of cricket but he came over and asked if I'd like to join the Cygnets (the name of their youth team). By that time, though, I'd already been training with Manchester United, and I knew I was close to signing schoolboy forms with them, so I had to turn John down. Mark had been with me up to United and he'd also been with me a little earlier when we went to Chelsea five or six times, as well as nine other clubs. One of the Chelsea scouts, Dave Bynon, was working at our boy's club and so about five of us went down. Mark and I kept getting invited – obviously, given the size of the club and the opportunity, we weren't going to say no and while I did enjoy it, I couldn't quite see myself committing to stay there. It was so noisy. It was noisy all the time, I couldn't hear myself think. The Cockney lads would be shouting all through the game and the Chelsea coaches would be talking through the entire game. The chief scout there was Eddie Heath. I was one of a number of young lads who had their legs slapped by him – that was something he did often – but even though we thought it was strange, and we all commented on it, the common consensus amongst us as teenagers was that we thought he was gay. Eddie was an imposing man; 6'4 with hands like shovels. It was revealed in late 2016 that he abused a number of young players from my generation. My time with him was relatively brief and I was clearly one of the very lucky ones who did not suffer at his hands. I actually remember that me and the other lads laughed about it and joked with each other. It makes me nauseous to think of what he put others through and what I might have gone through if I'd decided to go to Chelsea. I was thirteen or fourteen and if we were aware enough to know that it wasn't right, then it is quite unbelievable that he was allowed to get away with it for so long.

I had one trial at Leeds United, the club I supported, and I absolutely hated it. Pulling up to Leeds you would have thought it was all of my dreams coming true but I was unsettled from the start. It was once and done for me there – a four-day experience I didn't want to repeat. The football was okay but it felt like an escape from the daily routine of being there and where we were staying wasn't particularly pleasant. For any kid who has to move away, they have to be in a settled environment they enjoy and I knew that it wouldn't be the case at Leeds.

Back in Wales, it was a sign of just how talented our age group was when we'd play for the local team against Swansea City. Swansea were the big rivals for us, they had Dean Saunders in their team but apart from Mark and myself, just about everyone in our composite team from Neath and Port Talbot ended up with a professional club. Those games were the ones where the scouts from English clubs would come to visit and one of those scouts was Walter Robins, who lived in Swansea, but worked for Manchester United. He liked the look of me and recommended me to the club.

I was sold on the first trip there; there was just something about the club that helped me feel settled, like I belonged. We were taken to Old Trafford and treated to a fillet steak meal. It felt like they'd pulled out all the stops and really wanted me there so I was suitably impressed. Then, on a schoolboy trip for Wales, Mark Hughes - in the age group above me and already contracted at United - brought me down my very first club tracksuit. Black bottoms and a red top made of cotton. I remember it vividly and treasured it at the time. The football was good, too. The manager at the time was Dave Sexton but the person looking after the youth players was Sid Owen. Jimmy Curran was there and Norman Davies the kit man. I'd been playing in higher age brackets for a while but I could instantly tell the difference in standard between players everywhere else and Manchester United. Their touch was much better; I was instantly very nervous about my ability to fit in, though I was comforted a little by the fact that I was there at all. It showed that Manchester United had the faith in me to be alongside these very, very talented players. There were local lads like Mark Dempsey and Billy Garton and other boys who, like me, were coming in from all over the British Isles –Norman Whiteside from Northern Ireland for example. Norman was frightening, he was so good, but in those early days - though it's difficult to believe - he was quiet and shy, just the same as me. He'd have to fly over while for me it was a case of getting on a train up to Manchester from South Wales every week to play games on a Saturday. Many of the times I took the train alone. It really was a different time. Nervous as I was, those trips must have done me the world of good and, without really knowing it at the time, I developed a bit of character. I think I was too young to truly appreciate the size of Manchester United and their history but I wasn't too young to understand what the opportunity meant.

Mark Hughes was the best young player in Wales and he had gone to Manchester United. I found myself motivated by fear of failure. The idea of returning to South Wales and having to tell people I hadn't made it at United. Or, just as bad, them thinking I wasn't good enough. It's a funny thing. I never felt that about any other club but United, and the reality is, they're the biggest team, so not making it there shouldn't have felt like the idea of shame which it represented in my mind. I don't know if it's because of everything that's associated with it - the idea that you tried to be the best and failed - that worried this young teenage version of me. I only know it was a good thing because it kept me motivated. I went up a few times and then there was one occasion my parents went up without me - I never found out why they did but they came back with a pair of Puma King boots given to them for me by Joe Jordan. They were his but too small for him and they were the best pair of boots I ever wore. The club had sent me Admiral boots previously but they were too big and really uncomfortable.

I suppose it's not being too big-headed to say I was an intelligent footballer. I liked to play in midfield - when you're young and one of the better players, coaches tend to play you up front, but when I was with the better teams, I would play in midfield, or, as was the case with the Wales schoolboys team, I would play in defence, at right back, primarily because I was a bit small due to playing a year up.

Red in Reserve

WHEN I SIGNED AS AN APPRENTICE and moved to Manchester, I first lived in digs in Sale with Andy Hill who came from Sheffield. As someone who's worked with young players for the last fifteen years or so I've appreciated the courage it takes for these young kids to move away from home and relocate for football. Maybe the money makes it easier these days, it certainly didn't then! All that mattered to me was this chance to play football for Manchester United. With hindsight I can look back at the choices I was making and think of how brave I was; nights, at first, were very difficult, being away from my parents, not knowing when I would see them next.

Before I had even moved to Manchester I'd had a taste of a big occasion with the club. I hadn't played in any other youth team games but found myself called into the team to play Tottenham Hotspur in the Youth Cup semi-final at Old Trafford. It was a huge jump from playing in 'A' team games to suddenly getting a start in such an occasion. Fortunately we ended up winning - Mark Hughes scored a great goal - but I think it was more a statement of the problems with the youth system at United at the time and the few players we had, that I had to be drafted in, rather than it being a case of me having played so well they had to play me, however much I would have liked that to have been the case. I wasn't even at the club full time so it was a complete shock. On the other side, Tottenham not only had Mark Bowen in their team but they also had Terry Gibson who was only seventeen but had just made his senior debut. That's not to dismiss what I'd done entirely; I used my position with the Welsh team as a barometer for how I was doing. So, as long as I was playing up an age level, I was sure I was continuing to do the right things.

That said, even that wasn't straightforward. We had a game against Northern Ireland at Ballymena and Norman - who was developing, physically, at a frightening rate – scored a hat-trick in a 4-0 win for them. Our performance was so bad we were all back on trial, and the trial was a waste of time. I'm sure it was the same squad for the England game at Wembley, a game where we historically had a terrible record. We were doing well – Mark Bowen scored, and then Sparky hit an absolute screamer. The referee was English, though, and the goal was ruled out firstly for offside and then, after the game, it was apparently down to pushing. They scored a deflected free kick and got a 1-1 draw. It was a credible result in front of 60,000 supporters (which sounds intimidating, but most of them were kids, and there were screams rather than loud cheers) and we were all not 'on trial' anymore. The occasion was memorable – this was the old Wembley, with the Twin Towers, and we had the full experience; the long walk up the tunnel and all of that.

We did manage to defeat England in a 75th anniversary of English schoolboy football tournament – we had Holland and Switzerland in our group for that tournament as well as England, but we got through to the final at Maine Road. That was against Northern Ireland. And the scorer of the winning goal? Norman, of course. It was, nonetheless, an improvement on the 4-0 defeat. Around that time we played a five-a-side competition at Trafford Sports Centre; it was United against City, with Bobby Charlton and co playing first and the youth teams playing after. For the older players it was a bit of a kick about but for the likes of me, Norman and Billy Garton, it was a proper scrap. There was a makeshift stand on the sides and Norman walloped one of their players up a couple of rows back. He could handle himself.

My schoolboy contract included terms which stated that so long as I still wanted to be a footballer, I would automatically get offered an apprenticeship by United when I was of age. That of course doesn't guarantee that you will become a professional footballer nor does it guarantee you chances in the team, and nothing prepared me for the chance against Spurs in the Youth Cup. That wasn't just moving up one year but two, so it was pretty scary.

In the following season – 1981/1982 – I was given another boost. After starting that season playing for the 'A' team and youth team in the Lancashire League I was called up to the reserves to play at Burnley. The

United team included Jimmy Nicholl, Nikola Jovanovic, Billy Garton, Scott McGarvey and Garry Worrall. I was a substitute and it was a little intimidating to take in, watching all of these senior names so soon after joining up with the club on a permanent basis. Norman Whiteside was already flying and attracting the attention of Ron Atkinson, who had joined as first-team manager in the summer of 1981. I'd been used to playing with the older lads - men, even - and that stood me in good stead. When Dad was forty-two he was playing against a local team called the Royal Exchange. I'd always wanted to play a proper game with him so here was I, a fourteen year old kid against all of these men. Predictably one of their lads was a bit of a donkey and he ran right into me, knocking me over. About a minute later, this lad is on the ball and my dad went right into him with a proper shoulder barge! He hit the wall, then the floor. It's crazy to think about that sort of thing happening with a kid in today's game. You play them above their age level and you're instantly worried about them getting injured. It's crazy to think of me taking such a risk then, I was a fourteen year old who was a schoolboy at Manchester United.

That said it gave me some preparation for what to expect - in terms of physicality, if nothing else - when it came to playing for the reserves. After all, the reserve team back then was comprised of anyone who wasn't in the first team. There were a lot of big names at Manchester United then, players on the fringes of the first team, senior players whose careers at the club were winding down, and rather than be intimidating, they were welcoming, and, really, quite crucial in their assistance for players like me coming through.

The reserve fixtures would normally mirror the first team ones - so if United were playing Liverpool at Old Trafford, the reserves would be playing them at Anfield earlier in the day. When it came to big games like that, there was a real sense of belonging, a sense of us all contributing to the same cause. So it may have been the reserves but it felt like we were all part of the same thing. We were representing Manchester United and we appreciated those moments, it created this strange feeling of belonging and purpose. That is helped by the opposition team, who - even in the reserves - treated Manchester United as their cup final.

There is a prestige you can't manufacture and an aura you can't buy, which makes opposition players desperate to win against you.

People are quick to dismiss the United team of the 1980's as underachievers and that goes for those of us who came through the youth system at that time. Speak to anyone and they talk about the 1950s and 1990s as the two golden periods for Manchester United in terms of developing youth players and the implication is that no other players came through at any other time. Just take a look at United in the mid 90's – after the famous Class of '92 they got to the Youth Cup Final again in 1993 and won it again in 1995 and most of those players had good league careers. It was difficult for those players to break through when the likes of Ryan Giggs and David Beckham were not even at their peak.

In the late 70s and early 80s there were so many names who ended up playing hundreds of times for the club, it's an almost embarrassing list. Just before me there was Sammy McIlroy and I played alongside Arthur Albiston and Mike Duxbury. Players with hundreds of appearances for the biggest club in the world and that's before looking at the talent I was breaking through alongside. Norman and Mark were obvious names but there was also Paul McGrath and Kevin Moran. When I actually take the time to think about it, it staggers me to think we never won the league with that group of players but, of course, that's something I'll talk about later; the point is that compared to any other period of players being developed by British clubs, United probably don't get the praise they deserve. For me, Mark Hughes was the best in Britain and I was so happy he was on my side for club and country. He was frightening - even at a young age, he was so strong, and the variety of goals he was able to score was something I'd never seen. He could score from anywhere. He and Norman were a cut above and playing with players like that was something I knew would help me, as well as gaining experience from the likes of Martin Buchan, who was still the club captain.

The group of players I played with in the 1981/82 FA Youth Cup got to the final against Watford - our team included Mark and Norman, as well as Graeme Hogg and Billy Garton. Along with Mark Dempsey that made six of us from that side who ended up with first team experience afterwards. Watford had a lot of highly rated players themselves, although John Barnes missed the first leg. I scored in the first leg at Old Trafford – the goal was in the last few minutes, and pulled us back to 3-2. We thought we had a great chance in the second leg but we were up against it when Billy Garton scored an early own goal. We won 3-2 in normal time to take it into extra time but immediately scored another own goal through Andy Hill. It was still the best own goal I've ever seen – Phil Hughes, our goalkeeper, hit it against Andy from 25 yards out and it flew in! Norman equalised but a couple of minutes later, the big lad Jimmy Gilligan popped up with the decisive goal. It was topsy-turvy and we felt that if the game had gone on another ten minutes we would have won it but it wasn't to be.

We were coached by Eric Harrison – who, ten years after this defeat, would have his most famous success – who had joined the club a year earlier after being assistant manager at Everton. Anyone who worked under Eric will speak of the education they had and it was certainly a memorable experience. He came with a reputation – we'd heard stories of him head-butting one of his own players up at Everton – and we quickly discovered it to be true after losing a Lancashire Cup game 4-0 against Bolton. Eric was livid, he was screaming, 'What the fuck have I done coming here?' Even Norman Davies said that Eric was the most vicious he'd heard on the sideline. He really was. After Eric came, he was so aggressive that the thought did cross my mind to leave because it was getting unbearable. He would get in your face and it would get too much – I know that people say it is supposed to build character, and maybe it does, but I felt he crossed the line too often. It was how I imagined SAS training to be. Having played at Everton over the years, I always found it to be an aggressive place, so I can imagine how it would have been in training. To take their first team coach and put him in charge of the youth players, well… to some extent, obviously, it was brilliant because it did toughen us up, of that there can be no question. I'm just not so certain that for all of us it was necessary – I don't think Eric would get away with his more than liberal aggressive use of the F word in the modern game, that's for sure!

So, what doesn't kill you apparently makes you stronger, that could be said for how we were developed but the same motto could also be applied to defeat. That said, I don't think the learning curve we went on was so steep that it explained Norman Whiteside's summer – from playing in that defeat against Watford, making his first team debut and then playing in the World Cup in Spain and breaking Pelé's record to become the youngest ever player at the tournament.

His physical development had progressed so much that he was like a fully grown man at sixteen; I should also add the caveat that I think his frame was the primary reason for his selection for the World Cup. He had talent, of course, but if he'd had the stature of an average sixteen year old, it might have been a different question. Norman wasn't normal though and not only was he the right size, he also had the temperament to justify being selected.

For the rest of us watching back home it was a sizeable incentive. We'd been playing with him, playing against him in training (and at schoolboy level) and the idea, at least for me, was that if he was ready to make such a step up, then I might not be far away either. That was my first full year away from home and so I went back to Wales for the summer - my parents had only managed to get up a handful of times and I really missed them, so rather than feel any jealousy for what Norman had done, it was just genuinely exciting to see a friend achieve something like that and, if I was to be selfish, a part of that excitement was for what it could mean for the rest of us going forward. For us, there was an element of watching him and thinking he was representing Manchester United; I watched all the games hoping he would score.

I think by the end of that first year I had acclimatised well. I still had tough days, and going home was a bit of a reminder of that, but the fact was that there were similar lads in similar circumstances helped. Norman was one and Mark Hughes, although a little bit older, who I'd known from Welsh football, was another. Mark was also on the edge of playing in the first team. When he came back Norman was a first team regular so I'd only really see him in the mornings.

My footballing education in the 1982/83 season didn't happen in the same way as it did for them but it was no less enjoyable. A year into my time in Manchester I felt more like a member of the squad rather than a newcomer. Norman's breakthrough had the knock-on effect of people suddenly looking at United's youth team with keener eyes and that felt like a bit of a profile boost for those of us who hadn't enjoyed the experience of the World Cup.

For me, Norman's luckiest part of the summer was escaping Eric Harrison! That was something I wasn't looking forward to; his constant attacks about improving, having a go about trying harder, as if I wasn't trying my best anyway, were irritating. I suppose that was his motivational technique but the repetition of it was not something I enjoyed. I must say that a few hours away from it was clearly all I needed to be able to tolerate it again, so, as unbearable as it seemed, I was obviously able to get through it without it ever putting a real question mark on whether or not I could hack it at United but let's just say that I could understand how such an environment could prove too tough for some. I was motivated by fear, all right, but it was still that fear of going home and being seen as a failure, and that was a far greater force than any aggression Eric portrayed. Additionally, I didn't take it personally – it was clear to see that I was far from the only one suffering and that it had more to do with Eric's aggression than my attitude.

Thankfully I found myself surrounded by plenty of calmer, older heads who were perhaps a little more rational, throughout that year. On the first day of the season I played for the 'A' team and scored a hat-trick against Chorley. I was beginning to play a little further forward now, up front and in midfield, and the product of that positional move was that I scored a few goals. I was a good striker of the ball and in my pre-United days would regularly score one hundred goals a year in my local teams, so finding the net was no problem for me. To start the season in such fashion was obviously great but – and maybe this shows my naivety – I didn't instantly think that scoring three for the 'A' team meant I should now be a regular in the reserves. I was enjoying my football and I can't even say I was trying too hard not to focus on Norman's rise to prominence in terms of a comparison because, for me, it didn't register in the same way. I would watch reserve games and see the Manchester United team populated with first team players from the last five years and I would wonder if I could cut it at that level.

As it turned out, that hat-trick seemed to be the boost that was necessary to give me an opportunity in the reserves, though my introduction to life at that level left me in no doubt of how difficult it would be to make an impression at that level. My first game was against Stoke City and I scored, which was great, but that game would be best remembered for the impact of a young player called Peter Beardsley. He'd been playing in Canada and he was given a chance at United - in this game, he scored a hat-trick. Even then he was a fantastic player, he had a number of tricks in his locker to get past opponents - tricks he uses to this day. It was clear we had a talent on our hands and I'm obviously not the only one who thinks Ron Atkinson made an error by not giving him a greater opportunity in the first team. For whatever reason, Peter didn't get that chance; a message for us all that it would take something special to break through.

At least I settled into reserve team football pretty well. The worries about being able to fit in seemed to disappear once the games began. You learned at Manchester United that the biggest thing you had to get used to was the intensity from the opposition. Every game is a Cup Final for them and you're aware of that from the second you pull on a shirt at any level. The occasion, or the opponent, increases the intensity and then, as you go up the levels, it gets even tougher. As daunting as it is to make the step up to play alongside players who have rightfully earned the distinction of being called a Manchester United legend - the likes of Martin Buchan and Lou Macari - you are then thrust into games where for the opposition, they have the opportunity to win a match against those players. There are countless biographies and interviews of former Manchester United players who say the same things but for those of us who went and played for other clubs, we can vouch for it first-hand. There are players who mark the United game in the calendar and they're saving themselves for weeks. They all want to be fit for the United game. It's understandable, to an extent. If there's one team in the country teams are expected to lose against, it's Manchester United, so they give their all to try and make sure it doesn't happen. There are teams who celebrate draws against United as if it was a victory; there are teams who consider a narrow 1-0 defeat to be something they can brag about. You can feel it at every level.

So for those of us in the reserve team trying to prove ourselves, it was a bit of a minefield. Norman had fast tracked the entire experience but Mark Hughes was playing up front, not yet quite ready for the first team. Beardsley's short cameo had proven how difficult it was to make an impression and there was also the case of Scott McGarvey, a player who scored goals for fun in the reserves. Scott was about six foot tall and he had a good touch and instinct for scoring goals. But he wasn't the quickest and I think it's not doing Scott too much of a disservice to say his all-round game wasn't quite as strong as it needed to be in order to lead the line at United. You could look at Mark in comparison and see how strong he was then - he didn't score as many as Scott, even at that level, but he had this ability to bring other people into play that was to the overall benefit of the team. I'm not taking anything away from Scott, who was an excellent striker who obviously didn't have a problem scoring, but I look at Mark and he had qualities in his game that I haven't seen from anyone else before or since. Over time, the point was proven with the career Mark went on to have and his reputation as a player which is really quite unique in world football. He was a freak of nature. At the time, this was the kind of level we were competing with for our Manchester United careers.

It's pretty difficult for me to put an assessment on my own performance and ability in comparison to the other players at the time but I felt I was benefitting from the exposure to playing with and training against legends of the game. For most of my first year as an apprentice I was coming up against Sammy McIlroy every day in training. Obviously, it never quite reaches the same level of competitiveness as an actual game but it's not far off - and when you consider that the intensity of a regular United game is probably greater than the average game, then maybe that level of competition in training is worth first team games elsewhere. Careers can't necessarily be made but they can certainly be lost in such an environment; it's no place for shrinking violets.

And when you're talking about players who you can learn from when it comes to representing Manchester United, then there was arguably nobody better than Martin Buchan. He was club captain and in the last year of his time at the club but was playing reserve team football. He was called 'Skip' and we still call him this to this day. He wore Adidas 2000 boots, the leather was like chamois and cleaning them was a task. You had to wash them but once they went dry, the leather went rock hard, so you had to wet them again; Martin would hate it if his boots were hard. One day I went in to the changing room and he was the only one in – he said 'I didn't hear the door', so, I left and then knocked. He left me out there. I had to go off and clean someone else's boots. He was deadly serious and really professional – some of his older team-mates would joke about that but for us younger players it was a learning curve and an insight into the level of professionalism expected from the person chosen to be the club captain of Manchester United.

Ray Wilkins – a great passer of the ball – was another one who took his position seriously. Playing reserve team football with him was a great learning experience; we'd encountered each other before, down at Chelsea. I had a picture taken with him – the young kids on trial on the minibus alongside Ray who was only 18 but already club captain. I didn't know if he'd remember me but I bumped into him at The Cliff just after he signed in 1979 and he said, 'You've made the right decision.' Life with Lou Macari was less serious. His reputation preceded him and he was usually up to some prank or joke with Ashley Grimes and a few of the young players were often roped in as accomplices. Fortunately I was never on the receiving end; I think maybe I escaped because I was dead quiet. The noisiest one from our group was Mark Dempsey, a local lad. I was keeping my head down and playing football but being around such characters was helpful as we went from playing 'A' team games to reserve games which were sometimes in front of five or six thousand people (to put it into perspective, this was the average gate for some clubs in the Second Division). For the likes of Bury and Rochdale, save for the possibility of the FA Cup, these were the highest-level opportunities they had to take on Manchester United and you could certainly feel the animosity from the opposition in the stands. For those of us who played a fair amount of football down the flanks you would often find yourself enlightened with the personal opinion of the locals.

One game I was playing right back in a game at West Brom and there was one guy on the terraces who spent the entire half chirping away unprintable and unflattering remarks. I think I might have said a few things back to him! Likewise, when you went over to Liverpool and played against a team like Marine. It might not be Liverpool or Everton but the likelihood is that you're playing against someone who stands on the Kop every Saturday singing songs about hating United; they're only too happy to give you a kick, and the worst thing you want to do is lose to them. It wasn't an option.

I felt a sense of responsibility as far as it came to impressing Manchester United fans. They'd worked all week and they pay their money, they expect to see their team entertain and I carried that with my performance throughout my career. Even later on, when there was a year where I did receive a fair bit of stick from United fans, I respected their right to do it and understood that it was my responsibility to turn those opinions around.

I didn't have to worry about anything like that in my first full season in the reserves; I played in a variety of positions, mostly in midfield, and ended that year as second top scorer behind Scott. These days I suppose my development would be praised and that's what would be assessed but make no mistake, there was a very clear mandate at Manchester United in those days, and that was that we must win every game we played. We were getting that from all angles, whether it was Eric bawling at us if we didn't, the opposition dedicating every ounce of energy to it, or the rival supporters making it clear just how much they hated us. The one thing I understood from the younger players I was playing with was that United brought in the best kids that they could. The ability was there. These were the developing grounds, the places where our temperament and capability to handle pressure was tested and honed, and it was all done under the idea that Manchester United must win.

At first team level it had been sixteen years since they had won the League title but 1982-1983 was a successful year for the club. We finished third in the First Division and runners-up in the League Cup but we won the FA Cup for the first time since 1977, so there was every reason to be optimistic about what the future would bring. As a kid, the FA Cup had always been the one I wanted to win, the one trophy we coveted every year. There was something special about the occasion that was made out of the day, and even though I wasn't there, there was obviously a proud association.

I maintained my run of football in the reserves throughout the following year and found myself moving around – playing full back, in midfield, out wide and up front. I suppose there might be a worry for some people that they might not be getting a settled run in the side but as far as I was concerned I was growing in confidence every week, even with being moved around, because I saw it as a sign of faith in me to play anywhere. I knew that only counted for so much, though, and it was clear that winning the FA Cup for United was only seen as a springboard for the trophy they really wanted. It was supposed to have been that way in 1977 but Tommy Docherty was sacked and it had taken six years and two managers to get to a similar level. It was probably not a time that Ron could justify making wholesale changes; he would be looking to improve the team, of course, for them to be challenging Liverpool for the league title, but those changes were likely to come from outside. A case in point was the short term loan for Laurie Cunningham ahead of the Cup Final; one might argue that such an opportunity would have been better presented to Mark Hughes, though with Laurie coming from Real Madrid you can see what Ron was thinking in terms of it being a player he'd previously worked with and, in his mind, a greater guarantee than the risk of playing a young player at a crucial stage at the season.

As a player there's little you can do if the manager has a tendency to make those kind of short term signings. You have to do your best and hope that you will get your chance and then, when you do get it, take it. It sounds obvious when written like that, but there was reason for patience, because the manager was giving kids a chance. Norman had adapted to first team football with no problem and over the following year Sparky would get more and more opportunities. There was the disappointment of an FA Cup defeat to Bournemouth but we were doing so well in the league that there was no reason to make changes elsewhere.

There was a week in March where it seemed as if the club were about to achieve unbelievable things. We beat Arsenal 4-0 with Arnold Mühren scoring twice to put us top of the table with ten games to go. The following midweek we played against Barcelona at Old Trafford in the European Cup Winners' Cup. After losing 2-0 in the first leg, and against the best player in the world in Diego Maradona, we weren't given a chance. Standing in the terraces watching that game with the other apprentices was an unbelievable experience. The only kicks Maradona seemed to get were from Graeme Hogg and United, inspired by Bryan Robson, dominated the game to win 3-0. It was the loudest I'd ever heard the crowd; it was an onslaught from start to finish. Watching that game there was no explanation needed for why it was difficult to get into that midfield.

But then Robbo got injured, as did Mühren; there was a run of six league games where United failed to score in four which had a devastating impact on our chances. Around the same time I had a strong run scoring five goals in five reserve games - easily the best I was playing all season - and even though I know I was in the manager's thoughts for whatever reason I wasn't brought into the team when they were struggling.

The club were also eliminated from the Cup Winners' Cup in that rotten spell and so, having looked so promising in the middle of March, the season fizzled out to nothing. I was given my own Cup Final, however, when I was handed my first team debut in the last game of the season at Nottingham Forest. Try telling me that there was nothing riding on it; it could have been the FA Cup Final, it felt so important. I'd had the feeling it was getting closer, and that the chance was coming but I'd been feeling like that for so long that with it being the last game of the season, I was afraid I'd have to hold on until the next season. I can't really describe the feeling of going up to the team sheet on the Friday before the game and seeing my name there at number eight. There can be few tougher introductions to top flight football than playing against Stuart Pearce and it should be said that although the campaign had petered out, the game counted for a lot as Forest had to beat us to finish third. Unfortunately for us, they did just that. I was very disappointed afterwards; losing is never a nice feeling, but after having waited so long to make my debut, I was now faced with a summer of dwelling over the defeat.

Earning My Stripes

MY NEXT TASTE OF LEAGUE FOOTBALL was also at Nottingham Forest, and it also ended in defeat. So much for putting it right! I played left back this time and found the game much easier, though that obviously had little impact on the result. It was a difficult result to take this time because there was something on the game - we would have gone top with the win at a time when Everton, the leaders, were starting to stutter. We were 2-0 up at half time and strolling and I was thinking, 'this is easy!' We come in at full time and we've lost 3-2, conceding a goal in the last minute. Gordon McQueen was having a go at Gary Bailey in the dressing room afterwards saying he should have come out for the second goal; Gary confronted him and big Gordon lamped him one right on the forehead. I say big Gordon; Gary was big too, both of them were units. Robbo and Big Ron had to get in the middle of them to calm it down but it was a bit of an eye-opener for someone new to the pressures of this level of football for Manchester United. I just sat there thinking 'so this is what it means'.

Being on the fringes of the first team for the previous season, I didn't really feel part of the disappointment at not having won the league. That summer had been the first time there had been any suggestion of pressure on Ron to achieve in the league - the weight of expectation was always there but the disappointment of coming quite close was experienced, really, for the first time - and so it was the first time that there was any suggestion that he might not be the right man for the job. That's football, and any speculation was taken with a pinch of salt at that time but it was enough to make me think that, having now forced my way into his thinking, the last thing I wanted was a change in manager.

At least I was now being coached more by the late Brian Whitehouse than Eric Harrison; he was a little like Warren Joyce, with his emphasis on hard work and running. Everything seemed to be disguised as running so we'd complain about it, though it was obviously the best thing for us. Brian took it to extremes, to be fair. There was one time I literally collapsed. He had us doing a relay, a full lap of the Cliff after training, the grass was all cut up and muddy and I was dead on my feet. I went down and he came over barking in my face to get up. The training was a lot harder with Brian than it was with Eric but I would say that the most learning I ever did was when I was playing in the reserves at United. I learned more there than what I did when I was younger, because in those days there weren't coaches who were dedicated to any form of technical development. There were little bits such as crossing and timing of attacking runs and movement but there was a whole scope of things such as those I've mentioned that kids can't be expected to know instinctively. Brian didn't ease up; whereas Warren's emphasis is all about being fit for games, so he knows when to take the foot off, Brian was relentless. In those days player conditioning was not exactly identified as the priority that it perhaps should have been.

That said, though, I have to repeat that in those days where I was playing predominantly in the reserves, I felt as if my game came on leaps and bounds. Brian had us playing 1 v 1's the length of the Cliff. I remember playing against Paul McGrath; we'd put the ball on the half way spot, and race from the opposite penalty area to try and get to the ball first. Once we got the ball we then had to score in the other goal. I was never going to get there before Paul so it was a case of defending my goal, trying to get the ball and then running up the other end to score. It was always gruelling and really hard running. Even finishing drills were tough. We'd line four players on the byline, we would pass it along each other and run up the length of the pitch, with the idea that one would eventually cross the ball back up the other end and three would make runs and try to score. If the cross was no good, you've just run the entire length of the pitch for nothing. You didn't want to be the one to piss everybody else off so it makes you concentrate more when you were the one crossing the ball. It was useful individually and also had a practical use for when it came to games.

A couple of years prior, Alan Davies, the Welsh midfielder, kept going on about wanting to play in the middle, and Brian would always push him out to the right in training matches. Alan complained about it at the time but at the end of the season he was selected to play in the FA Cup Final when a space became available on the right hand side of midfield. I don't know if Brian had had the foresight to envisage that Alan might be needed there one time or whether he just identified that Alan had the capabilities to play in that position despite what the player himself thought but that was a useful lesson to the rest of us about accepting what the coaches were saying. If an opportunity was to come up in the team, it goes without saying that you'd want to give yourself the best chance of being the one who gets picked, and you certainly don't want to be doing anything which may count against you. Alan was a nice player – he moved really smoothly with the ball and he was a good crosser. As a fellow Welshman, and an international, he was somebody I looked up to, a player I thought I had to become as good as. He was a really quiet guy but still, the shock of finding out he'd taken his own life a few years later, when he was at Swansea, was incredibly sad.

I'd begun the 1984/85 season in positive form, scoring a few times for the reserves. I didn't go into it with any expectations – well, at least, not the expectation that I would now be with the first team all the time just because I'd made my debut. For most of my career I'd played above my age groups and I think the summer of 1984 was probably the first time I was not 'ahead' of what I might have expected or what might have been expected of me.

It helped that I was seeing progression in other areas; I'd played eighteen times for the Welsh schoolboys and had also been called up into the under-18's. It was a big thing because generally just about everyone who was called up for the under-21's was going up to the senior squad, so there was a natural progression. That's not to say that I was taking it for granted, even as a Manchester United player, but because Wales is a smaller country and their pool of players isn't so big, there was a feeling that naturally it would all fall into place.

Competition was much fiercer at United and that point was proven by the players Ron brought in to improve the side in 1984; Gordon Strachan and Jesper Olsen were bought to improve the creativity in midfield and Alan Brazil was signed to play up front, although Sparky's emergence had an impact on that. Alan didn't get much of a chance at United and was given a fair bit of criticism but I always thought he was a great player. That season I ended up playing a lot of football with him in the reserves. In the week before we played Liverpool in the FA Cup semi-final there was a friendly game between the reserves and the first team at the Cliff, with Alan and I both in the reserve side. We were 3-0 down at half time but came back to draw 3-3 and Baz scored a hat-trick. He was throwing dummies everywhere and sending the defence all over the gaff; I couldn't understand why he wasn't playing more.

By that point I was also a little frustrated with the sporadic nature of my own appearances. Those games against Forest sandwiched a League Cup game against Burnley but those were my only first team appearances of the season and it didn't seem as if I was going to get a fair crack of the whip so I could put a run of form together. The only thing that kept me from really worrying about it, insofar as questioning my future, was that I was far from the only one. The same was happening with many of the other lads such as Mark Dempsey; they'd get a little taste of first team football and then they'd be out again.

Some didn't even get that. I mentioned Peter Beardsley earlier but there was also the famous case of David Platt who played for our reserves that year but didn't get a sniff of first team action. Another case of one that got away but at the time he was playing up front and, considering we had Alan - a first team signing that season - in our reserve team, opportunities at that level were hard to come by. Even I was in front of David in terms of front player choices, probably because of my goal return. He went to Crewe Alexandra, moved a bit further back into midfield, and carved out an exceptional career for himself; he was very similar as a player to Frank Lampard, with the timing of his late runs into the box and ability to score goals. It's all very well saying United missed out but things work out as they do for a reason and would David have moved into midfield if he hadn't left Old Trafford? With Bryan Robson in there, would he have found opportunities any easier to come by? I know from experience that was not something that could be reasonably suggested. So while I think maybe Beardsley could have been given a fairer chance, I think things worked out as they should for David, and it obviously had a positive effect on his career. That season even Robbo played in the reserves, as he was on the way back from an injury, and he played with exactly the same intensity as you would expect to see in a first-team game. It was only a short period - three games - but, after being around the likes of Buchan, Macari and McQueen, standard bearers for the club in the past, Bryan was very much showing the standard of the present and what was expected. He was the best in the country and led by example. Expectations were high but, with the club going well in the FA Cup again in 1985, so was morale around the club. Ron's problem was that United had failed to do quite so well in the league; a bad run of results over Christmas had ended realistic hopes of a title challenge. Because I wasn't in the first team at that point I don't know if I'm qualified as an expert to say why we didn't win the league but I can only offer my opinion as someone who looked at our players the same as everybody else - I couldn't understand how we didn't end up with a league title with the players at our disposal.

That belief was justified by the FA Cup Final result where we defeated Everton. I'd ended the season in good form for the reserves but didn't expect to play because my first-team chances had been few and far between. And yet I was given the suggestion from Ron that there was a chance. He said that he had to choose between me and Gordon McQueen for a place in the squad but he had to select Gordon because he might not get another chance. And as it turned out Gordon didn't make the squad either. I travelled down with Robbo's brother, Gary, and we got drunk on the train. I understood what Ron was getting at but I was still disappointed because there was no guarantee I would get another chance to play in an FA Cup Final. A few years later, after I was fortunate enough to have a winner's medal, I was at a dinner with Martin Peters, the former West Ham player who of course won the World Cup. I took it for granted that he'd won the FA Cup and mentioned how good the winner's medal was. I was mortified when he told me he hadn't won it!

So I didn't play or make the bench but I was sitting in the stand right behind Norman with a perfect view of that incredible goal he scored to win the game in extra-time. The game had gone through so many twists and turns, with the sending off of Kevin Moran, that I don't think I was alone in thinking that we wouldn't be able to win it. Just before Norman struck the ball, from that position, I couldn't see the net; and somehow, he found it. The celebrations afterwards were fantastic and, being around it, I naturally dreamed of one day getting back there and really being a part of it. I would be lying if I said I wasn't jealous of the lads.

There was no doubting that Ron had his favourites and he also liked joining in the five-a-sides with the team and I suppose that it's only natural that if he saw more of a player and became more aware of what they could do, then they stood a greater chance of getting regular football. I don't think I did it with this in mind but I would take part in a few of those small games in the gym at the Cliff - for players like me, who'd come from out of town, playing football and being at United was my entire life. Ron would bring his friends in or invite random players; around this time, Gordon Hill, the former United winger who'd suffered a serious knee injury and had played in America, was without a club, so he came along. He looked like he had the old magic and was really sharp and Ron was talking about offering him a contract. That never happened but it was the sort of thing you might expect from Ron, and around that time our wide options were not exactly set in stone.

I don't think it's being conceited to say that I wasn't done any favours when my chances finally started to look like they would come. Following the FA Cup win I went to Jamaica on a post-season tour with the club and scored in one of the friendlies there, a long range effort into the top corner from 25 yards. That was a crazy game; our opponents were so aggressive and were smashing our players all over the place. I had a 50/50 with one of them and in the heat of the moment I went over the ball and did the player deliberately.

Despite the on-pitch aggression it was a relaxing trip, just the tonic after a long season. Well, once we'd got the hotel sorted - we turned up at one place which wasn't the best. They'd put a banner up which said 'Welcome Manchester United' but we turned around and left, and went in one down the road. When Ron found out, he realised our hotel was now better than the one he had booked himself in, so he came and stayed with us! Mick Brown was scared to death of a peacock that was running the grounds of the hotel. A group of us, including the chairman, Martin Edwards, got a bunch of branches together and tied them up. We put them under Mick's bed in his room and attached a rope to it, which we hid and fed through to the next room. When he was in bed we started pulling the ropes so that he would think there was this peacock under his bed! The year after we went to Israel to play a friendly and that was the location of another prank on Mick; a few of us found a giant dead turtle on the beach and somehow smuggled it back in the back of a local's car and then into Mick's room without him knowing. We put it in the bath put a flower on its head and one of Mick's cigars in its mouth. We went down the long corridor to the bar and we could smell the turtle – it was rank. We were helped by one of the hotel staff who said he was going to 'take care' of it later. Micky Duxbury tells the story in his book and I'm afraid to say I'm none the wiser about what the ultimate fate of that turtle was!

After the peacock incident Mick wouldn't speak to anyone. I was the victim of a practical joke myself; I was given something to smoke – me as a non-smoker – and let's just say a little local produce had been added to it. I was giggling the rest of the evening. The next morning Big Ron pulls me out of the pool and said, 'See that son, they put that there especially for you!' and pointed to a sign. 'Keep Off The Grass.'

We were supposed to go to Montego Bay the night after the game but we couldn't because there were bandits on the road, so we were offered to be put up for an extra two days. Only four of us took up the offer – Alan Brazil, Gordon McQueen, John Gidman and myself. Mark Hughes had to fly back because he had an international game against Norway and, at the end of those extra two days, I was approached by Martin Edwards who told me I had been called up too and I had to fly back immediately. I flew to Gatwick and straight to Norway and it was all a bit of a blur as I was named on the bench at Brann Stadion; I came on at half time, and the game was already beyond us at 3-1. We were three down after eighteen minutes. At least we drew the second half

1-1, the hosts winning 4-2.

The call up for Wales was completely unexpected. I was twenty years old, and I had gone from playing and representing Manchester United in Jamaica to then flying back halfway across the world to play for my country. It felt like life was one big adventure. It was a disappointment - it meant I'd lost my debut for club and country - but being part of a team that didn't lose the second half, as stupid as it sounds, did feel like a big deal to me. The summer of 1985, then, had unexpectedly turned into a confidence builder.

Breaking Through

RETURNING TO PRE-SEASON for the 1985/86 campaign as a full international clearly helped my credibility as far as Ron was concerned, though it still took a while for me to get my chance in the side. Perhaps in the case of Mark Hughes and Norman Whiteside, the buzz around them and their quick ascent at international level facilitated the speed at which they were given first team chances. Norman was a veteran compared to me now, despite being the same age! I can't say I was truly frustrated because I knew it was a case of earning my stripes and playing for Wales against Norway was apparently part of that process. That was proof for Ron that I was capable and worthy of a longer opportunity in the Manchester United first team and the standard to get there was so high that I understood his reluctance and wariness to just give those opportunities. His job was on the line, after all, and so in that light it's probably understandable that he made a lot of short-term signings of players who were established names.

There are a number of truths in football and a few ideas and theories about the best time to give kids a run in the team. If the team are doing well, why make the change? If the team aren't doing well, is it the right environment to throw a youngster in? There are so many players who don't get the chance they perhaps deserved because of circumstances or the opinion of others. Beardsley and Platt are prime examples, players who were obviously good enough for top teams but couldn't force their way in at United because of circumstances and opinions.

For a little while at the start of the season I did have a slight worry about ever getting a chance because the team were playing so well. They were winning all their games and playing some incredible football; everything was clicking with the bigger names and even those who weren't automatic starters were playing in the form of their life.

Peter Barnes on the left wing was probably the stand out player in that infamous run where United won their first ten games. He was sharp; beating people for fun and putting in a constant supply of good crosses. Gordon Strachan was a different type of winger on the other side – he liked to deliberate with his crosses and tease his marker. At the time, he was on the top of his game, so it was the perfect complement. We were direct and ruthless and with a fully fit team we were top of the league. Barnesy was almost the stereotypical Ron signing, that player who had enjoyed a great career and developed a fine reputation for himself elsewhere but a player whose best days were supposedly behind him. He was proving people wrong and for me he was the catalyst of that incredible run United enjoyed.

It was difficult to see where my chance would come. I had started the season in good form in the reserves and scored twice from left back in a 4-2 win against Everton. I was then part of a reserve team that played at Kettering Town on Friday, 20th September – so you can imagine how surprised I was to find out I was a substitute for the game the next day, at another of Ron's old teams, WBA. My legs were gone from playing on the heavy pitch the night before but there was obviously no way I was going to talk myself out of a chance of playing in the first team. I was brought on and it felt like hell at first; I just felt lucky I was brought on when the score was 3-0. My reactions can't have been too bad though – it was here I scored my first goal for the club, getting onto a rebound from a Robson shot to tap in. Frank Stapleton scored a minute later to make it five and I huffed and puffed my way through the rest of the game, wondering if it was me who was out of shape or if I was suffering so badly with nerves and not really realising it. It didn't even cross my mind, at the time, that it was due to the fact I'd played the night before.

I'd done enough to earn a start on the right wing in the next game, a League Cup game against Crystal Palace at Selhurst Park, but it wasn't until a couple of months later that I got another chance, in the same competition. Clearly, then, using the League Cup as a competition for introducing younger players into the team is nothing new. It was an opportunity for managers then, just as it is now, to use their squad and, this season in particular, game time was even harder to come by because of the ban on English clubs playing in European competition because of the Heysel disaster. As a young man at the time I confess to my thoughts on the matter being insular and selfish; I was just concerned about breaking into the United team and the idea of the opportunities that had been denied me didn't even register. In more recent years I look at that time and think of how we were denied playing in European competition and how difficult that must have been for some of the players who were in their prime. Spare a thought for Everton, who had one of their best ever teams and weren't able to compete in the European Cup. Honestly, I didn't think it was fair to ban all English clubs because of the actions of one set of supporters.

That next League Cup appearance for me, funnily enough, was at Anfield. Yes, the atmosphere was intense and it was aggressive but that was the same of most grounds you went to. It was a part of the game and it didn't bother me too much; it made the atmosphere better and made me more motivated. Not that it counted for much on this occasion as we suffered defeat and elimination from the Cup.

We played them again later that season in February. As the bus pulled up outside Anfield I remember thinking that I just didn't want to get off behind Norman. The Liverpool fans hated all of us but he was Public Enemy number one. I managed to get out on my own, but as I was making my way to the ground a Liverpool fan sprayed me in the eyes with gas, which I later found out was ammonia. The spray also went into the eyes of some other Liverpool fans stood on the other side of me. We ended up with around eight or ten Liverpool fans in our dressing room, pouring water on their eyes to try and help them.

I obviously missed the game and watched it from the stands - no pun intended but it was a bit of an eye opener to witness the abuse that gets hurled towards the director's box from the Kop. When you're on the pitch you are sort of protected; you hear some of it but not all. In the stand you really notice how much every little action is amplified. Every tackle, every minor foul, almost every incident, the Kop would go mental screaming at our directors.

The previous season I'd travelled with the team but didn't play - as the bus turned into Anfield, it was in a bit of a bottleneck and it was surrounded by Liverpool fans. They were shouting abuse, as they would, and all of a sudden a huge brick smashed against the window right where Sparky was sitting. Fortunately the brick just bounced off the window and fell to the floor, leaving just a dirty mark. For some reason the driver never washed it for the rest of the season – maybe it was a badge of honour! Instead of arresting the fan, the police just grabbed him and threw him back into the crowd. It made me concerned for the United fans who were running the gauntlet out in the streets.

The pepper spray was a big story even by United and Liverpool's rivalry standards. It was national news, and I was a 'gong' on the News at Ten that night, though I think they said 'Manchester United player is CS gassed at Liverpool' rather than my name.

By then we'd had a wobble in the league – defeats at Sheffield Wednesday and Leicester City prompted Ron to ring the changes and I was now the beneficiary, coming back in for a game at Villa Park in mid-December. It's a game that always sticks out to me because of my mind playing tricks and making me think this was where I scored my first goal but I think that's simply because it was my first goal as a starter. The goal itself was a little more memorable than the one I scored at the Hawthorns. In the team-talk beforehand Ron's given me a man-marking job, which was something I hadn't expected, nor had ever done before. I was told to get around Steve Hodge; 'stop him and you stop Villa' was Big Ron's theory. That obviously went well – both of us were on the scoresheet inside half an hour! Breaking from a corner, one of the Villa players was trying to control the bouncing ball near the halfway line; I nipped in, robbed the ball and raced away. I was clean through but was brought down by big Allan Evans about twenty-five yards from goal. It was the kind of foul that would definitely be an automatic red these days. The free kick was teed up for me, and I struck it from distance into the left hand corner. I was pretty pleased with that one, not just for the quality of the strike but few players can say they effectively assisted themselves!

Hodge scored ten minutes later; thankfully, in the second half, Strachan and Hughes scored to give us a 3-1 win. It was the boost we needed after losing our previous two away games.

Without wanting to do Ron a disservice there wasn't a huge emphasis on tactics; my instruction was simply to stay tight to Hodge. Most of those sorts of instructions were dealt with by the players anyway. If you see someone scoring headers on Match of the Day every week then it's probably a good idea to stick your tall players near them. If you're playing against Chris Waddle you'll be expected to help the full back if you're playing wide midfield. We were schooled with a basic thought – we knew we had to work at least as hard as the opposition in order to win the right to play our football. If anything, I'd say that in the post-Sir Alex Ferguson years, that's been the most obvious thing that has been lacking, though hopefully there are signs of that returning. More often than not, Manchester United teams will have the necessary quality in their team to win a game but, considering how big the game is seen by their opponents, if they are not putting in the work, they'll quickly be found out. That was an ethic that isn't perhaps associated with Ron and that would be unfair; it was certainly instilled by him via the staff he employed at the club.

For the start of that season we had substance and style; the way we'd played was as good and exciting as any Manchester United team and the way it is perceived from the outside is that the wheels came off but I wonder if it's more true to suggest that it was a run of form that was never really sustainable. Or even that the change in form was due to the condition of the pitches - especially at Old Trafford - as the weather worsened.

I remember playing a reserve game with Peter Barnes and he turned round midway and asked, 'How am I doing?' I thought 'Fuck off Barnesy, you're an England international, you don't need reassurance in a reserve game!' As I've said, Peter's form is my enduring memory of that run of wins. He wasn't as confident as he should have been in his own ability - he was brilliant. When confident, and on song, he should have been first choice. The problem, if we played Strachan and Olsen, was that both of them liked to feint so often that they weren't only

tricking the defenders, I can imagine the frustration of Mark Hughes
and Frank Stapleton in the box, trying to second guess when the cross
was coming in. Funnily enough I thought Jesper would have made a
good centre forward, though his size probably counted against him.
He was so good on the ball and if he had it in the box it was near
on impossible for opposition defenders to get it off him. Peter, on the
other hand, was direct and consistent and it made the difference. Not
that I'm suggesting United's run fell apart because Peter Barnes wasn't
arrogant enough. The biggest problem with Peter was that he wasn't
selected as often as he should have been. Gordon was very much like
Jesper - a player who looked good, and got fans off their seat with his
skill but the end product was lacking too often for us, in my opinion.
The best comparison was just up the road at Everton, where they had
clinical delivery in the combination of Gary Stevens and Trevor Steven
down the right, supplying Andy Gray and Graeme Sharp in the middle.
Looking back, it just seems nonsensical to me that we had the right
players but just didn't use them as much. It was ruthless and it brought
results and medals. In addition to all of this, Robbo picked up an injury
and missed a few games and that had a big impact on us.

We played Arsenal just before Christmas and should have been in
front but Norman missed a penalty in the first half; fifteen minutes from
the end Charlie Nicholas scored to inflict our first home defeat of the
season. It was the first of six defeats in ten league games which obviously
hurt us and I admit it was very difficult to play over that period. This
spell of prolonged exposure in the United first team opened my eyes
to the many things that you need to go for you if you're going to
challenge. In addition to the defeat against Arsenal we were also beaten
by Everton but generally we had a good record against the bigger teams
and it begged the question why we could win at Anfield and then
struggle - with all due respect - down at places like Carrow Road.
Maybe there's some truth in the suggestion that there was no need for
any extra motivation up at Anfield, while against a team like Norwich
or QPR, we would struggle as the pitches were a lot smaller than at
Old Trafford but I would say that was just one of many factors. I felt we
struggled on smaller pitches because our game plan didn't change; the

difference in the amount of time you got on the ball at Old Trafford compared to Goodison Park or Carrow Road was just incredible. And, that said, particularly in the 80's, we didn't adapt either because the state of the pitch at Old Trafford would be horrendous after November.

In spite of that, we had started the season so well that we were expected to win the league and at the time we weren't thinking about the year turning out so badly, we were hoping that it was the sort of hiccup every team goes through in a season. But then Bryan picked up a shoulder injury a couple of minutes into an FA Cup game at Upton Park - we drew that but West Ham beat us in the replay and then we were also defeated by Queen's Park Rangers. We were suddenly six points behind the leaders, Everton, and had dropped down to third in the table. I can't emphasise enough what a huge miss Robbo was for us. For me he was the best midfielder in the world; he was up and down the entire pitch, throwing himself into tackles at both ends and he was a good goalscorer too. His on-pitch leadership was exceptional - we used to call him Son of Ron, because they'd both come from West Brom but he really was like the on-pitch manager, recognising danger and snuffing it out. Any team would miss a player with his quality but it was more than that, he was the heartbeat of that United team and not having him there emphasised just what we were missing.

The ironic thing of all of this is that when Robbo was injured, I was one of the players to come in and wear the number seven shirt. I was confident in my ability but I was a very different kind of player to Bryan. I'd have much preferred to have been playing alongside him, though to be fair I don't think anyone expected me to do the things he did, though naturally, I felt the pressure simply from being the player who was in for him. I thought my general level of performance was good enough to justify selection.

As the season came to a close the mood around the club wasn't great. There were rumours about Terry Venables arriving from Barcelona or Alex Ferguson coming down from Aberdeen but Ron was kept on through the rest of the campaign. I started in our last home game, scoring a half volley at the Stretford end in a 4-0 win over Leicester City. It was a good performance, sealed with a goal to make the manager think that I could be selected when Robbo was fit. I tried to take those things in my stride but it was a difficult and uncertain time for me too. The anti-climax of that final home game - a game we were expected to be parading the Division One trophy in - was deflating but honestly, my thoughts at the time were selfish, and about my place in the team. I worried if my versatility was counting against me. Ron had made a number of short term signings which did nothing to benefit us - to outsiders, it may have looked like panic, and to the senior players who hadn't been playing it was a bit of a kick in the teeth which had a damaging effect on morale. You get those kind of situations at the best of times at football clubs - someone is always going to be unhappy that they aren't playing but when things aren't going well, then obviously the spotlight is on you.

Instead of someone coming to United from Barcelona, we ended up losing Mark Hughes to the Spanish club and that for me was one of the most disappointing things of the entire season. He was my roommate for club and country and had recently signed a five-year contract. I suppose with hindsight that was something done by the club to maximise the fee they got from Barcelona; it was a shame he left, but it was also a pity as his friend that it didn't work out for him in Spain. It was an understandable move. United were underachieving, Barcelona weren't, they were able to offer more money and they offered him a chance of proving himself in European competition. And, from Barcelona's point of view, Mark was as good as any striker they could hope to buy. He scored two headers on the opening day of that season, against Aston Villa, which demonstrated everything you needed to know about his capability to score any kind of goal. The first was a diving header and the second was a thunderous one where his timing was spot on. Ultimately the move didn't work out for him and he went on loan to Bayern Munich before eventually returning to us but I know he took a lot from the experience. The writing was probably on the wall from that point because Ron wasn't given the money from the sale to reinvest in the squad. Maybe we should have seen it coming but when Ron returned to take charge for the following season, there was every reason for us to believe that the club were backing him.

The disappointment of 1985/86 wasn't just confined to matters at Manchester United. Following my international debut I was involved in the latter part of Wales' World Cup qualifying campaign, which concluded with an infamous game at Ninian Park against Scotland - we had to win to qualify, whereas Scotland needed just a point. Wales and Scotland had faced off in similar circumstances in 1977, though our 'home' ground on that occasion was Anfield. In the 78th minute of that game Scotland were awarded a penalty even though you could clearly see Joe Jordan's blue sleeve rise up as he handled the ball — Don Masson scored, then ten minutes later Kenny Dalglish did, and they qualified at our expense. Eight years on and it felt as if our response was going to be perfect; we were playing well in the game, and took the lead through a Sparky goal. It was instinctive and smartly taken first time - his sixth goal in ten caps, emphasising his quality.

With seven minutes to go, the ball was played into our box and David Speedie tried to hit it on the turn; his effort was going well wide but struck the elbow of David Phillips, who was so tight to Speedie that he couldn't get out of the way. The referee, Jan Keizer, awarded a penalty, despite it clearly being accidental. Davie Cooper scored. The reaction of Mike England, our manager, was to bring me on to try and help us get the goal we needed. It was only seven minutes or so but I can vividly remember being breathless the entire time. I didn't stop running; I, like every Welsh player, was desperate. It was a blur, with so much on the line. To be minutes away from qualifying from the World Cup… well, I try to be diplomatic about it, because at the time it was out of my hands (no pun intended). As a substitute you're watching these events unfold and there's nothing you can do to affect it; my assessment in those situations would be to analyse where I would be likely to come on, if I did, and study my opponent and see if there was anything I might exploit. Though, of course, in this situation, with so much riding on it, there was certainly an additional spark in the atmosphere. Afterwards, I was as disappointed as anyone that we didn't qualify, though it has to be said that at the time the idea of it being since 1958 since we'd qualified for a major tournament wasn't something that weighed particularly heavily on my mind; it was the acute disappointment, the idea we were so close. We also had a certain sense of injustice, even if it wasn't quite as controversial as 1977, because there was nothing David could have done.

After the game I bumped into Strach outside the dressing rooms and he completely blanked me. I thought it was odd but I wasn't aware of the far more important event of the night. It was some time after the game before we found out Jock Stein had died and obviously it redefined the perspective with which we viewed our disappointment.

I made my first international start the following February, against Saudi Arabia in the Prince Saud Bin Jalawi Sport City Stadium. There were three other debutants in the game – Mark Aizlewood, who started, and David Williams and Malcolm Allen, who came on. Malcolm was a bit of a joker and even though we won the game 2-0 – with both goals scored before he came on with a few minutes to go – it was he who provided the strongest memory of the game for me. There was a pipe going around the pitch and before the game Malcolm a bit of a joker, says to the boys, 'watch this.' He walks over to the pipe and trips over it deliberately – the stadium erupted, and I looked up to see the Saudi supporters dressed in white robes laughing their heads off. It's strange, the things that come to mind – I mean, I do remember some of the game, it was tough, they were very quick, athletic and strong and made it difficult for us but whenever I think back to making my first start, it's Malcolm making the crowd laugh which comes to mind.

Our next game after that was at Lansdowne Road against the Republic of Ireland; neither nation had qualified for Mexico. We won again, but again the game is more memorable to me for the fact that Neville Southall broke his ankle after landing awkwardly on a very bumpy rugby pitch. Despite being a friendly, it was just as competitive as any domestic game, considering the number of players we were familiar with playing with and against every week. Add to that the spice of Welsh players playing for Ireland – Kevin Sheedy – and the atmosphere became that bit spicier. Jokes aside, I have to admit I'm not a big fan of players who choose to play for another country than the one they were born in. I'm still not convinced that Vinny Jones didn't get selected for us simply because his surname sounded Welsh!

We played against Uruguay in April; they had been drawn with Scotland in their World Cup group so we were seen as good opposition to prepare them. That is a fairly frustrating thing for a professional footballer to go through nor is it something you ever really get used to. We did have some good memories which came from those kind of situations, though; in 1988, we went to Italy to play against them before Euro '88. They hadn't been defeated at home for three years and then we went and won, with a goal from Ian Rush. It was a proud moment and another tiring game playing against Roberto Donadoni.

We played against Uruguay at Wrexham and I remember Mike warning us about Enzo Francescoli. He was one of the best players in the world but he was always using his elbows. As luck would have it, I came up against him, trying to get the ball from him, and lo and behold he swings his arm at me. He just missed; he passed the ball and got it back, and I went straight through him. Anybody can be dirty. Seconds later I'm surrounded by a group of Uruguayans screaming in my face, eyes piercing through me. It was a scrap on a muddy pitch and finished 0-0; they came with a vicious reputation but they left knowing we were their match as far as aggression was concerned.

We weren't the only home nation who had handball controversy connected with the 1986 World Cup but I remain convinced that if Bryan Robson hadn't suffered an aggravation of the shoulder injury that had done so much damage to his and our season at United, then England's game with Argentina might have gone down in history for very different reasons. He was as important to England as he was to United and they missed him more than anything in that game. If he's there, I doubt Diego Maradona gets the opportunity to get in the position where he handles the ball into the net and he certainly doesn't get the opportunity to waltz past Robbo the same way he did everyone else for that second goal. The thing about Robbo is that the heat didn't bother him, he could play at exactly the same pace and intensity for the match even in difficult situations like that. I'm not saying Diego Maradona wasn't brilliant, he obviously was, and brilliant players can embarrass other brilliant players and make them look foolish. Whichever way you look at it, though, that England–Argentina game is one of the landmark games from Maradona's career and he scored - probably - his two most famous goals in it. Likewise, I think missing that kind of game and missing that opportunity to really make the same kind of name for himself, is probably the biggest reason why Robbo doesn't get the credit he deserves when people are talking about the greatest players of all time.

There's a similar thing with Ryan Giggs and Wales; there was a time when he was the best player in the world but, for circumstances beyond his control, he didn't get the recognition he deserved. Ryan was ripping defences apart across Europe and almost of all of the top players across the continent were saying the same thing. But Wales never qualified for anything while he was playing and at the time when David Beckham was voted third best player in the world there was no doubting which of the two, for me, was the better player. I'm not saying Beckham wasn't a great player, he was; but Ryan, for me, for that period of time was the best around. For Bryan, well, in their head to head at Old Trafford, he'd come out head and shoulders above Maradona in that game against Barcelona so, naturally, there's reason to believe he could have done it again for England.

All Change

BRYAN'S INJURY KEPT HIM OUT of the start of the 1986/87 season and so I kept my place in the team in our pre-season which kicked off with a tournament in Holland against Fluminese, Dynamo Kyiv and Ajax. A few of us in the squad got in hot water out there; we'd been out drinking and the papers had taken pictures and called us the 'Magnificent Seven'. Ron had decided to have dinner at 7pm and I didn't get back in until 7.30 - four of the group didn't even get back until four in the morning. Ron called the police. Terry Gibson, Micky Duxbury and I arrived back at the hotel to be confronted by Mick Brown who was going out of his mind. He goes, 'Where've you been, where've you been, he's called the police!'

'Where is the fat bastard?!' answered a drunken Micky.

So, for the Kyiv game, a few of us were punished and made to be subs - watching from the sidelines, we should have been four or five goals down in the first half because they were absolutely all over us. It was only 1-0. We were told to warm up but they looked that good we didn't fancy coming on. I came on in the second half and scored one of my best ever goals in a red shirt. The ball was played to me direct from a corner and I volleyed it from the edge of the box, in off the post in the top corner. We drew 1-1 and were very lucky. In fact, I was the only scorer for us that pre-season - I got our other goal, a header, in a friendly at home to Real Sociedad. That game also finished 1-1.

Looking back and writing this down, it does appear to be fairly obvious that there were significant problems at the club, and perhaps some of the players who weren't exactly fans of Ron weren't exactly shy of showing it. However, if there was any dissatisfaction among certain players, I want to make it clear that it was never the case that the players were trying to get the manager out. There might have been frustration about not getting opportunities or how things were going but there was never any suggestion that we would down tools or not put in one hundred percent commitment to get results for Manchester United. That said, it is well known in football that morale and momentum are just as important as talent and dedication and the mood around the club wasn't great. Our form from the back end of the previous season continued into the 1986/87 campaign as we lost our opening three games. As always, the results only tell part of the story. We were defeated at Highbury on the opening day in a tight game, coming towards the end of the game I hit the bar from 25 yards - within five or ten minutes Charlie Nicholas scored for them and they won 1-0. We then played West Ham at home - we're a goal down within a minute and went 2-0 down but managed to pull it back to 2-2 and there's déjà vu as I hit the crossbar again with a long range effort late on. Within minutes Frank McAvennie's scored at the other end and I'm left rueing the fine margins between strikes which could have won us six points and instead we've ended up with none.

Despite the disappointment, I felt I was playing well - a feeling justified by Mike England selecting me for the Wales squad after seeing me play against Charlton at Old Trafford. No crossbar shot for me this time but another defeat as we lose 1-0. I was good enough for Wales but seemingly not good enough for United; Ron dropped me for our next game, against Leicester City. At the age of 21 and with only one season of regular first team football behind me I wasn't so arrogant that I felt I was an automatic choice but I thought I was playing well enough to deserve my place in the team so when I wasn't selected for our next game, at home to Southampton, I went to find Ron to ask him why I wasn't in the team. I found him in the car park on the way to one of his five-a-sides and his response to me was, 'Well, Bryan Robson's back, he's the England captain and it's a big boost to the players and the club to have him back.' Young, naive and on the spot, I nodded meekly and accepted the explanation. Only afterwards did I think I should have said, well, what about the other three midfield places, it's not as if Bryan's the only player. Against Charlton, Strach had somehow misplaced a pass to me and I was only ten yards away from him; that incident stuck in my mind when it came down to it, I thought I was in better form than some of the other players.

Ron was right, in a way. Bryan coming back in was the lift he'd predicted – we battered Southampton 5-1 and even though I was back in for the next game, a defeat to Watford I was soon dropped again. We then lost our next two, against Everton and Chelsea – six out of eight league games lost – to put us second from bottom. Liverpool, the reigning champions, had lost just six times the previous season. Ron was clearly on borrowed time but even though I, as much as anyone, had reason to grumble about his management, I still felt he might get it right with time. Home wins over Sheffield Wednesday and Luton Town were welcome but did little to improve the mood.

I was back in the reserves and, because I was in the reserve changing room, I wasn't present when Ron announced to the players that he had been sacked. It was a weird set up whenever I was selected for the first team, it always felt like I was just visiting. News filtered down to us second hand. I was surprised, I must admit. Yes, things were tough, and perhaps all the signs were there when the board didn't give him money to spend that summer but I expected that he would stay and like I said, I thought he could turn it around.

I know a lot of people blame what's come to be known as the 'drinking culture' at the club and I can see what they mean. Bryan was a big drinker but the difference with him was that it didn't affect his performance or at least it didn't seem to. The others often associated with him were big Gordon McQueen, Norman Whiteside, Paul McGrath. I don't know if it's fair to say these were all favourites of Ron so they got away with it – he liked to have big lads in his side and they all fit into that category too. They weren't the only ones drinking. I could be just as bad and so could Arthur Albiston; we certainly kept up with them as well as we could. Since retiring, Arthur doesn't drink – there are obviously cases in football where the habit becomes an addiction but I think Arthur's case proves that it was simply a routine that we were in. Robbo's rule was no drinking forty-eight hours before a game and at the time we thought it was sensible but look, there's just no other way of saying, that kind of lifestyle is obviously going to affect your body and it is going to have a negative impact on you if you're a professional sportsman. Sure, we tried our best, and for players like Bryan the effects weren't obvious but you just can't be at full tilt.

Under Ron I think that United had all the tools to win the league - he just perhaps didn't have them all at the same time and in a league as competitive as the First Division, and a team as big as Manchester United, you need everything to fall into place. I look again and think about how we defeated Liverpool on such a regular basis and scratch my head how that didn't translate into league winning form over a season. Apart from the things I've said, a major thing Liverpool had that we didn't seem to have was tall and strong defenders. We had Paul McGrath - a player definitely good enough to build a title-winning defence around but he was injured too often. The only season he played 40 games was 1985/86 and, sod's law, that's when Robbo missed so many games and then Paul was 6ft dead on and Liverpool had the likes of Alan Hansen and Gary Gillespie at well over six foot, which made them more capable of going to some clubs who were, shall we say, less apologetic about their style of football, and defending the long ball game. I'm moving forward a little here but that is why I attribute a lot of the success which was to follow to Gary Pallister. Pally was even taller than the Liverpool players and we were instantly more at ease with going to grounds where we had previously struggled.

In addition to that they Liverpool had Ian Rush up front. I obviously knew Ian from the Welsh team and saw how good he was at close quarters but the main thing for me was what he brought off the ball. He was defending from the front, closing down opponents and not giving them time on the ball. It's a bit of a rare thing in football to see hard-working forwards. Too rare, for me, because the teams that have them tend to be successful. A large part of Leicester City's unexpected success in 2015/16 was that they had Jamie Vardy up front, a quick striker who was working throughout the game. Leicester also had two big and tough centre halves and these are the individual qualities players bring to systems which determine how successful that system is going to be. Leicester's style of football wasn't the prettiest - I didn't think Liverpool's was either - but it was effective to the point where it won them silverware.

I also maintain that the quality of the pitch plays a huge part. Anfield was like a bowling green, perfect for playing on. Perhaps the case in point is when Liverpool lost the FA Cup Final to Wimbledon, a team who matched their combativeness and physicality. The Wembley pitch had longer grass which made the ball roll slower when dry, meaning Liverpool couldn't pass the ball the way they were used to on that shorter grass at home. In 2004 I went to Middlesbrough's league game at Old Trafford which they won 3-2. I bumped into Juninho afterwards – I was trying to get tickets from him for Boro's upcoming League Cup Final against Bolton – and he was saying, 'Shitty pitch, shitty pitch.' I said, 'Well it suited you because you scored two goals!' After the game I was doing some punditry on television talking about why United lost and I explained the state of the pitch meant that the players were not capable of passing the ball the way they were used to. The groundsman pulled me on that – he wasn't happy. He said "the manager hasn't moaned, the players haven't moaned." The next week, Fergie and some of the players were in the press complaining about the pitch. To be fair, the groundsman has done an excellent job at the club ever since. There can be few complaints about the field these days. Talking about Cup upsets, I think that's a reason why you don't see as many of them these days, or at least, not on the scale they used to be – and really, I think the standard of lower league and non-league teams has improved so much. They're much fitter, they're better technically, but the problem they have is that their pitches are much better than they used to be. So top teams can play their natural game on them, they aren't such a leveller anymore.

Then of course there is the Manchester United factor and the way our games are seen as Cup Finals for whoever we're playing, as I said earlier. I know this from experience because when I went away from United the first thing anyone did when the fixtures came out was to look when they were playing United or playing at Old Trafford. I'm not saying that Liverpool or Everton or Arsenal didn't deserve the titles that they won but it would have been nice to have played against teams who had the same application as they sometimes seemed to have when I was playing at Middlesbrough. I would have appreciated the breather! I remember a few years ago, back in 2003, when Shrewsbury knocked

Everton out of the FA Cup, they barely won a league game afterwards for the rest of the season because they were now seen as a 'scalp' by other teams in the division. You have to be mentally prepared for that sort of thing; the challenges which come with success, or representing the biggest club in the world.

The managers are obviously included in that too and I think to be fair to Ron, even though results at the end were horrible, he mostly lived up to what is expected from a Manchester United manager. It is one of the most difficult jobs in football because not only are you expected to win every game, you are also expected to do it a certain way, and adhere to certain ideals which are held by the club and its supporters. Dave Sexton won his last seven games as United manager and it wasn't good enough to keep him in a job. He had four years at the club and was deemed a failure because of the style of football and the fact he didn't win anything. Frank O'Farrell had a similar fate – he didn't even have Wilf McGuinness's 'I had the job for four seasons – summer, autumn, winter, spring' joke to fall back on. The era of David Moyes is still fresh in the memory and Louis van Gaal's time at the club showed that you can win something and still be seen as a failure because the supporters just did not enjoy watching the football. Under Ron, the club won two FA Cups and played football that got the fans off their seats and I think he is remembered favourably in comparison to some others because of that. He also did okay after leaving Old Trafford – winning two league cups against United, of course!

Tackling the drinking was the first big impact felt by the player under Ron Atkinson's successor. There had been links for a few months with Fergie so even if there was shock at Ron going, there wasn't at his replacement. There wasn't really any time to consider alternatives or hear any speculation – I'd barely found out that Ron was gone before I heard Fergie had come in.

It was clear that the new manager had ideas about how we should look after ourselves. As well as a ban on drinking we were also forbidden from playing golf, something that was pretty annoying at the time and disappointing for me as I loved playing. Then the next time I played golf, by the time I got to the fourteenth hole, I was starting to feel pretty exhausted and could see the manager's point. You think that it's just walking but that's like saying four or five hours shopping with the wife is just walking! The boss was right, again. Our way around that was to use the golf buggies. We could still have put our backs out with the swinging so we shouldn't really have been doing that either.

In my opinion, the problems ran deeper than the drinking culture or our sporting hobbies away from football; it wouldn't have been an easy fix for Ron to turn it around and it wasn't an easy job the new manager was walking into. It was easier for the players that the transition was resolved as quickly as it was and I think I'm not alone in saying I had been very impressed with what the gaffer had done up in Scotland. To break the dominance of the Old Firm – at a time when the Scottish league was really strong – is something that has never been done since so it puts what he accomplished into perspective; when you add to that the European triumph they enjoyed over Real Madrid and the fact that all of those accomplishments placed the gaffer as the best ever manager in Aberdeen's history, his record was unquestionable. Beyond the trophies, what had become clear was that Fergie was a manager who knew how to implement a successful strategy.

The gaffer himself has said that in the first few weeks he was never at the Cliff but that's not my memory of it. As I recall he was there all the time, working around the clock – maybe he was working so hard and putting in so many hours away from the training ground as well as on it, that he feels he was barely there. His presence was certainly felt. He was first there, always early and he always last to go home and I can believe that in those first few years for sure, he would have felt like he was never at home. The fruits of his labour would take some time to bear; and maybe some people might look back over the history of the club and how things turned around for us in the 1990s and attribute that success down to some smart signings at the right time, or even fortune that so many good young players blossomed at the right time but to do that is to completely neglect the time the manager put in.

To give an indication of how closely he was involved, and of how far ahead he was of anybody else in management, the day after games he would take over from the physiotherapists and do the rub-downs on the players himself! He would stress that the players needed to get rid of the lactic acid. Nobody knew about lactic acid back then, it was certainly the first time I had heard of it. Initially we moaned about having to come in on Sundays but the manager was all about recovering for the next game and many a time I was laid there having him washing and rubbing my legs with hot soapy water. I've got to say he wasn't the best masseur I've ever had – I had to tell him he'd missed a bit – but it was clear that the point he was making was to be more thorough and more professional in order for the players to be at their optimum condition. When you consider that these things are problems the managers don't even have to think about these days because they have specialists and managers to do those kinds of jobs, just shows how revolutionary it was to be doing it over thirty years ago. Most famously of course, that included addressing the drinking.

Ron said in his autobiography that Norman and Paul were the biggest culprits and also that Norman would only be really bad if he was out injured. Obviously that must have affected his recovery time from those injuries but to me it felt like he just drank too fast and the other lads couldn't keep up. Paul wasn't being deliberately unprofessional, he had an illness. He would be out drinking two days before games and we'd all hear stories about the extent of how bad it was getting – there was a line and the manager had to draw it. He didn't want us drinking at all; most of us stuck to Robbo's rule of no drinking for two days before a game. Really, we were wrong to even think that, we needed more recovery time. It's funny how attitudes change though, isn't it – in 2016, Wayne Rooney got hammered in the press for having a drink when he didn't have a game for three or four days!

By and large there was no real resistance to the new manager's drastic way of changing things. There was a lot of talk about chips being banned from the menu after David Moyes took over, which was a bit farcical. Chips have carbohydrates which you need – Moyes stopped it through the week but it was made out that the club had always had chips on the menu before then, which clearly wasn't the case in the build up to games. I remember the big changes for us were that we started having pasta without sauce and with chicken instead to give it flavour. Under Ron it wasn't uncommon that we would have steak before a game and that's clearly not the best preparation; conversely, when we won the FA Cup in 1990, I remember that every round we seemed to be playing on Sunday at 1pm and so the pre-match meal was bacon and eggs!

Many might look at United at the time and say we weren't far off under Ron and they'd have a point because looking at it for what it was - we'd won two FA Cups in recent years and with mostly the same squad as we still had and we'd won those ten games in a row. You could argue that we had most of the things that we needed. I stand by my belief that our team should have been good enough to win at least one title but our collective mentality would take years to be right. I don't think even he foresaw the incredible number of league titles he would win but his objective at the outset wasn't simply to win one league title, it was to break the Liverpool dominance in the same way he'd done up in Scotland. When he originally planned to retire in 2002 he could safely say he'd accomplished that and laid the groundwork for a successor to overtake the total titles Liverpool had won. Typical Fergie, he changed his mind and did that himself too.

In those weeks after he first came to the club, with the changes in attitude, training became even more competitive than it had been previously. For players like myself, who had enjoyed a bit of a run but had now returned to the reserves, there was the opportunity to impress the new manager. Training matches consequently became Manchester United versus Manchester United, players giving their all in order to demonstrate that a) we were committed to the club and b) we were committed to giving our all, just like the manager. A major problem for us as a side effect was that level of intensity was not sustainable and something had to give; for me, what gave was our performances on the Saturday through tiredness after midweek games, which was obviously the most disappointing thing. In those days, when you're in the thick of it, you don't know any better. I was later told it takes two full days to recover from a game. It's like having steak before a game. You don't question it and, as a young player who had seen chances come and go, I simply couldn't afford not to give absolutely everything in training. That meant on a Friday morning, if I felt I wasn't going to be in the manager's plans for the game the next day, I had to throw myself into everything in order to get that chance. The day before a game you should be easing up but the environment around United was such that not showing that commitment wasn't an option. After all, for some of us, it wasn't just a case of turning up and getting to play, it was the idea of our very future at the club being at stake.

That said, the gaffer didn't make any big changes to the team. Formation-wise, 4-4-2 was pretty much the domestic standard - only on the continent would you find teams playing with three or five at the back - and as such, it really was a case of the qualities of individuals and the way they complemented one another that made the difference. That sounds like an obvious point but I go back to the combinations at Everton which had such a big influence on them winning the league, or the attributes certain players had at Liverpool which set them apart.

I remember the first team-talk the gaffer delivered after he'd named the side that would play at Oxford. We were all at the Cliff and he's going round telling the players what he expected of them individually. He got to me and I was really struggling to understand what he was saying! My takeaway from it was to simply do what I do and be sensible. Honestly, I was a bit worried to say I couldn't understand him! On a fundamental level football is very basic and it's all about decision making. As a player there are two points; can you make the right decision and can you execute it in the right way. The one thing that happens when you can't understand the manager is that you become more acutely aware of being responsible with those decisions, until of course I got to grips with his accent.

The game against Oxford United has assumed great importance as the start of the Ferguson era. The team-sheet has been sold for thousands at auction - wish I'd picked up a couple - and there are stories about the driver of the coach ending up on our bench and the gaffer barking at him to get off. That was a strange one, to be honest, but the manager was right again. We played alright in the game but one thing that is often forgotten when looking back at our 2-0 defeat is that Oxford had one of the best sides in the country back then. At the time they were taking everyone by surprise – they'd won the League Cup earlier that year. Their stadium was comprised of seven little stands and you wonder what you've walked into because it was unconventional to say the least. They had Ray Houghton and John Aldridge in their team. In any time in history, though, Manchester United losing at Oxford is an upset and we should have beaten them. Aldridge scored early on and they scored near the end to make it a terrible first game in charge for the manager. Our midfield comprised of me, Remi Moses, Paul McGrath and Peter Barnes, which was pretty unfamiliar.

One thing that was clear was that the manager was at least giving the players at the club an opportunity to prove themselves and, after a spell in the reserves, I was relieved to be among those getting early chances, even though they were trying times. We drew at Norwich before getting a pretty unconvincing win at home against QPR. Next up for us a trip to Wimbledon, who had been promoted to the First Division for the first time in their history. The club had only been in league football for a few years and their style of football had obviously caught a lot of opponents on the hop as they had even been top of the league in September. The manager prepared a dossier which detailed all of their players and to be fair, I think the reporting was a little bit generous about their ability because I remember reading the reports and expecting to come up against a better footballing side than what the reality. The Dons played to their strengths and were very unapologetic about it. I don't see how anyone could complain about it, no matter how difficult it was to play against. It's good management - maximising the best of what you have. They seemed to have big lads all over the pitch, the only small player was Dennis Wise, and he was the one crossing the balls in. I was playing against Vinny Jones on the day but no matter how unappealing that task might have been, going down to Plough Lane was never a game for midfielders anyway. The ball was in the air the entire time - I actually remember an occasion where one of their players dared to take two touches and the other players and management coming out to scream at the players to hook it on behind our defence. The intent was to lump it in to John Fashanu so he was either challenging in the air with a defender who was almost certain to be shorter than him or to play it behind so Fashanu could have a race. He was quick, tall, athletic and had a black belt in karate! The odds were almost always going to be in his favour.

Vinny Jones scored the goal that gave Wimbledon a 1-0 win from a corner and I was on the post, so I'm unsure who was supposed to be picking him up. They all came charging in like rhinos, like they tended to do. It was maybe one of two or three touches he had in the entire game which gives you an indication of how the game was played. I know a lot of people compared the Stoke City team under Tony Pulis to the classic Wimbledon side but I think that is firstly a little disrespectful to Stoke and Tony and secondly glossing over how Wimbledon actually played. Those games against Wimbledon were primarily scraps and secondly about the sport. They used what they had and if you weren't sufficiently prepared you would be beaten and, for some teams, beaten heavily. Nottingham Forest had a horrendous record down there – they had small centre halves which were like cannon fodder to Fashanu and company. Forest would be defending in their own box from Wimbledon's goal kicks; it was ridiculous. Before we got Pally in and were able to stand up to their size, our best result there was a draw. The gaffer just played it cute in that game and told us to play offside; to our credit, we implemented it pretty well. It didn't help us in the return fixture though as they won at Old Trafford too, scoring in the last minute through Dennis Wise.

Another thing which made the first six months under the new manager a little more tough than it might have been were that teams would have that extra element of aggression and clearly when the confidence of the group is down and teams are always bringing their 'A' game to United anyway, sensing that we were perhaps a little more vulnerable and their chances were just that little bit greater, strengthened the resolve of our opponents. They would tackle to win the ball and tackle to hurt; that's how the game was back then – you had to get up and pretend it didn't hurt or they'd sense you were weak and they'd come back at you. Another example of how the game has changed.

That said, our only loss in the next thirteen games following that Wimbledon game was at home to Norwich City, the day after Boxing Day, when we'd gone to Anfield and won our only away game of the season. Six of those thirteen games were draws which stabilised things a bit but left us miles off the pace.

After a while the reality of the situation we were in returned and the novelty of a new manager wore off. It certainly did for me. I was back in the reserves after that Wimbledon game, barely playing in the first team for most of the season apart from two games in January when Robbo was injured. I wasn't given a reason. I was less annoyed than I had been with Ron earlier in the season because I understood that the new manager had to give everyone a chance. I didn't feel as if I'd had a fair run but I knew that it was up to me to improve the manager's impression of me and I think I did that by the application and form I showed in the reserves. A run of four goals in six games in March and April put me back in contention and I made two substitute appearances in our last two away games at Tottenham and Coventry City. By this time we had at least climbed in to mid-table, with no danger of relegation and no chance of success elsewhere. In the League Cup, Southampton's 4-1 win over us had spelt the end for Ron and one of those January games I'd played in was the very disappointing FA Cup defeat at home to Coventry. I was however given a start in our last game and we finished the season on a high - I scored our first goal in a 3-1 win, hooking in a goal in front of the Stretford End.

The last thing I wanted in those circumstances was to be in a situation where I was out of the team again but I'd unwittingly created one by agreeing to get married. It had been arranged when Ron was at the club and I'd organised the date of the honeymoon so it didn't clash with pre-season training. Of course, as you have probably predicted, when Fergie came in he changed the pre-season dates to two weeks earlier. He said it wouldn't be a problem but I'm not too sure it didn't have some influence on his decision to not even consider me for selection until we played Tottenham at the end of September. The hours spent running to keep my fitness up on honeymoon clearly didn't count for much which was ironic when I look back and think that I was probably influenced by the manager talking about settling down and how it would be better for us if we were.

I'd been seeing a Salford girl called Jackie and I got it into my head that getting married would be the best thing. Looking back, I don't think I was ready. I'd been with her since from pretty soon after moving up from Wales and I think what was in my head was making that sort of commitment would perhaps show that I was more settled and mature. There was no real practical way of rebooking the honeymoon because we were getting married and then going away – to rearrange would mean to reschedule it for the following summer. That said, if he had suggested that I would have done what he said and put it back until the following summer a year. Punctuality was a huge thing for Fergie; you had to be there early or on the dot at the latest. It's a good trait to have and it leaves a lasting impression. There is the story of Roy Keane behaving exactly the same way when he was at Sunderland and Pascal Chimbonda – who he'd just signed – turning up late. That was it, the bus left without him, and he was dropped. The message was clear, if you're late, you'll miss the bus, and sometimes in more ways than one.

Despite the gaffer's reassurance that it would be okay, I started the 1987/88 season in the reserves. Now he had spent half a year with the squad he was probably fully aware of what we all brought to the team. He was also aware of what was lacking and tried to address that by bringing in Brian McClair from Celtic. 'Choccy' had scored 126 goals in just four years at Celtic – and came to us on the back of a 41-goal season. He was 24, so was only going to get better, and he gave a prominent goal threat that we'd been missing since Sparky had gone.

However the boss's first signing was Viv Anderson, the experienced Arsenal defender, who arguably had a bigger impact as far as the dressing room went. With our form not really pulling up any trees since Ron had been sacked, a positive atmosphere had instead become one that was maybe too competitive. Viv's arrival immediately changed that. He was loud, sociable and friendly, and it immediately brought the laughs and jokes back to the group. We all contributed to that as much as Viv, although he relaxed everyone around him. When we played Arsenal in the league game I'd played in January, it all kicked off – I clipped David

Rocastle in a tackle and he then went straight into Norman with a two-footer. Rocastle was sent off and Viv was right up in Norman's face, screaming at him. All the while Norman's not saying a dicky bird. So when Viv arrived we cleared all the tables in the dressing room and said to them both, 'Right, let's get that fight on now!' He took it in good humour. I think it's fair to say that Viv isn't really recognised as a signing who was pivotal to transforming our fortunes on the pitch (though that is not to say that his experience didn't improve us) but his personality and attitude had an impact on morale that is unquantifiable. It's why, a few years later, one of Robbo's first acts as Middlesbrough manager was to bring in Viv as his assistant. He had been manager at Barnsley and when he came to Boro he didn't do an awful lot of coaching but he had a similar impact there as he did when he came to United. He improved the atmosphere in the dressing room.

Brian McClair, on the other hand, was quiet and reserved – he was incredibly intelligent and had a very, very dry sense of humour. He had just won the Golden Boot with Celtic and his arrival essentially said that United were there to compete for the best names which was a big boost considering there'd been a while where we'd bought poorly and lost our big name striker. Above almost all else, I think the most important aspect of Manchester United's title-winning teams has been those players who are capable of breaking through defences. Players like Andrei Kanchelskis, Lee Sharpe, Ryan Giggs, David Beckham and Cristiano Ronaldo. It only matters so much if you have good strikers in your team – because you need the delivery and you need penetration. We apparently almost had that in the summer of 1987; it has come to light in recent years that we were offered the opportunity to sign John Barnes from Watford. John had all of the attributes to have made a great winger for us, just as he did eventually for Liverpool. The gaffer said that he turned the chance to sign Barnes down because he still had faith in Jesper Olsen; that's fair enough, although I don't think I'm alone in wondering just how quickly a league title might have returned to Old Trafford if the manager had believed differently.

The Hairdryer

THE 1987/88 SEASON brought with it an increase in the number of substitutions from one to two, meaning that in theory there would be greater opportunities for game time for those of us on the fringes of the squad. Not that it helped me in the first quarter of the season as I didn't get a sniff! I always found the advent of substitutes to be a curious thing. I support it in terms of conditioning and keeping players fit and healthy but it makes me wonder how it came to be seen as necessary - surely there should have been some sort of endemic of games finishing with eight and seven players because of all of the players who got injured and couldn't continue. Even with the extra subs allowed, I wasn't getting in the squad, but I started the season well for the reserves, scoring twice in the first three games - my goal return was generally pretty good at that level, I'd scored 37 times in 130 reserve appearances by the end of that season, though going into it, I'd only played 33 first team games.

Just as it began to feel as if I was being phased out, I was suddenly recalled into the squad to play against Tottenham and as luck would have it Viv Anderson was forced off at half time and I was in at right back. I stayed in the team for the draw down on the Astroturf at Luton and was back on the bench against Sheffield Wednesday. Robbo had scored at both ends in the first half and I came on for Kevin Moran at half time - McClair scored a few minutes into the second half before I made the game secure for us on the hour mark; it was a pretty nice goal, I overlapped Gordon, he rolled me in and I struck it well.

So, just like that I was back in the side with no explanation offered - or sought - and I was enjoying my football in a team that were gaining some kind of momentum. We had lost just once in our first fifteen games - at Everton, the reigning Champions - but we'd drawn eight games and that would prove to be our downfall. Down at Wimbledon

My dad (captain in the centre of the middle row) in Britons Ferry Boys Club under-18s. He was 17 at the time, he went on to play against the likes of John Charles in a great amateur career..

And here's my old man (far right) meeting Hopalong Cassidy!

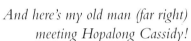

Me and mum, 1965; El Matador; with a lion cub and at a BBQ with my mum and dad.

TOP: *Wearing QPR colours as a young lad, with my grandparents and my cousin Gary; Football daft as I practice in our back garden in Neath.*

LEFT: *With Dave Bynon, the Chelsea scout and Adrian Mills who went to Swansea City.*

BELOW: *Recognise the driver? Ray 'Butch' Wilkins, then of Chelsea, soon to be Man United midfielder! This was taken from when I had trials down at Stamford Bridge*

TOP: With Mark Bowen, Darren Gale and on the right, Mike Smith, then Welsh team manager.

MIDDLE: With a young Sparky after we lost 2-3 to West Germany; Enjoying a laugh onboard a ferry with some of the Welsh lads: Mark Bowen, Darren Gale and 'Bonzo' Jones.

BOTTOM: With the Welsh schoolboys - I'm the 14 year old sat among the 18 year-olds.

TOP: *A proud day, signing for Manchester United, as my Mum and Granddad watch on; Suited and booted in official club blazer;*

MIDDLE: *My old man took this pic as I was preparing to play for United's reserves. His smile was as wide as mine.; No words are neccessary!*

LEFT: *With fellow United reserves Stephen Pears and Mark Dempsey.*

MANCHESTER UNITED YOUTH TEAM 1981-82

GOOD LUCK ON MONDAY NIGHT

On Monday night Eric Harrison takes the Youth team to the North East for the FA Youth Cup semi-final second leg against Sunderland at Roker Park.

A draw will be sufficient to take United into the Final where they will meet the successful team from the other semi-final, Watford.

It is 18 years since we reached the Final, so in wishing the youngsters all the best for Monday we take this opportunity to have a look at the players on which our hopes rest.

PHILIP HUGHES (Goalkeeper) Philip's record in this season's FA Youth Cup speaks for itself, for he has conceded just one goal in the eight games so far. Belfast-born he is a former Northern Ireland Schoolboy international who has also gained Youth honours for his country.

BILLY GARTON (Defender) Local boy born in Salford he is in his second year as an apprentice with United. A former Salford Boys defender, he made his Central League debut on the opening day of this season against Wolves. Billy has played in all this season's Youth games.

ANDY HILL (Defender) Born Sheffield. Played for Sheffield Boys before joining United as an apprentice. A tall, strong defender he has filled the right-back berth in six of the ties. Has turned out regularly for the 'A' and 'B' sides this season.

GRAEME HOGG (Defender) Born Aberdeen. Graeme is the Youth team captain and together with Billy Garton forms a central defence of considerable height and strength. Another ever present, he made his Central League debut last month in the 3-1 win at Stoke City.

ANDREW ROBINSON (Defender) Another local product who was born in Oldham. An England Schoolboy international he has played most of his games for United in the 'B' team but occasionally has stepped up to appear for the 'A' team. Has played in five of the Youth Cup games, including three as substitute.

KEN SCOTT (Defender) Born Belfast. Ken missed the opening match against Walsall but was selected for the third round tie against Liverpool and has been a fixture at left back ever since. He is a Northern Ireland Schoolboy international.

CLAYTON BLACKMORE (Midfield) Former Welsh Schoolboy international he was born in Neath, South Wales. Currently a member of the Welsh Youth team he made his FA Youth Cup bow against Tottenham Hotspur in the second leg of last season's semi-final. Central League experience has been limited to one substitute appearance against Burnley last November.

MARK DEMPSEY (Midfield) The only Manchester born member of the Youth team. He has made great strides since signing apprentice forms almost two years ago. An ever-present in the team he scored the winner against Leeds United in the fourth round replay. February, this year, was a good month for Mark, he became a full-time professional and also made his Central League debut at Derby.

LAWRENCE PEARSON (Midfield) Although his birthplace was Newcastle-upon-Tyne, Lawrence played his Schoolboy representative football for Sheffield, in the same side as Andy Hill. An elegant midfield player he has also appeared as a winger. He is United's top scorer in the competition with three goals.

MICHAEL ROWBOTHAM (Midfield) Michael is the second member of the squad whose birthplace is Sheffield and the third to win Schoolboy honours for that city. Has only made one appearance in the Youth team to date and that was against Leeds United in the fourth round at Elland Road.

SEAN WILLIAMS (Midfield) Sean began his United career as a full-back but has recently moved into midfield with a good deal of success. A tenacious little player, he has appeared in all, but one, of the games. He was a member of last years team.

PETER DOCHERTY (Forward) Born London and younger son of former manager Tommy. Peter hit the headlines following his surprise selection for the semi-final first leg, a fortnight ago. Prior to that he had only made a handful of appearances in the Lancashire League sides. He is a left winger of whom a great future is expected.

MARK HUGHES (Forward) Born Wrexham, North Wales. Played for his country as a Schoolboy and is at present a Youth international. Like Graeme Hogg, he has appeared in every FA Youth Cup tie over the last two seasons. He topped the United scorers list in the competition last season. Made his Central League debut against Coventry City in March 1981 and just recently scored four goals for the 'B' team in a match at Preston.

NORMAN WHITESIDE (Forward) The third Belfast-born member of the team. Norman has played for Northern Ireland Schoolboys and is a current Youth international for his country. He is yet another who has already made his debut for the Central League side. That was against Nottingham Forest in February. In his second Reserve game he scored twice in a 4-1 victory at Sheffield Wednesday.

NICK WOOD (Forward) Born Oldham. He has played for his home town as a Schoolboy and Nick has made a number of appearances for United's 'A' team this season, but in the main his outings have been with the 'B' side. Made his debut in the Youth team as a substitute against Walsall last November.

11   (CLIFF BUTLER)

ABOVE: A proud Welshman with his first cap following a 4-2 defeat in Norway; Me and Big Norm when we were apprentices. Norman went on to break all kinds of records as a teenager when we cheered him on during the 1982 World Cup.
LEFT: An article in The United Review about our upcoming FA Youth Cup semi-final against Sunderland.
The squad was: Phillip Hughes, Billy Garton, Andy Hill, Graeme Hogg, Andrew Robinson, Ken Scott, myself, Mark Dempsey, Lawrence Pearson, Michael Rowbotham, Sean Williams, Peter Docherty, Mark Hughes, Norman Whiteside and Nicky Wood.

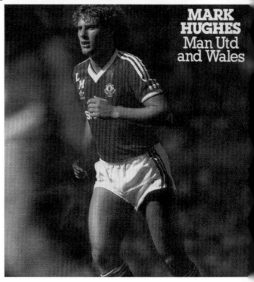

TOP: *A newspaper picture story about United's multi-national (but still all British Isles) team.*

MIDDLE: *My first team debut at Nottingham Forest sandwiched between European Cup winners Ian Bowyer and Viv Anderson in May 1985; Here I am taking on a very good West Ham team who very nearly won the title in 1986 following a late surge. We lost this cup tie 2-1.*

RIGHT: *A case of mistaken identity!*

ABOVE: 'Sunbed' is not a nickname I enjoy but I suppose it's well earned here as the lads relax on a summer break to the Carribean with Sparky, Steve Pears, Mickey Duxbury and Alan Davies in Montego Bay.

RIGHT: It was an honour to be Sparky's best man.

BELOW: Sparky's new Audi Quattro was a bit of an upgrade on his Vauxhall Viva Mexico that he used to drive us to Welsh games in. One time he had been pushing the pedal down that hard for 3 hours straight that he ended up with a hamstring injury!

TOP: *Fergie's first training session - at first I couldn't understand him!*
LEFT: *The change of manager turned out to be good news for me as I was soon making more first team appearances including this encounter with former Welsh schoolboys team mate Mark Bowen at Norwich.*
BELOW: *More drinking! This time with Sparky and Micky Duxbury.*

on 21st November, I scored a free kick midway through the second half but they quickly equalised and it looked as if the game was petering out into a stalemate. With three minutes to go the gaffer brought off Deiniol Graham, a young forward, for Liam O'Brien, a midfielder. Wimbledon's response was immediate; they pumped the ball forward, throwing everything at us, and they benefitted right away, scoring in the 88th minute to win the game.

It was disappointing, obviously, to lose but we maintained our momentum and I was feeling much better about how things were going. I was back in the first team on New Year's Day, coming on as a substitute midway through the second half in a 0-0 home draw with Charlton Athletic. By that time we'd strengthened our squad further still; after trying and failing to sign Terry Butcher we brought in a rhino in the box of our very own, Steve Bruce from Norwich. When he was younger he'd played some games up front and so he was a very dominant force in both boxes. He was also a great organiser and talker on the pitch and settled in showing his authority straight away.

Our league form continued to be pretty good and a run of four league wins gave us great momentum going into an FA Cup 5th round tie with Arsenal. In Division One, we were twelve points behind Liverpool who were still unbeaten from the start of the season but with our form improving and the fact we still had to play at Anfield, I think the manager believed that we might have half a chance. Then we lost that Arsenal game and the knock-on effect on our league form wasn't great as we drew at Spurs and lost at Norwich to give Liverpool a huge seventeen point advantage. The defeat against Norwich was difficult to take but it felt as if there was a collective anxiety among the players. We were on a good run but it seemed even our best might not be good enough to catch Liverpool. And when you become worried about things like that, you begin to worry about the decisions you're making in a game. You become more cautious of losing and more hesitant in your attacking. Maybe, if I'm honest, we were also haunted by the memory of what normally happened to us whenever we hit a good run of form. The ten game run was the perfect example - we win ten, then worry about losing our record of wins, draw a couple because we are creating our own problems and that invites pressure.

Our next game was against Sheffield Wednesday and the manager was in a fiery mood. 'Do your own fucking team-talk!' he said before the match – we'd had the famous 'hairdryer' before (I think we might have had one in the first couple of months) but they were usually in reaction to a bad result not before a home game. We were obviously disappointed and we didn't need telling. We all had our heads down, sheepishly looking across at Robbo to stand up and be the one and to be fair to him, he did it. 'You pick him up, you do this, you remember to do that.' He finishes and says to us all to get changed. The gaffer steps back in and yells, 'Is that fucking it? Is that fucking it?'

Our response was strong – we got a corner in the first minute, and Strachan took it low to me. As it came across my body, I struck it well into the top corner; it was probably one of the best shots I've ever hit. McClair scored after seven minutes to give us a really strong start and we took the 2-0 lead into half-time, when the manager went berserk again, apparently it was just a coincidence we played well. We won that one 4-1.

I don't know if it's because the pressure of the expectation to chase Liverpool's lead had gone but we went unbeaten for the rest of the season, winning eight and drawing two of our last ten games, starting with that win over Wednesday. We achieved comfortable wins at home against West Ham and Derby before we went to Anfield in a game in which Liverpool could effectively win the title. We didn't need a team talk to fire us up on that occasion and we took the lead early on again when Robbo scored in front of our fans. In the space of ten minutes either side of the break Liverpool turned it around to get a 3-1 lead and to make matters worse Colin Gibson was shown a second yellow shortly after and it looked as if the game was up. Me and Dux were brought off for Whiteside and Olsen with the gaffer going bold to chase the game; Norman was straight into the thick of it taking out Steve McMahon and John Barnes. The substitutes were involved in the build up to the goal that got us back in the game, Robson's effort from 25 yards deflected in. Gordon Strachan was then sent through to equalise and celebrated with that cigar pose, as if it had all been a piece of cake.

There was absolutely no level of football that we could accept losing to Liverpool at, regardless of whether it was a game like this, where they could wrap up the title at our expense, or a reserve game – and I found reserve games against Liverpool to be as intense as first team games for other clubs.

They didn't have too long to wait to win the league but we still enjoyed a good end to the season, winning all of our five remaining games. We played Wimbledon at home in our last game; the problem with playing against them was that the games were so confrontational and full-on that you would quickly be dragged down to their level. They'd qualified for the FA Cup Final and I remember the lads saying in the changing room that if we were in their situation and we were down at Plough Lane, they'd be preparing to kick lumps out of us. We subsequently kicked lumps out of them and won 2-1.

My contract was due for renewal and as I was negotiating with the club, I was approached by Manchester City manager Mel Machin who asked if I might be interested in moving to Maine Road. He asked me to meet him down at a hotel near West Brom's ground. I don't know why but I agreed to do it out of courtesy, even though I had no real intention of leaving United, even for more money. I knew they had players on a couple of grand a week and that was a lot more than I was on at the time. Maybe that's a case of more fool me for not having an agent. He talked about making me captain and how it would be great if I did move to City but I obviously can't have looked too keen because he finished the meeting with an offer.

'Let's play a round of golf and if you beat me, you stay at United, and if I beat you, you come to City,' he said.

I called him the next day and thanked him for his offer but said I wanted to stay where I was. Everybody in football knows just how different Manchester United are compared to any club in Britain. After Old Trafford all the other stadiums just aren't as big. You don't ever want to leave, really. And, at that time, there was reason to be genuinely excited about the future, a huge turn around from just twelve months before. In the November, I had been in Denmark to play a European Championship qualifier and so I was obviously rooming with Sparky; I was told by the gaffer, who'd come to watch the game, to subtly suggest we would be interested in bringing him back. Mark was so good and had been sorely missed. By the end of the season, the deal was done, and nobody was more delighted than me.

Return of the Radar

THE BOSS BROUGHT IN ANOTHER familiar face for the 1988/89 season, Jim Leighton. At the time I remember Scottish goalkeepers getting a fair bit of stick and I didn't think it was totally unwarranted. The gaffer knew Jim from their days together at Aberdeen and to be fair to Jim, he was better than I expected. He was a better shot stopper, anyway. He wasn't brilliant with his feet - with the way the game has gone, I don't think he would have been a top goalkeeper now because you need to be a better footballer since the law change. Before he came down his reputation had preceded him; I heard stories about how opposition teams would put two players on the edge of his penalty area when Aberdeen were taking goal kicks. He had a strange technique where his left knee would go low down, like he didn't know how to kick properly. There was also a question mark over his ability to claim crosses. He just didn't move his feet quickly enough and that affected his ability to spring high enough so he would just take a step and dive because he couldn't do anything else. Good distribution wasn't something that was commonly seen as a major thing for keepers in those days but I'd been used to playing with Neville Southall for Wales and could tell the difference it made. We later signed Peter Schmeichel who took it to a whole other level and in recent years United have had the luxury of having David De Gea who for my money is one of the best ever with his feet. We also had Fabien Barthez for a time who was brilliant - he just liked to take too many risks though to be fair it did take him a year before those risks started to cost us. If the gaffer thought, in 1988, that we needed a new goalkeeper because Gary Bailey and Chris Turner weren't good enough then fair enough, I just wasn't sure Jim was the necessary upgrade.

He got off to a good start with five clean sheets in his first six games - the only goal he conceded was a penalty in our second league game, at Anfield, which we frustratingly lost. We'd kicked the season off at home to QPR but were held to a 0-0 draw; Paul Parker, who would later come to United, was all over Sparky like a rash. At least, after going to Liverpool, we won five games out of the next six to get the season up and running. I was getting games, alternating between the full back positions. My longest runs in the team either came on right midfield or at left back which, when you think about it, is a pretty odd one. Most players will say they enjoy attacking more than defending and I was no different. I enjoyed being in a position where I could be creative with the way I crossed the ball – I think I had good technique on my crosses (Beckham had to learn from somebody, right!) and had developed an instinct for the timing of Sparky's movement. What stood me in good stead was that instinct was strong wherever I was on the pitch and even from left back I was usually able to find Mark or know the runs he was going to make. He called it 'radar'; I'd been playing with him for almost a decade and I'd like to think it showed. In late October of his first season back I set up a goal for him at Everton which summed up our relationship; I floated the ball into an area I just expected him to get to, and once he did arrive, he finished in the acrobatic way that only he could.

Mark took to life back at the club like he'd never been away and struck up a very good partnership with McClair. Choccy was a great predator and many of his goals from the previous season (he scored 31) seemed to be tap-ins from rebounds of Peter Davenport shots. He would always stand in front of the goalkeeper at set-pieces because, instinctively, most shots in a game go towards the goalie. So he'd be there for the diversion or deflection. I wouldn't say he was the most clinical finisher but he had an assurance about his play that meant it didn't matter if he missed one, he'd be comfortable taking the next chance on. It was a great attitude to have. There's a saying in football of players either being a great goalscorer or a scorer of great goals and we were fortunate enough to have one of each in our front line. Mark also had a knack of being there when it mattered. I always used to say to him that he should have brought out a video of '100 ridiculous goals' because there were so many he scored that only he could have. His thighs gave him the ability to hit with such power – there were goals he scored with his left foot from outside of the area which flew into the top corner. He was an absolute freak. Psychologically, though, he was always up for the big games and he was always there for the big moments – he didn't shy away and that's a quality you need to have if you want to enjoy the sort of career he had, and also, if you are to go down in history for a club like Manchester United.

Having kept the club's wallet closed for so long the gaffer was now spending quite a bit and he brought in Ralph Milne, another player he'd known from Scotland, to bolster the left hand side, having already brought in young Lee Sharpe from Torquay United earlier in the year. Ralph received a lot of criticism and maybe Old Trafford was too big a stage for him; I thought he did okay but maybe he was expected to go on and be better than he was at Dundee United and for whatever reason it didn't happen. Being at United you don't get much of an opportunity to hide away; the press were quickly on his back and he was unable to turn it around.

As great as it was to have bounced back from the loss at Anfield our form was a bit of a red herring; two of those five wins came against Rotherham United in the League Cup and, despite Mark's return, in those first few weeks we weren't scoring more than one or two goals per game. Those one or two goals were generally shared between the strikers.

The gaffer was a great thinker and I'm inclined to believe that he didn't know ahead of time just how good Mark was. He hadn't witnessed at close quarters the number of qualities to his game, so he hadn't been able to appreciate the things he could do that could improve the team. His ability to bring others into play, for me, had a huge influence on the way the gaffer would build our team moving forward. He played McClair a bit deeper because he knew he would be able to join up with Mark when he was holding the ball up but the best way to exploit him was to send two or three other players up too.

I think it would be fair to say that with all the changes that were starting to impact the team, we were struggling to discover our own identity. After beating Rotherham we went more than two months without a win, although we drew a lot of those games. I've said a lot about the things I thought we could have done better but it was a tough division and if you were not at your best for whatever reason then results would be hard to come by. I remember playing a game in the middle of that run down at Derby County's Baseball Ground. We drew 2-2 and there was a lot of pressure on Sharpey who was coming back from injury and expected to immediately transform our form. He was just eighteen and that ground had a notoriously boggy pitch. It was shocking. It makes it easier to stop somebody playing. Lee had made an immediate impact down the left because he was so direct – I think it was his form which convinced the gaffer to sell Jesper that November – but in the time Sharpey had been out of the side, it seemed as if the rest of the division had become wary of the news that we had a winger with frightening pace and so they were determined to stop him at all costs. He'd only been in the side a few weeks and it was a lot of pressure for him to come back into but, fair play to him, he dealt with it quite quickly. I got the impression – probably from the gaffer being a centre forward in his playing days – that he was keen to see more crosses played into the area and I don't think it's a coincidence that he went out and bought a few wingers, another was Giuliano Maiorana who came in around the time Jesper left, although his journey to United was a lot steeper than most others, coming from non-league Histon. Jules was a bit different to Sharpey, he would keep his head down and use his skill to beat a number of players. Lee was more of an athlete, he'd run for forty or fifty yards with or without the ball and play the ball in.

Sharpe had played his way into the first team set up but that winter we were also hit by an injury crisis which wiped out most of our midfield. I was the most senior midfielder left standing and even I missed a few games over Christmas. A lot of youngsters came into the team way before they expected their opportunity. Deiniol Graham and Lee Martin had played a handful of games between them but the likes of Russell Beardsmore, Tony Gill and David Wilson were thrust into the limelight with Jules and the group were dubbed 'Fergie's Fledglings' in the press. I knew from my own journey that it took some time before I felt as if I was part of the first team squad – maybe I didn't even until

Fergie arrived, and that was a fair while after I'd made my debut. I couldn't imagine how these guys felt coming in, in the middle of a season, as young as they were. Strangely enough, being the senior player in the middle of the park gave me a new found self-confidence and against all odds we enjoyed our best run of the entire season in very trying circumstances. I scored the goal which kicked off the first of six consecutive wins - a 3-0 win against Millwall, a nice strike from the edge of the area after good play between Mark and Brian.

It's ironic that our best run that season came with the kids in, particularly considering the transition period the club was in. As well as letting Jesper go, the gaffer sold Peter Davenport, Gordon Strachan, and was also looking for buyers for Paul McGrath and Norman Whiteside. The manager was probably getting calls left, right and centre about Paul's activities the day before most games and he decided that enough was enough, he didn't need the headache. The frustrating thing was that when he was sold, at the start of the following season, he came back from the summer looking the best he had in years. It was like the message had got through he was at the front of every race in training, he was looking sharp, and I was imagining how things would be with him alongside Steve Bruce for a full season but it was too late for him. For Norman it wasn't his drinking but the fact he suffered a terrible Achilles injury the previous year and when he came back he was struggling to get around the pitch. It was deflating to see that he couldn't do the same things which had previously made him such an outstanding player - particularly as he was so combative off the ball and had such quality on it. Paul suffered with knee injuries too but I think he got away with it a little more because of where he played. It's not to say it's an easy position but in midfield, where you are expected to be aggressive - and Norman had been - it was difficult for all of us to see that he couldn't be anymore. For me, Norman's best position was up front. I thought he was a better finisher than Mark. For him to have come through the inevitable comparisons to George Best and then establish a name for himself in his own right illustrated the kind of character he was. He was up for sale at the club for a year before Everton signed him and it was very difficult to see him go - this was a lad I'd grown up at the club with in similar circumstances and it was obviously very sad it had to end the way it did.

The manager had made it clear from day one that he wasn't going to stand for people crossing the line and with two years at the club under his belt, he clearly felt secure enough in the third year that he could make such huge changes. To get rid of five first team players simply put weight behind the threat, though strangely enough, with the run of games I was getting, I was the most secure I had ever been. Maybe the gaffer felt he had no option but to make those changes, or he would have undermined himself by saying he wouldn't stand for it but letting the players get away with it. It didn't matter their profile - and the profile doesn't come any bigger than being a Manchester United first teamer - for one reason or another, five of that team were gone in the space of a year. Selfishly, with so many of them being midfielders, that theoretically meant even more chances for me.

Off the pitch the manager might have been feeling more comfortable in making the big decisions - he must have had assurances from the board - but on it things did not go well for us at all in the second half of the season. The results were dreadful, as we lost eight of our last thirteen games to finish 11th - sandwiched between Millwall and Wimbledon, which was simply not good enough. It was also four years without a trophy as we suffered defeat in two controversial Cup games - first in the League Cup at Wimbledon, which got so nasty Viv Anderson received a ban afterwards, and then in the FA Cup, when Brian McClair scored against Nottingham Forest in the Sixth Round but the referee said it didn't cross the line. It had been a very unlucky and difficult year all round, packed with tough decisions for the manager. Of the kids who came in and did well, once the early momentum had fizzled out and the reality of playing at that level week in, week out hit home, the gaffer then had to make the tough call of who to phase in, who to phase out and who to continue giving opportunities to. I was part of that cycle too, playing in some reserve games as the manager was trying to get the right system towards the end of the season. Because of the difficulty of that situation and the quite drastic turnaround of players, it meant a lot of players were coming back into the team with the injury they'd gone out with. You want to play and that means grinning and bearing it and sometimes faking it a little in order to get in the team. I once rushed back from a medial ligament injury and every single time I was tackled I felt as if I was being shot in the knee. That knee still gives me grief thirty years later from time to time. It's the short term sacrifice you make to prove yourself without thinking of the long-term consequences.

As far as the season went as a whole, we never got a chance to get into our stride and our hopes of building on our second place finish of the previous year were quite clearly misplaced. Regardless of the circumstances which had contrived to make that the case, the pressure was definitely on the gaffer going into the season that would turn out to be pivotal for many reasons.

The Real Saviour

FOOTBALLERS START EVERY SEASON with a blank page and the most obvious thing is you are hoping for the perfect season; ideally you'd love to win every game and win every trophy, while realistically, at Manchester United, you're at least expect to be challenging for a trophy, ideally the league. There were so many changes and transitions with personnel, attitudes and philosophies, that we probably should have expected a little more turbulence to affect us before we settled down. And, did I mention the pitch! That was still an issue left unresolved. Some changes were temporary - players who came in to do a job but didn't stay for a long while. Others were a little more permanent and while difficult to get used to at first, were obviously going to help us in the long run. The diet, as I've discussed, was a big thing, but the gaffer also did things differently in training. Just about every club starts training with boxes these days - you make a box of ten yards by ten yards, put seven or eight players around the edge of it and one or two in the middle and their objective is to try and win the ball. The outside players are only allowed one touch. I think something as relatively simple as that helped us improve massively because it improved our awareness and ability in receiving and distributing the ball.

I've taken that into my own coaching with the Welsh schoolboys and I can remember some of the other coaches complaining to make the box bigger because, to them, it wasn't working. At first they struggled. They had to get used to it; you can't expect them to do it straight away. The benefits from that form of training would stay with them for long afterwards.

There was a lot of speculation about a takeover of the club from Michael Knighton. He came down to the Cliff to introduce say hello. He was walking around with his hand in his blazer as if he was Napoleon; it was all very strange. It got stranger still as he turned up on the opening day of the season for our game against the Champions, Arsenal. I remember that the gaffer was annoyed with us because we'd played golf on the Thursday but it didn't seem to affect our performance too much as we won the game, convincingly, 4-1 - if anything, after that, the boss was probably more pissed off with Knighton who got the headlines for changing into a United kit, doing kick-ups and volleying the ball into the empty net at the Stretford end. It was a bit like a circus, a little boy realising a childhood dream. Perhaps Fergie was annoyed because he had an inkling of what was revealed by Graeme Souness in 2016 when the then Rangers boss claimed that Knighton had told him he would make him United manager. I'm not sure how welcome he would have been with his Liverpool history, and considering how he did at Liverpool when he succeeded Kenny Dalglish as manager but it makes you think just how close the club came to ditching Fergie.

With so many senior players having departed during the 1988/89 season (and Paul and Norman going in the August of 1989) it was obvious that the gaffer would bring in senior replacements. In 1995 when he did a similar turnover and didn't bring anyone in, that was because he clearly had faith in the youngsters breaking through at the time but in 1989, that wasn't the case, so Mike Phelan and Neil Webb came in. Webb scored a great goal on his debut in that game against Arsenal. Both were midfielders but Mike could also play at full back. It was more competition for places but I didn't see it as my place being under threat as, since that run in January, I'd started to feel as if I was one of the more established players in the squad. Obviously, it crossed my mind that they played in similar positions but all that did was resolve my focus to keep my performance levels as high as I could. I was in at left back from the start of the season - but any inflated hopes of glory were quickly let down by the fact that we brought our terrible form from the old season into the new one. Maybe that much was predictable because of the continued transition but we had hoped the problems had been confined to just one awful season. The Arsenal result could possibly be put down to the fact that we had a lot of time to dwell about what had happened to us in the last season, a lot of time to be frustrated, and a lot of determination to put it right. The fact that it was them, considering our difficult recent history with them, might have helped.

We continued to strengthen, bringing in Gary Pallister from Middlesbrough. It might have seemed like a strange move bringing in a centre-half from a team that were relegated – especially breaking the transfer record for a defender – but Pally had won the Player of the Year award for his own performances despite their troubles and that goes some way to saying how impressive he was. As I mentioned earlier, I credit Pally with being one of the most important signings we ever made. I would go as far as to say he was potentially more crucial than Eric Cantona. The reason for that is, by the time things turned around to the point we won the league, I think we more or less had everything in place. I'll talk about this later but when we lost the title to Leeds in 1992 nobody could convince me we weren't the better side. Eric provided the spark and the confidence that improved the side further but Pallister coming in addressed our main issue and helped us achieve results in games where we had struggled previously because of our lack of height. But even he needed some time to settle in. People remember that Nemanja Vidic and Patrice Evra struggled when they initially came to United and that was the same for Pally; some say he had a nightmare in his debut, against Norwich City, giving away a penalty but I don't think he was that bad. Those kind of things look bad but you have to understand that they do happen when a player moves to a new club. Look at Jaap Stam's first game for United – the Charity Shield against Arsenal. He got the run around from Nicolas Anelka that day but it didn't happen too often again after that. When a player comes in they have to get used to their new surroundings, there's a bit of anxiety to do your best, to not make a mistake… it was made worse by the fact that we were already losing and chasing the game, so you're making more rash decisions than you normally would.

We won against Millwall and then down at Portsmouth but even the victory at Fratton Park was underlined with concern; Jim Leighton came for a cross and palmed it into his own net, which didn't exactly instil confidence and was the worst thing possible for a defence who were trying to get to know one another. I had been out of the side for a couple of weeks – I missed that League Cup win at Portsmouth but

I was on the bench when we went to Maine Road in September and couldn't believe my eyes as we went in to half-time three-nil down. Lee Sharpe was a sub with me on the day and we expected to come on right there and then but the manager went ballistic at half-time telling the lads who started that they better get out there and fix the damage themselves. It didn't happen and we lost 5-1. I keep on talking about the transition we were going through but it was emphasised in this result – we had just signed Paul Ince and Danny Wallace and for them, as well as for most of that team, it was their first derby as City had been out of the top flight for a couple of seasons. City, on the other hand, was packed full of young local lads who were up for their biggest game for a few seasons.

The signing of Paul Ince ruffled a few feathers. His arrival from West Ham had been protracted. It was well known that the gaffer was trying to give his midfield a strong identity and had failed to convince Paul Gascoigne to sign the previous year. We had played against him for Newcastle and he gave us the run-around but he chose Spurs – I did eventually play with Gazza briefly up at Middlesbrough and it really would have been something if he had come to United. He didn't and, really, his talent was so rare that it was pointless trying to find someone like him. Ince wasn't like Gazza but he had a good reputation for his performances at West Ham but he arrived at United with a lot of confidence, 'I'm coming for your shirt,' he said to Bryan Robson, of all people, on his very first day at the club! That's confidence alright but it was hard to take him too seriously because of the enormity of that ambition. He told us he wanted to be called 'The Guvnor'. We all called him Incey – I think only the kit man called him 'Guv'. Despite that difficult first impression I generally got on alright with him. We did have a little wrestle once in the cafeteria at training. Out of nowhere he tried to bite me on the neck – we ended up scuffling all the way out into the corridor. It got quite aggressive although neither of us threw a punch. It was crazy. Maybe my own reaction was a little bit sensitive but he had previously bitten Jim McGregor on the arm and turned it black and blue. Within a week or two he's trying to biting me. He'd only been at the club a couple of months! In his defence, I would say that by that time we were bonding closely as a squad, developing the sort of spirit that would help us in later months and years and he and I did get on. We'd go out for a few drinks and there'd be no problems.

In all the time I was at United there was only that and one other time where I had any real disagreement with any of my team-mates. A few years prior, in a practice match, I went to tackle Remi Moses. Out of nowhere, Graeme Hogg came charging in on Remi and kicked him. There were three or four players around us and when the dust settled it was me and Remi looking at each other – he thought I'd been the one who kicked him so threw a punch and caught me flush on the cheekbone. Hoggy came clean and Remi apologised. Not bad, I suppose, to only have those two moments as being really negative ones and they're not really that negative, either.

Incey was a good player, not as good as he thought he was, in my opinion, but there were still elements of his game that I felt were under-rated by many. He was a very, very quick player. He had a race with Ryan Giggs once in training and beat him – quicker, on that occasion, without the ball, although Ryan of course could run that faster with the ball. Ince used that speed in his tackles and I thought that added a great dimension to our midfield. If there was one area of his game where he did compare to Robbo it was in his tackling because he was ferocious, committed, brave and quick. I remember he once went into a tackle with Vinny Jones and he wiped him out. I wasn't surprised at that so much as the speed at which he did it. Danny Wallace also had a great turn of pace – I used to hate playing against him when he was at Southampton – and I was pleased with his arrival as I thought he could add an extra direction to our forward play.

We followed up that loss at City with four wins from six games. I scored in the last of those wins, getting the winner at Luton Town to put us ninth. Apart from the first two games of the season, which don't really count, that was the highest we would get in the league all year. It was a good result to come back to because that week I'd suffered a miserable end to Wales' World Cup qualifying campaign for Italy 1990. We didn't stand much of a chance, really, in a group with Holland and West Germany but we went into the last game still capable of making life tough for the Germans, who had to beat us to be certain of qualification. We actually took the lead but they turned it around to 2-1, although in the last minute Mark Aizlewood – a defender – went into their box and got his head on a ball that seemed destined to fall for Mark Hughes. Aizlewood went close but couldn't put it in. Not that it mattered for us, really, but a point would have seen us at least finish third in the group instead of bottom. Germany went on to win it of course.

With the Heysel ban still in effect, international football was our only chance of playing against continental opposition and so I was able to test myself against the likes of Ruud Gullit and Thomas Hassler. It should have been enjoyable but because we weren't used to playing in Europe, we weren't used to European referees, and it became frustrating as they'd blow up for every little thing. I got booked in that Germany game for nothing. There were some benefits. I played for Manchester United which to me was a fair trade-off – I wouldn't have swapped that for European football elsewhere – but most of our players were internationals and so that experience helped us when we returned to play continental opposition. If anything, European teams were often caught by surprise by the work rate of British teams.

Beating Luton after the international break should have helped us carry on our momentum into the winter fixtures and I was on a high, as the goal was one of my better ones. McClair crossed it and I let it go across my body before hitting it on the volley with my left foot. Instead of giving us the impetus to improve, instead we hit our roughest period of the season losing four and drawing four of our next eight games, dropping to fifteenth going into the 1990s.

One of those draws came at Anfield – you could always count on us to get something there. The night before the Liverpool game a couple of days before Christmas we were winding down after our evening meal at the hotel and me, Pally and Sparky went to the shop to pick up some snacks. Pally was a bit of a chocoholic so was stocking up. We were making our way through a New Year's party – loads of people in dicky bows, that sort of thing – and Pally accidentally nudged some lad who was as tall as him. The guy turns around and for a split second I thought he must have known Gary because he started following Pally back to the lift. When he caught up with him he knocked his bottle of Ribena to the floor – I'm still thinking it must be his mate – but Pally turns around and is obviously as shocked as anyone would be. He didn't react, though, and instead bent down to pick up his bottle, and the lad kicks it away from him. Pally picks it up and walks back to the lifts, where Sparky had already pressed the button. When the lift came, we got in, and the lad's tried to get in.

'You're not coming in here,' Pally said.

'I am!'

'No you're not,' Pally says again as the guy is trying to force his way in. Gary punched him on the forehead and this guy is easily the same size as him but bigger – obviously not as athletic, shall we say. The guy gets hold of him and the two start wrestling outside the lift. They land against the wall inches away from one of the glass cabinets. If they'd hit it, it would have cut them to shreds. I jumped on the big guy to try and pull him off Pally and quickly I'm off the floor, with my arms wrapped around his. Pally could have leathered him but resisted the temptation and within seconds the hotel manager had come along trying to find out what had happened. This guy's wife is suddenly on the scene saying we started it but the gaffer arrived. I told him what happened, and he spoke to the hotel manager who kicked them out of the party. It wasn't ideal preparation for one of the biggest games of the season but we coped with it pretty well and got a goalless draw. Not a bad result but it's part of a run of five games in six without scoring a goal.

At this point it's only fair to look back on the comments I've made about transition and look at it in a different way. Pundits often mention that a club is 'in transition' as if all that is needed is time. Robbo was missing large chunks of that season through injury again but any time you get injuries to key players, it's going to affect your performances. The manager had been there for three years and there was speculation gathering in the press about his future. I, personally, didn't think he would be fired but I thought if the season finished badly then the following year he'd definitely be on borrowed time. I'm sure the gaffer benefitted from the support of the Chairman because to be fair to him, Fergie didn't panic, he did things just as he always had.

There's no getting away from the idea that every tie in the FA Cup that season felt like a final in itself. The first game in that run has almost become as famous as the final itself over the years. Just as many people remember that Mark Robins scored at Nottingham Forest in the third round as they remember Lee Martin scoring the winner in the final. Mark was a very good back up to have to Hughes and McClair. The one thing we lacked was an aerial threat up front and Mark didn't bring that; in fact, I couldn't really say that there was an area of his game where he excelled in comparison to our first choice forward line but his goalscoring instincts made him a very capable back up for either of them. He had a great knack of being able to score with both feet from inside the box.

In the build up to that game I can remember that the manager had been on Sparky's back about his tendency to hit passes with the outside of his foot. He was hammering him for it all of the time; and of course, what does Sparky do? He plays in Mark Robins with a superbly hit pass with the outside of his foot. We all gave the gaffer a bit of stick afterwards. Mark's winner at the City Ground gets a lot of press attention though, to be fair, losing to Nottingham Forest would hardly have been the disgrace that would have tipped the balance against the gaffer. We'd been beaten by the same team at home in the cup the previous season, after all. However, later that month, perhaps the pressure was very real. We lost our next two league games against Derby County and Norwich City before our fourth round tie at Fourth Division Hereford United.

I've complained about the state of pitches from this era but imagine a fourth-tier team who, in their wisdom, allowed a bull to run riot on the pitch before the game. I think it was the only game I've ever played that might be classed as having been played underwater! It was as bad as the fields I used to play on as a kid that had been damaged by a herd of horses. It was a terrible game and make no mistake about it, going into the last five minutes, with the game goalless, the manager was going to face some serious questions if Hereford had managed to snatch it. As it turned out Brian McClair dug the ball out of a puddle to find Mark Hughes and Micky Duxbury had made a late run into the penalty area - Sparky played the ball to him and Dux played it to me.

I had the fairly simple task of scoring a very important goal, although the state of the pitch meant even that wasn't as straightforward as you might expect. Being down at Hereford, my mum and dad had come to visit, though I don't think they would have enjoyed the stick me and Sparky were getting from the stands - "SHEEP, SHEEP, SHEEP SHAGGER". It made the goal all the sweeter - especially as they'd just broke out into a chorus of 'You'll Never Walk Alone' - I celebrated putting two V's up (for victory) in front of their supporters. No more 'sheep shagger', no more Liverpool songs. That was the heat of the moment and I immediately grimaced, worried about the repercussions from the FA. I dreaded looking at the newspapers the next day but all of the back pages had my arms outstretched, and my hands cut off. I have been a little critical of Jim Leighton so I have to also give a lot of credit to him - earlier in that game there had been a whistle blown in the crowd. We all stopped, thinking the referee had blown, but Hereford played on and Jim maintained his concentration and made two good saves. A whistle from the crowd could have cost us the game and the manager his job.

Talk of Hereford reminds me of a strange team-bonding exercise the boss had us on a few years later. It all started when we had a reserve game in Cornwall and the club would always take five or six first team players along wherever possible so that the club could get a bigger crowd and raise more money. We were flown in on a big red and white search and rescue RAF helicopter.

Ned Kelly, our head of security, kept saying he was one of the SAS boys in the Iranian Embassy Siege. We kept on at him, saying it was rubbish and there was no way he could prove it, and then he took us down to the SAS camp in Hereford. There were only about eleven of us and the manager. We actually stayed on the camp overnight. We had a go with the machine guns and then they threw some stun grenades into a room, the 'killing room'. The soldiers were talking to us about the stealth side of it, that you don't just run into the room and go mad. The room was set up like a normal room, a settee, and some wooden statues as human figures. They were talking to us about the room beforehand; because they always use live ammo, sometimes things don't go according to plan, and apparently some lad had been shot in the leg and died because they couldn't stop the bleeding. As the soldier is talking, he switches the light off and straight back on within two seconds. Two soldiers are stood right in front of us, out of nowhere, with their masks on. Ryan nearly jumped out of his skin, he absolutely shit himself. More of them burst in and shout to get our heads down; impulsively, the Gaffer lifts his head up to look and they banged it under the table! They were using live bullets!

We also went up in a helicopter with them, the same ones they used in the Falklands. They were showing us how they would bank when the engine stalled. It was absolutely terrifying. Incey went up and fair play to him because he was scared of flying. That night we went out for a drink with them and we drunk them under the table. At least we could beat them at that.

Fun and games aside, although those days were difficult there just wasn't the feeling on a game-by-game basis that the manager was under threat. It came to light that a section of the support weren't behind him but when it came to supporting the team they were always 100% there. They were amazing, especially on the road. Considering that all of our FA Cup games that season were played away from Old Trafford, maybe it was the fans, and not Mark, me, or Jim, who deserve the credit for turning things around. Their support away from home was the best.

I continued my goalscoring form in the next game – a diving header against City, from a Danny Wallace cross – I took a boot to the face in the process. I didn't feel it though, such was the euphoria of the goal. I could have snapped my leg and not known! To add insult to injury, though, they scored less than five minutes later to get a point. I played in our next game – a win at Millwall – and, just as things were picking up again, I picked up an injury in that game and was back in the reserves for a few weeks.

Still, it was exciting watching the team win at Newcastle in the 5th round and then Sheffield United in the sixth to set up the semi-final with Oldham Athletic. Those games too have gone down in folklore due to how back and forth the games went and the fact it took extra time in the replay to finally separate the sides. I think my form for the reserves hadn't gone unnoticed – I'd scored a couple of goals, again from full back – and I was back in the first team the week after the semi-final replay. It had been five years since our last trip to Wembley – proof positive that Ron's words of my 'time coming again' wasn't something I could take for granted, even if, technically, he was right – and I was desperate to make sure I was included this time. I always felt that the distribution of medals was a little bit unfair because it didn't always include all of those players who might have made a contribution earlier in the Cup run. It's the same as league medals, you have to play twelve games to qualify for a medal. They say it's a squad game so it's madness that some can miss out if they play, for example, eleven games and don't get one at the side of someone who does get one for playing twelve appearances. Federico Macheda didn't get one in 2009 but had such a huge influence on where the title went. It's also tough for reserve goalkeepers who rarely play but sit on the bench every game. I know the rules are a little looser these days and that's good news for those players but what for everyone else in the past? In the end, it came down to a choice between me and Mick Duxbury for a place on the bench. I was clearly delighted for myself but it was tough on Mick, who was leaving the club that summer. He's another example of a player who perhaps deserved a medal from that run, having set up my goal at Hereford and played in a few of the Cup games.

There was no indication beforehand that I was going to be involved. Our patchy form barely improved towards the end of the season and my appearances came mainly from the bench. I was a sub in our goalless draw with Wimbledon a couple of weeks before the final but that team included the likes of Mark Bosnich in goal, Viv Anderson – who, after giving good service to the club, was about to leave, too – and Colin Gibson, who hadn't been first choice for a while. Luckily Wimbledon didn't take the approach we had a couple of years earlier and we all came through it unscathed. Form-wise, I don't think there were many of us in the squad who were able to take our place for granted after such a miserable season in the league, which probably meant those of us who had made a contribution in the Cup were extra hopeful that it would be recognised when it came to the selection.

I was disappointed not to start but relieved to be named as a substitute. We'd finished above Crystal Palace - just - although when we'd both qualified for the final they had been above us. It was going to be a tough game and that was proven when their strengths and our weaknesses were exploited for the opening goal. They hit a free-kick in and Jim Leighton came off his line but didn't come for the ball - Gary O'Reilly was able to head over him into the net. Robson and Hughes scored for us before Palace brought on Ian Wright. He immediately made an impact, scoring an equaliser to take it to extra time. Almost immediately a cross came in from the left and Ian Wright had lost Bruce in the box. He was unmarked and finished the chance well. In the second half of extra time we played a short corner, Webb to Wallace, he passed it to me and I hit it first time from about 25 yards out. It just skimmed the crossbar. Then Sparky scored to earn us a replay when all seemed lost.

With a second chance at the trophy the manager clearly felt he had to be ruthless. He left out Jim and brought in Les Sealey, who had been brought in a couple of months back as cover. Les was a bit of a car salesman and he was forever rattling my cage. Every morning he came in hassling me about buying my Rolex watch. 'What do you want for your watch?' he asked every day. I gave in and he ended up buying it off me for £500. Les was a great character and a very experienced goalkeeper with a long spell at Luton Town. He had good feet as well. He maybe didn't have the stature of those who would follow him but he certainly had a presence about him and I think we needed that sort of confidence in order to not be as vulnerable as we had been in the first game. He was a great character to have around, a proper Cockney - in many respects, he had a similar impact to Viv Anderson.

In all, there were just two players who were in that FA Cup Final team who had been involved in our last trophy win in 1985 - Robson and Hughes, and even Hughes had left and come back. There had been a huge turnover of players in the intervening years and I was perhaps one of the best examples. The substitute appearance in the FA Cup Final was my 130th for the club and I'd played in lots of different positions. I had a good relationship with Mark Hughes but aside from that, it was very difficult to generate consistency when for whatever reason the team was changing from week to week. The most crucial part of success – and I have spoken a lot about external factors – is knowing your team-mates and I don't think it would be unfair to say that in 1990 our best eleven wasn't obvious to anyone.

For reasons that I explained earlier, even though I didn't get on in the replay, I still felt as if I'd earned my winner's medal. I still treasure it for what it is and I feel as if I was a part of that success. The most honest thing I can say about it is that I felt as if I'd accomplished that childhood dream of winning the FA Cup – it had been something I'd longed for as a kid, watching the full day coverage, waiting for the team news, watching the helicopters follow the coaches to the old Wembley Stadium and winning it at the old Wembley made it all the more sweet. To make the big walk up the tunnel on Cup Final day was very special, after the week's build up to it. The manager made some tough decisions and it becomes equally tough, as someone who missed out, to complain if he's proven right to have made those decisions. Jim couldn't complain because defensively we were sound in the replay and Les kept a clean sheet. I couldn't complain because Lee Martin, who I could feasibly have been playing instead of, scored the winning goal. And I say with complete sincerity that I was delighted when he scored. The success of players' careers is defined by the trophies they win.

Annus Mirabilis

CONSIDERING THE WAY the last two seasons had gone, even ending 1989/90 with the FA Cup didn't automatically generate the huge shift in mood and momentum that you might think. It gave us all a lift but we were not any surer of how the team would blend together long term and the knock-on effect from that was that none of us were guaranteed places in the team - bar, of course, a couple of notable exceptions. That was a good thing because we now had to justify our place in a winning team which presents a different sort of motivation. So when Denis Irwin signed from Oldham Athletic, I wasn't worried about my place in the team being under threat because of his arrival. Denis was an exceptional player but came in at right back and, though I had played there a little, it hadn't been very often.

I started that season in midfield - in Robbo's number seven shirt as he'd picked up another injury at the World Cup - but I eventually made my way back to left back where I enjoyed my best run and, most would say, my best form at United. I wouldn't disagree. I started in the best way possible, scoring at Wembley against Liverpool in the Charity Shield. We drew on the day, sharing the trophy - it makes me laugh when I hear people dismiss the Charity Shield, or Community Shield, as a game that doesn't matter. Every game is important, you add that to a chance of a medal, and add in that the game is played at Wembley and you can't take those occasions for granted. I can't understand the mentality of a player who would take it for granted. You see it with the League Cup and today with the Europa League. There are only so many trophies you can win. For Champions League clubs, it's understandable that you would use your squad for the League Cup games but for everyone else, I just don't get it. This is what you're playing football for. You spend all year trying to qualify for Europe and when you get there you rest your players for the league. That said, I can understand that it is difficult for managers these days. For some clubs it can take nineteen games to win the Europa League. Nineteen games! That's half a season! We're meant to be making it easier for players. But, anyway. Manchester United versus Liverpool at Wembley? There was no chance of it being a friendly. Even drawing against them was a bit of a disappointment, even though I was buzzing to have scored.

We won on the opening day - not quite the fanfare of the last season, against Arsenal - but a 2-0 win over Coventry City was a nice way to kick off. Still, missing Robson was bound to have an effect (and, to add to that, Sparky was missing a few games, too) and we dropped points over our next two games at Leeds and Sunderland. We drew at Elland Road and then suffered the blow of a last minute defeat at Roker Park. I played left wing in both of those games and I would guess that my work rate impressed the gaffer enough to think he could play me at left back. That's where I played down on Luton's plastic pitch and even though we won 1-0 on the day, we were one of the first casualties of the rule changes in the game over the summer when Steve Bruce was sent off for pulling an opponent down in what was deemed to be a goalscoring position. Before the season we'd all been gathered in the gym at the Cliff to go through the new rules and we listened and took it all in but the frustrating thing as a player was that these rules would come in and then halfway through the season they'd just stop. If you're going to book a player for pulling a shirt, fine. If you're going to send off a player for denying a goalscoring opportunity, fine. But at least be consistent and do it throughout the whole season. But as usual they didn't, and what you would find - especially in the 80s and 90s - was that at the start of the season, there would be a bunch of players who were made examples of, and then it would die down. It wasn't like players suddenly stopped pulling shirts or fouling. There was the ten yards for dissent rule. I thought that was brilliant - if a player is having a go at the ref, move the ball forward ten yards, don't book him. They stopped that too; why? That's one of the easiest ways of helping to get players to respect referees.

On that subject, the standard of referees is always a matter for debate.

In the modern game I think referees should disclose who they support. A few years back, in 2009, Everton played United in the FA Cup semi final when David Moyes was still manager at the Toffees. Before the game he comes out and says that referee Mike Riley is a Manchester United fan! I said at the time that there was just no way Riley should have been allowed to referee the game with those comments fresh in everyone's minds. What happens? Danny Welbeck goes around the keeper, he's got an open goal to slide the ball into but gets brought down. Riley doesn't give it because he knows he will get hung in the press. United lose the game – ironically enough, on penalties – but they don't just lose that, they lose the opportunity to become the first English team to win the domestic treble. They went on to play Barcelona in Rome in the Champions League Final as well. I'm not saying they would have won the FA Cup Final or against Barcelona but they had Wayne Rooney, Carlos Tevez, Dimitar Berbatov and Cristiano Ronaldo and they had the momentum of equalling Liverpool's league title record. There's just no way of knowing but those players had their chance of making even more history taken away from them because of unfair pressure put on the referee. Having said that, maybe my idea of more referees admitting who they support isn't the answer, I know of one who says he supports Rotherham but has season tickets at Leeds!

Brucey was made an example of but that didn't dampen his spirits for the season. He'd scored our first league goal of the season, and, like me, that gave him a good kick start for momentum that season. He went on to score nineteen goals – nineteen, for a centre back! – in all competitions and even though some were penalties he got his fair share from open play. He was always a goal threat because of the way he attacked the ball and to have that from a central defender was a huge bonus. Pally was less of a goal threat but was very good on the ball. Denis was an exceptional footballer, good on both sides, and I would like to think that I was a good complement for that on the left hand side. For the first time in a few years even our back-line was full of potent attacking threat, though I would also say that with Bruce and Pallister having played together for a year, they had developed a good understanding and were able to organise the defence efficiently. We had a great offside trap and quickly developed a strong awareness of our responsibilities in the unit, in front of Les Sealey, who was now first choice after his FA Cup Final performance. Robbo was still missing but his words rung in my ears whenever I was closing an opponent down, 'Go all the way to the ball. Don't just close him down to five yards. Don't give him time to play. Make him make a decision.' Paul Scholes got so much stick throughout his career for the way he tackled but at least he was trying to win the ball; and, he was getting in the face of the opponent, not giving them the time to do what they wanted. Unfortunately for Scholesy there were a few people in the media who made a bit of a fuss about it and that meant that he was one of that very rare breed of footballers who were never allowed a first indiscretion from a referee – he went straight in the book.

In one of our very first games as a unit - that being Sealey, Denis, Brucey, Pally and me - we went to Anfield. After spending so long here singing our praises, you know we obviously lost that one 4-0, with Peter Beardsley scoring a hat-trick. Anyone watching that game would think that maybe the goalkeeper could have done better; I wouldn't disagree with that. Like I said, Les wasn't the best goalkeeper in the world, we just weren't as unsure of him coming to collect the ball as we were with Jim. I don't mean to sound hyper-critical of either of them, I admit to being spoilt first with working with Big Nev and then later on with Peter Schmeichel who were the best two goalkeepers around at the time. That was a frustrating game. We thought we'd proved that we were their equal at Wembley and so, with them as Champions and us as FA Cup holders, this was our first chance to get one over on them in the league. Obviously that didn't happen. By the end of the game I was so wound up I went in on Ray Houghton and wasn't exactly hiding the fact I was trying to get the man rather than the ball. They went and scored from that move. Our problem was never recovering from the early two goals - we were chasing the game and left ourselves open, creating a scoreline that was in no way reflective of the gap between the sides. I felt responsible, culpable. I felt as if I'd set up their goal. So much in football is about mentality and a part of that is how you react to defeat or disadvantage. That defeat against Liverpool was one of the worst days of my career but my personal response was as strong as our collective response.

Next up came one of the proudest moments of my career. In April of that year it had been decided that English clubs would be allowed to re-enter the European club competitions so our reward for beating Crystal Palace, as well as the FA Cup, was a place in the European Cup Winners' Cup. Our first game was against Hungarian side Pesci Munkas at Old Trafford. I started an attack and joined up with the play as Choccy and Ince combined on the left. Incey played the ball inside to me and I took a touch which opened up the play inside of my marker. From around twenty-five yards, with the ball rolling across my path, I decided to have a shot at goal. I don't think I would have taken it on if we hadn't been playing with the old Adidas Tango balls but because I knew the bend you could generate with them I just fancied having a pop - the ball swerved a great deal, away from the goalkeeper who was stood near his right hand post. He didn't move, there was no point, as the ball flew into the top corner on the other side. Consider the factors - it was my first ever European game for the club, it was our first game in Europe for five years and it was at the Stretford End and it was one of my finest ever strikes; it was an absolutely perfect moment and a perfect response to the weekend.

I set Webby up to score a few minutes later and we achieved a 2-0 win to take into the second leg. I found playing in European football to be much the same as I found international footballer - it was easier because it was much less frenetic which is the perfect word to describe our next game, on a rainy day at Old Trafford against Southampton. I was playing left wing, and so I was able to read Neil Webb's flighted cross to head in our second goal to help us to a 3-2 win. I scored another good goal at Halifax in the League Cup to make it three in three but they made it really difficult for us, as we needed two goals in the last couple of minutes to get a 3-1 win to take into the home leg. Like Hereford the previous season, Halifax were fourth tier opponents which adds further justification to my belief that sometimes, particularly in that era, anything could happen if the opposition worked hard enough on a poor pitch. Our quality and concentration won out in the end but it just served as illustration that no game for United is easy, especially as the Shaymen were coached by former Red Jim McCalliog. I was really happy with my goal – it was a free kick that Denis was over, as well as Paul Ince and Neil Webb. It reminded me of a goal Denis scored at Anfield a few years later, where nobody from our team was in the box. It was a spur of the moment decision; I suppose I claimed seniority and I was pleased to have hit it so well. We won the second legs against Halifax and Pesci Munkas and enjoyed progression in those competitions by overcoming Liverpool in the League Cup and Wrexham in Europe respectively. Mark and I got a lot of stick from the Wrexham fans so it was nice to shut them up. We had ambitions, as holders of the FA Cup, to retain it as well as final reach the 'holy grail' – the league title.

We were expected to challenge for the league but we weren't used to competing on four fronts and something had to give; frustratingly it was our league form, as home defeats to Arsenal, Nottingham Forest and Chelsea before December left us off the pace. After fourteen games we were in seventh but a mammoth eighteen points behind Liverpool who were unbeaten, we'd lost five. The gaffer was probably getting somewhere near deciding his strongest eleven at the time and it was unreasonable to suggest we could all play three times a week.

After years of needle against Arsenal, our home loss against them was infamous – with the 21-player brawl (more like handbags, to be fair – only one person threw a proper punch, and that was Incey) which resulted in both teams being deducted points. I thought the one with Norman from a few years back was more ferocious but maybe because of all that had gone before this one got the most attention. At the centre of it was Nigel Winterburn, who dived in on a tackle on Denis and it all kicked off from there. Winterburn had been in Choccy's face a couple of years earlier when he missed a penalty down at Highbury; Brian had just laughed it off but it was something that didn't go down well with the rest of us. So when Winterburn went in on Irwin – obviously thinking because Denis is a smaller player, he can leave a mark – the lads got really wound up. Everyone that is apart from me, I was too far away to get involved. I was there to play football and I'd forgotten my handbag anyway! We lost our heads and lost the game that day (later that season Arsenal were deducted two points and we were deducted one) but had an opportunity to let our football do the talking when we were drawn against them down at Highbury in the League Cup five weeks later.

In games like that how you start is so important. I received the ball right from kick off and pinged one into Sparky. The ball felt beautiful to strike and when we were awarded a free kick after just three minutes I was determined to take it. It was so far out but I said, 'I'm gonna shoot.' To be fair, it was a good strike, not brilliant – they look better when they go in the top corner – but to beat Seaman from such a distance was obviously very pleasing. That was a game which belonged to Lee Sharpe; he was all over the pitch and even now I can't remember where he was supposed to be playing because he popped up everywhere. It was 3-0 at half time but they came out and scored two to pull it back – in their desperation for an equaliser we ended up picking them apart on the break and scored three more, Lee got a hat-trick. Slowly but surely we were getting into our groove and to get five goals before Christmas, mostly from left back, was a sign that my own form was going well, too.

To prove the point we got our first win at Plough Lane. It was no coincidence that it came when we had Pallister and Bruce at the back. When we had Davenport and McClair up front a couple of years back, we decided to go route one ourselves a little bit, lumping balls up to Peter and having Choccy and the midfielders picking up the scraps. It worked for us for a while but it clearly wasn't something that came naturally to us. The gaffer had talked about the importance of spreading goals around the team and how much closer you'll be to winning silverware if that is the case and I think that was something that definitely helped us in the 1990/91 season. Although, over Christmas, it seemed as if the only three players capable of getting the goals for us were Choccy, Mark Hughes and Steve Bruce. The Arsenal win kick-started a run of fifteen games unbeaten, which included FA Cup wins over QPR and Bolton Wanderers. During that time we were boosted by the return of Bryan Robson but, what would ordinarily have been a bit of a no-brainer was probably a conundrum for the gaffer. Robson was going to come back into the team because even at 34 he was our engine but the question of who he would replace wasn't obvious – we'd been playing well and there was a risk of upsetting the balance. As it turned out Neil Webb, who was arguably better at passing than Robbo, found himself missing games. The first time Neil was dropped he didn't take it well; I remember him being upset and bringing his own drink on the team bus, something the gaffer didn't take too kindly to.

Our unbeaten run had to end, even with Robbo back, and the defeat came in the fifth round of the FA Cup to Norwich City. It was the worst possible preparation for the second leg of our League Cup semi final second leg against Leeds at Elland Road. We'd won the first leg 2–1 so it was finely balanced with them needing just a goal to win it. It was goalless going into injury time and they piled everyone forward; Hughesie managed to clear it to McClair, who was on the halfway line. He played a long ball wide to the other side and the Leeds defence stopped, thinking they could catch Lee Sharpe offside. He was on – and he had to run from just inside their half, then their goalkeeper came out and made himself big and Lee rounded him and pushed himself wide. I thought it was too wide. And yet somehow he struck it perfectly across goal and into the top corner to seal the tie for us.

Our cup success was bound to have some repercussions and one of those was being forced to play at Bramall Lane forty-eight hours after the game at Elland Road. Leeds' pitch was like a farmer's field – we were getting to that period where pretty much the same could be said for most grounds – and Sheffield United's wasn't much better. I had a rare game up front because Sparky was injured. Steve Bruce was also out of the side so when we were awarded a penalty I stepped up to score. That drew us level but we went on to lose. We also lost against Everton and Chelsea either side of the first leg against French side Montpellier as European football resumed. Montpellier had the very distinctive Colombian midfielder Carlos Valderrama who was very good. He was by far the most recognisable of that team with his big hair but we quickly learned that their team was full of good players. We started well at Old Trafford – McClair scored in the first minute – but they drew level through a Lee Martin own goal and it meant that the second leg was going to be very difficult.

And it was. It was every bit as tough as we expected but just before half time we were awarded a free kick even further out than the one I'd scored at Arsenal. It must have been close to forty yards out. If it was a Mitre ball I wouldn't have gone for goal but it was a Tango and we hadn't had many shots so I thought I may as well hit it. I was almost too eager, wanting to strike it before the referee blew his whistle. I connected with it well but it was going straight at the goalkeeper. I mean, there was a little bit of swerve but my hope was that he would spill it and someone would be there to pick up the pieces. As it turned out he wasn't able to get hold of it and, although he got a hand to it, he fumbled it and it went in. Aesthetically it wasn't quite as pleasing as the one I'd scored at Halifax but the result was the same. And, to be fair, the way people have talked about that goal since, you would think it flew in off the bar. It's always one of the first goals people ask me about but sometimes there are these memories that are more about the moment than the quality of the goal. Ole Gunnar Solskjær scored over one hundred times for United and plenty of those goals were better in terms of quality than the toe poke which won the European Cup in 1999. None were more famous, or fondly remembered, and everyone remembers the moment.

Going into half time on the back of a pretty average first half performance, Montpellier were probably confident of going through. As it stood before I took the free kick they led the tie on away goals but that strike came at such an important time - it not only killed their momentum but it gave them something to dwell on for fifteen minutes before being able to put it right. They had to prepare to chase the game, from previously controlling it, and having the added anxiety of having to do that in front of their own fans. In contrast, we went into the break knowing exactly what the goal meant. While celebrating I looked over to the bench and they were all going nuts, it showed how important the goal was. It had been reported before the game that they were on £35,000 a man to beat us. Our bonus if we won the entire thing was £5,000 before tax! After the interval it seemed as if they lost their heads; Micky Phelan crossed one in from the right and I made a near post run –I ran across the defender and the temptation to tackle me was too much for him. I saw him coming, got my body between the player and the ball and waited for the contact. I was begging him to take me out. He kicked me and I went down and I knew as I was on my way to the ground that we'd got a penalty. Instinctively when I got up I thought I might take it but Brucey had come back into the side and hadn't missed one. He scored and the French side really lost it. I remembering them clattering into Incey a few times and then one of their defenders, Jean-Manuel Thetis, was sent off for spitting at Sparky. I wasn't worried about how aggressive the atmosphere was getting – in fact, I was revelling in it. We got another free kick from quite wide, a perfect position for a cross but I thought I'd try my luck anyway. The keeper fisted that one away. I played one ball into Phelan and his cross was intercepted by the defender, but I jumped on to the rebound and smashed it first time – it ricocheted off of the post and back into play. Despite it being a really tough game, clearly it was one I had a lot of positive involvement in and I'm always proud when people mention that game.

It inspired another great run of form going into our League Cup Final where we would face Sheffield Wednesday, now managed by Ron Atkinson. Before that Wembley date we had won five of our next six which included a 3-1 victory in the first leg of the European Cup Winners' Cup semi-final at Legia Warsaw to give us an incredible chance of qualifying for the final. I scored my ninth goal of the season in a 3-1 win against Derby County the week before Wembley, a good half-volley from the edge of the area. We were fourth in the table but seventeen points behind leaders Arsenal.

The game against Sheffield Wednesday was a complete non-event. They did their homework and worked hard to snuff us out and they completely nullified the threat of Lee Sharpe. On such a big pitch we could have done with that pace but it wasn't to be. It was my first taste of defeat at Wembley and it was so disappointing. We never got going in the game, even though their goal came in the first half and we had the entire second half to get an equaliser. There were so many similarities between our game and the Liverpool/Wimbledon Cup Final of 1988. The underdogs score a goal, they have something to defend and hold on to, and gradually the confidence and energy of the favourites ebbs

90

away. You start to think it's just not going to be your day. You start making rash choices, wrong decisions. You're over-hitting passes and playing balls into areas you just normally wouldn't. I should be fair to Wednesday after that Wimbledon comparison, they did have some good players. They were in the Second Division - which rubbed the salt in the wound a little bit more - but the gap wasn't as big as it seemed. Roland Nilsson, Nigel Worthington, Nigel Pearson, John Sheridan and David Hirst were all players who would contribute to Wednesday finishing third in the First Division the following year and also getting to two Cup Finals the year after that. It doesn't make it any easier to deal with and I don't think it's fair to use Les Sealey's leg injury in that game as an excuse. It was a bad injury, you could see the bone. There was hardly any blood, the cut had gone so deep - I called right away for a stretcher and couldn't see how he could stay on - Les is telling Jim McGregor to strap him up so he can get back on, then the next minute I'm thinking, well, I'm definitely going to have to take the goal kicks for him. Les is in shock, yelling at me, 'Fuck off, get up the field!' The injury was pretty bad and I can only think he was worried that this would be his last game for the club. He was stitched up in the changing rooms while he was smoking. When we got to the airport Les collapsed in front of me; we were told if he had got on the plane he would have lost his leg, or worse.

Gary Walsh came in as his deputy with the rational thinking being that Les wouldn't be fit to play against Legia Warsaw in Europe, so, we needed to give Gary as much time as possible. It's hard to see why Gary didn't get as much time as he perhaps deserved because he was a very good goalkeeper. Maybe he wasn't the quickest with his feet but he was an excellent shot stopper and was also quite confident taking crosses.

Our comfortable result in the first leg against Legia might have had a bearing on how we played in the second - you could use Manchester United's League Cup semi-final with Hull City in 2017 as a perfect example - but I was never a fan of using that as an excuse. Sharpey scored in the first half to give us a 4-1 aggregate lead at half-time. Manchester United had never lost at home in Europe, never mind by two goals, so we were in the driver's seat, and at that point I think there were a few of us who did allow ourselves to dream at that point. We were just forty-five minutes from a European final. They got an equaliser but even as the game entered its latter stages they didn't exactly attack with the same level of ferocity as, for example, we faced when we played Leeds in the semi-final of the League Cup. In British football, teams throw players forward and it gets a bit chaotic but the more methodical pace of the European game helped us (as did the fact that Robbo was back from injury) to close the tie out.

Despite having Arsenal and Manchester City as our opponents in two of our last four league games we ended the domestic season with that subdued lull which sometimes affects teams who have qualified for a Cup Final and are unable to really make an impact on the league. In our game at Highbury we had to give a guard of honour to them as Arsenal had just won the league. Though that was obviously unpleasant our minds had already turned to Rotterdam, where we would be facing Barcelona in the final. We lost 3-1 to the new champions but the game had little of the resentment of recent encounters - our biggest disappointment was losing Robbo early on, with our worries immediately centred upon whether he would be fit for Rotterdam.

As nondescript as the end of that league season was otherwise, two new players were added to the Manchester United squad whose impact on the first team was to be significant. There had been a lot of buzz around Ryan Giggs for a couple of years and it was easy to see why as soon as you saw him move with the ball. Bear in mind, we already had Sharpey who was able to move at blistering speed - he could even match Ryan - but the difference was that Ryan could change direction with the ball and still be moving as quickly. I would go and watch the reserves and youth team play as the manager liked us to do that and he was the one player regularly standing out - this, against seasoned professionals from other clubs. They couldn't handle him - it was obvious we had a very special talent on our hands. When he was moved up to training with the senior players at United, and I saw how easily he adapted, my immediate thought was - I wouldn't want to be playing against him. I didn't even fancy it in training.

Giggs made it into the first team against Everton in March and, come the next season, he was pretty much first choice, as he would be for the next 23 years. Around the same time, we signed the Russian winger Andrei Kanchelskis. He doesn't always get the recognition he deserves. It's probably due to the controversial circumstances regarding his exit from the club but Andrei, for me - especially at £650,000 - was one of the gaffer's best signings. He was two-footed, exceptionally quick and a very good finisher. He was strong on the ball, which was pretty rare for a winger. So strong in fact that I think he could have played as a centre forward. At the time I don't think anyone at the club realised just how much our fortunes would be transformed by the extra dimension our wingers would add. Andrei didn't speak a lot of English but football is a universal language, as they say, and we quickly learned that all we had to do was give him the ball and get in the box.

Kanchelskis made his debut in our penultimate league game of the season - the last game before the Barcelona match - at Crystal Palace. I was left out of that one with the manager playing Mal Donaghy instead and I admit to being slightly worried that I might not be selected in Rotterdam.

Rotterdam

UNDER JOHAN CRUYFF, Barcelona were in the early stages of their first 'revolution'. They were just about to win the Spanish League, after Real Madrid had won it five times in a row and they had a reputation of having big time players who played excellent football and were strong favourites for the final of the European Cup Winners' Cup.

There was a mixture of excitement and nerves for this, the biggest match of our careers to date, but a quiet confidence, too. Not so much confidence that we were better than Barcelona but a confidence that had developed throughout the competition, especially in the away games. We always thought we could beat anybody, home or away; it wouldn't bother British teams whether you played home or away as European teams gave you time on the ball. It made a change from the claustrophobic pitches of Goodison Park, Carrow Road and Plough Lane. It meant that we were looking forward to playing football against another of the world's best teams.

The climate was different, then, too – it is rare that Manchester United enjoy the support of neutral supporters (and there were probably a fair few wanting us to lose) but it did feel as if British football had been behind us on this amazing adventure back into European football. To go away from home and win in the Quarter Final and Semi Final captured the imagination of not only United supporters, though, of course, our primary aim was to make sure that it was our supporters who were rewarded for their excellent dedication. It added to the romance that we were playing the final in a foreign country, too. That's not to take anything away from the 1968 win at Wembley which clearly had its own romance but to go away from home, in this, our first venture back into Europe, felt extra special. If I had any wishes about how it could have been different, well, I just look at the final the year afterwards, which was won by Werder Bremen and was held at Benfica's Estádio de Luz when the capacity was 120,000. We sold out in Holland and I'm sure we would have easily done so in Portugal as well. I'm sure we could have done that with United supporters alone.

The build up for the final was perfect. It felt as if we were in our own little bubble; the disappointment of our recent league form felt like a completely separate entity to our European run. The first time reality struck us was when we walked out on to the pitch at De Kuip and realised we were about to go toe-to-toe with one of the best teams in the world as underdogs. I had been used to the feeling for Wales but this was the first time in 186 appearances that I'd ever gone into a game as a Manchester United player and been an underdog. It was an unusual feeling – in this bizarre situation, where it felt as if we were the ones with something to prove, we were given an extra sense of motivation that may have given us the edge. I also think that the loss against Sheffield Wednesday helped us. It was fresh in our minds and even though we always gave everything, it helped refine our concentration.

The European Cup Winners' Cup was actually a very close rival to the European Cup. As well as winning their domestic league, this Barcelona team would also go on to win the European Cup the following year. I think that goes some way to explaining the strength of the team, the strength of the competition and the size of the task awaiting us.

There were enough distractions beforehand to take my mind away from the enormity of it on a personal level. I found myself concerned with Les Sealey, who the club were trying to get fit for the final. I thought back to the times I'd rushed back from injury to get back into the team or the times I'd seen it with others and known that a team-mate might not be at their best. There was nothing to convince me that Les was ready because he still wasn't moving right in training and, in fact, right up until the team was named, I was sure he shouldn't have been playing. I couldn't understand taking such a risk. A few days before the final we were doing shooting drills and he was really struggling to move. Almost anywhere else on the field you might get away with carrying a player and it might be worth it if they are capable of the spectacular or a moment that changes the game but if you take a risk with a goalkeeper there are rarely positive consequences.

As it transpired the team worked so hard that Les didn't have much to do. Throughout the game, I think if we'd had a fit Les we would have won and kept a clean sheet. The game was closely fought – one of those types of games where it was going to take a set piece or an individual moment of quality to turn it. McClair had a decent chance early on but it bobbled and he wasn't able to get it on target. We got a free kick midway through the second half around forty yards from their goal. Robbo put it down but I went over to size it up. I wondered if they'd done their homework. They were bound to have seen the Montpellier goal. Did they think it was a one off or did they know I had done that a few times before that season? These thoughts went through my head, but I was definitely prepared to take it on. It wasn't a case of not doing it because it was the final. Before I'd even made my mind up, Robson saw Brucey make a run in behind the defence and clipped the ball into the box. Bruce got there in front of his marker and headed the ball past Carlos Busquets who had come out of his goal. There was still time to pause and consider what was unfolding in front of us – Mark Hughes nipped in to divert the ball into the unguarded net. There has been a little bit of debate over whose goal it was – Mark definitely got the last touch before it crossed the line, which ends the debate anyway, although I still think that it probably needed it as there was no guarantee that the ball wouldn't hit the post or go just wide. Brucey has joked about it since. 'Have a look at the lads, look at who they all celebrated with!' Sorry Brucey but you were closer than Sparky that's why I ran to you!

The goal unleashed a number of different emotions; relief that we had made a breakthrough. The most dominant, though, was confidence. Scoring that goal made me feel so confident that we could win the game. I won't say that I felt as if we were inferior but with their reputation being so large you wanted to prove yourself, you wanted to justify yourself. You wanted to prove that you are part of one of the best Manchester United teams and that you are every bit the match of Barcelona. The supporters must have had the same thoughts and we could hear their own confidence and jubilation by the sudden deafening increase in volume. Less than ten minutes later they went crazy when Sparky scored again. There was no debate this time.

I was thirteen or fourteen the first time I ever saw Mark play. It was up at Wrexham and he was on the opposite team. Even then he had freakishly sized thighs. All you could see for ninety minutes was this pair of legs running around the pitch, dominating the game. It's a team sport and in an entire career you end up with just a few moments where your individual ability stands out as having made the difference. You need composure alongside your natural ability to not let the moment pass you by and, as Mark rounded Busquets to chase onto a through ball from Robson, even though he was pushed wide, I fancied him to score. He was at an angle and two defenders were running back to cover the goal. Really, he had no right to get a goal from that position but this was Mark Hughes and he struck the ball with such precision and force that it flew into the far corner. I struggle to think of any player at the time or even since, who would be able to have physically accomplished such a goal. Maybe Cristiano Ronaldo because he has powerful legs too but the number capable of finishing from there would be very small. If it had been anybody else on the team we wouldn't have scored. If anyone else had taken it on, we would have been moaning at them for not crossing it to Sharpey. When you watch it back and hear Brian Moore on commentary he thinks the chance has gone when Hughes has pushed wide. It was remarkable and yet unsurprising - even though, as I watched it unfold, I thought he'd gone too wide.

At 2-0 relief outweighed confidence. People say two-nil is a dangerous lead but believe me, it's a lot better than 1-0. With quarter of an hour left we knew that in order to win we just had to keep playing the same way we had. Close them down, attack when we can. Attack is the best form of defence and in that situation having Sparky who could hold the ball up and Sharpey who would run with it were crucial weapons for running down the clock.

It was inevitable that such a good team would come back and have some good moments. All in all I thought I had a good game against Andoni Goikoetxea - he threw a dummy and got past me once, but generally, I played well. The adrenalin of being so close to glory kept us from exhaustion. With a two goal lead to protect I was full of energy. That could be said for the rest of the team – Robbo said after that it was one of his best performances and I would agree with that. He played a big part in both goals but just as crucial was his work rate and application, which I think we all mirrored on the day. A potentially difficult game had been made much easier by everyone putting in an incredible shift and it actually made it a fairly enjoyable one to play in, despite the intensity of the occasion.

Our two goal lead seemed like it lasted a lifetime but in reality it lasted just five minutes. Ronald Koeman had a tremendous reputation from free kicks and added to it by scoring to set up a nervous finish. He was fortunate to say the least. Les may not have been the best goalkeeper in the world but if he was fit I think he would have got across quickly enough to tip it around the post. He was just short - he got a hand to it, it hit the post, and then rebounded into Les' back and went into the goal. It was a dreadful moment of bad luck which causes you to momentarily wonder. But that's all it was; bad luck. It wasn't bad goalkeeping and I didn't blame Les. I didn't blame him for not getting there or for playing when he was injured. I would have done exactly the same. He'd played a big role in us getting there and deserved to be a part of it.

I don't know if nerves got the better of Brucey but with seconds remaining, against the backdrop of a chorus of whistles from the terraces, he hesitated in possession on the edge of the area, and Antonio Pinilla stole in. Les went out to try and smother the ball but Pinilla turned and played it towards Michael Laudrup who had raced into the penalty area. The only thing running through my mind is that I had to get back and so I ran onto the line in Les' absence. I'm not normally a fan of doing that - I think in those circumstances you should try and close the player down - but Laudrup was too far away for me to have tried that. Nobody else was picking him up and he had a free shot. I was not only able to block it on the line but also get enough purchase to get it away from danger.

It was their last chance.

It's easy to conclude that the clearance was as important as any goal I ever scored. I scored twenty-six times for United. The Montpellier goal was probably the most important one because of what it meant in the game, and our fate in the competition, coming at the time it did. But, by far, that goal-line clearance was my most important contribution during my Manchester United career because it meant we won the game. The moment the whistle went was one of the most euphoric of my life. I had been at United for more than a decade and had lived with the tag and privilege of being at the biggest club in the world. Forget the ifs and buts, we had never had a team that achieved something to justify being described as the best. To finally be able to hold our heads high and to have an achievement worthy of the club was a moment of satisfaction we all allowed ourselves to indulge in. The celebrations were great. I smoked a cigar with Mick Hucknall and Mark Hughes - well, again, I say, I smoked it, but as a non-smoker, it was all a bit of a joke. I didn't know how to and ended up just blowing smoke through my nose; being pissed at the time I thought it was quite clever, the word doughnut comes to mind. It was all for the effect, we were largeing it.

I said that the year before I had felt part of the celebrations because I'd played in the first final against Palace and also played my part in the Cup run and I stand by that, and my opinion that all who participate in some form in a trophy success should be rewarded, even if it's in a previous or early round. Still, it's hard to shy away from the truth that I felt even more satisfied with my contribution not only in Rotterdam but throughout that competition. I'd scored the first goal back in Europe, I'd had one of my best games against Montpellier and now played a big role on the second biggest night in the club's history.

In more recent years the night has taken on a life of its own. The supporters hold a special fondness for it, even accounting for the fact that it was followed by two European Cups under the gaffer.

Pride Of All Europe

THAT SEASON, 1990/91, is remembered is fondly remembered because we beat Barcelona. That one night upgraded it from what I suppose we would have classed as a good season – finishing sixth, and getting to the League Cup Final. The league finish had been an improvement on the year before but was still disappointing and, following two major trophy victories, it was clear that we needed to deliver a league title. It was the only thing missing.

Rotterdam was a big turning point for the confidence of us as a group. Compared to how it had been in the winter of 1990, the difference was night and day. The best compliment anyone had given our team before was that we were the best Cup team in the country. It's obvious what was implied by that and the results suggested they weren't wrong. We were capable of beating anyone in the country but we just couldn't do it over thirty-eight or forty-two games. We didn't need to be told that, we knew it. We had taken Arsenal apart on a few occasions when they were either Champions or Champions-elect. We had a great record against Liverpool.

Maybe the difference had been that we were underdogs in Rotterdam. Even against Liverpool and Arsenal, we were their Cup Final just like we were everyone else's. I don't think anyone's attitude had ever been a problem nor could you ever question our application but there was an extra buzz about our performance against Barcelona and the achievement that night. If we could replicate that in our domestic form, we would surely be unstoppable. What we didn't know at the time was that we had two amazing wingers about to come into the side and that elevated us on to the next level, there is no questioning that. However I think the rest of us also benefitted from a new-found confidence of not only believing we could compete with the best but we were among the best.

We also signed Peter Schmeichel and Paul Parker whose qualities were a little more obvious and straightforward. I was curious about Parks and why we brought him in. I had been delighted with my season – not only in the more notable contributions but my all around game had been pretty good which I felt was a good indicator of what I was capable of if I was given a run in the team, in one position. Denis had been outstanding on the right hand side. Paul had played on the right for England but at QPR he had made his name as a centre-half and although he had neither the height or physicality of Bruce or Pallister, he was a brilliant man-marker. We called him 'the leech'. He was a stopper and dead sharp. I've no problem admitting that he was a better defender than I was, though I do think I had more to my game in terms of what I brought to the team with attacking, build up play and my range of passing.

I think it was partly for his defensive quality but also due to the 'foreigner' rule that he was selected against Atletico Madrid in the first leg of our second round of our Cup Winners' Cup defence in October 1991. It was a harsh rule which particularly punished British clubs. We had Peter Schmeichel who was Danish, fair enough but the rest of our 'foreigners' in that game were Denis Irwin, Brian McClair and Mark Hughes. It meant I wasn't even on the bench and I was doubly gutted to not be a part and to see us capitulate late on and concede two goals – it meant instead of a manageable 1-0, we were facing a 3-0 deficit in the return. I played in that one – Peter and Denis came out and Ryan and myself came in to add a more attacking threat. Sparky scored in the first five minutes to have the fans dreaming of a comeback to better the one that was achieved against Barcelona in 1985 but that was an unrealistic ambition. We were frustrated for most of the game and conceded an equaliser in the second half. I couldn't help but think – naturally, and selfishly – that we might have stood a better chance if the defence which won the competition had been kept together.

It was a very disappointing exit but our domestic form at the start of the season had been exceptional. Before going to Madrid we had drawn against Arsenal at Old Trafford but we were top of the table after going unbeaten in our first twelve league games. Some of us had been around long enough not get too carried away but even though the style of football wasn't quite the exhilarating brand that had been on show at the start of the 1985/86 season, there were small indications that we were getting there. I scored in an early season win at Wimbledon. We had Bruce and Pallister at the heart of our defence so that was no surprise but our midfield on the day - Phelan, Webb, Robson and me - showed that we were still trying to get that perfect blend. The gaffer seemed unsure about playing both Kanchelskis and Giggs early on in the season and I suppose that was a sensible decision. It wasn't a risk that the manager needed to take because defensively the cohesion between us, as well as the new players, helped to make us really strong. We kept eleven clean sheets in our opening fourteen matches - finally we had developed a consistency which showed we were difficult to break down and hard to beat. The good feeling about our league form was not before time considering how frustrating it was to constantly hear people talk about how it was coming up to twenty-five years, a quarter of a century since we'd won the league. At 27 I was approaching my peak but I was starting to wonder if I would be one of those players to win a league title with United. I'd seen and played with too many great players who had never won a league medal.

A couple of weeks after we were eliminated from Europe we came up against Red Star Belgrade in the European Super Cup; it was a perfect opportunity to restore any lost confidence, not that we got it from the performance. There weren't many people who got the better of Paul Ince but Dejan Savicevic was something else. He completely gave Incey the run-around and put on a masterclass of a performance, one of the best I've ever seen from a visiting player at Old Trafford, and probably the best I played against. It helped that he was left footed and everything just looked that little bit more graceful. To do that on the pitch we had at Old Trafford at the time was extra special. Even with Savicevic, though, Red Star couldn't score - and maybe I'm as guilty as anyone for helping to romanticise what was still a very good side. The only games I can really remember watching Savicevic in, after all, was this one I played against him and the Champions League final between AC Milan and Barcelona. I saw Lionel Messi come to Old Trafford with Barcelona in 2008 and he dribbled a lot but couldn't influence the result. Diego Maradona didn't even get that amount of joy back in 1984. Red Star were a brilliant side and it was a very tough game but we had enough chances to justify our status as deserved winners even beyond the indisputable currency of football – Brian McClair scored and they couldn't equalise. The level of competitiveness in the game left us buzzing afterwards because it felt as if, by beating the European champions, we now had the right to believe we were the best side in Europe.

Shortly after Choccy's goal Lee Martin came off for Ryan Giggs and I moved back into defence having started on the left wing. Giggs and Kanchelskis had rarely played at the same time but from this point onwards it was almost impossible to leave them out. I talk of Messi and Maradona and in Giggs and Kanchelskis we had two players just as brilliant at dribbling. Those are the players that win you games and titles because of how rare their ability is. It's the best thing to see in football and I can't understand why it isn't encouraged more amongst youngsters. In fact, it's actively getting coached out of them – it's all pass, pass, pass. It helped that both of our wingers had pace to burn and for the rest of 1991 we scored goals for fun. We scored three at Palace, three at Chelsea, four at home to Coventry and then six at Oldham on Boxing Day. Kanchelskis and Giggs were running riot and teams didn't have an answer to it. Instead of having one player to deal with, one danger man you might could double up on, we had speed on both flanks to add to our goal threat in the middle. At this stage they were so fresh that to opponents they were completely unpredictable. The only time I've seen United play a vibrancy and speed that caught everyone so off guard was at points in the 2006/07 season when Ryan was still running up and down that left hand side but there was also Cristiano Ronaldo, Wayne Rooney and Alan Smith causing problems. The most famous example of it all coming together was that 7-1 win over Roma but there was also a blistering counter attack goal against Bolton around the same time that was executed by Rooney and Ronaldo. The win at Oldham was similar to the Roma game in that it seemed as if we'd score with every attack. We were a point clear with two games in hand as we closed out 1991 against Leeds United, our closest competitors for the league. They scored a late penalty to get a point at Elland Road which didn't seem like it was the worst result at the time.

It wouldn't be far off the mark to say that at that period I was probably the most popular I'd ever been in regards to the supporters. In our tough times I'd endured a little bit of stick from the fans but my form over the last couple of years had changed their opinion. It's amazing to think of how much it's changed over the years. I would read every letter sent to me and reply to as many as I could – normally a signed picture, occasionally a little note, which we'd post ourselves. It doesn't happen so much these days – I think clubs just get players to sign a bunch of pictures which are sent in response, so the personal factor is gone from it. That said, that may be the wisest thing, as security is such a big thing these days. Back then it helped cement an already very strong bond between the players and fans. There was a unity growing and a belief that we were on the cusp of achieving greater things. For many managers winning in Europe would be a pinnacle, and rightly so, but Fergie's ambition was greater.

Our confidence was boosted even further by the fact that we went back to Elland Road twice in the next two weeks and won in both Cup competitions. Leeds were our closest opponents and as far as I was concerned our team had proven we were much better. I thought, especially with our goalkeeper and wingers added to our European side, we were by far the best team in the league, playing the most entertaining football.

We had one big hiccup, against QPR at Old Trafford. Hiccup is a kind word for it. We lost 4-1 and got hammered in the press for apparently going out drinking the night before. Me and Sparky had two beers each in our rooms in the Holiday Inn. I put our defeat down to something else. Our midfield was Phelan, Webb, Ince and Sharpe. We'd been playing with pace for weeks and had restricted ourselves to just one quick outlet – and even Sharpey was coming back from injury, so we couldn't expect him to be flying from the start. We were caught cold, as they were up for it as usual, and scored twice in the first five minutes. For the second goal I couldn't quite get in front of Dennis

Bailey and his shot looked to have been saved by Schmeichel but it bounced horribly and went in. It was clearly going to be one of those days. Our response was dreadful and they could have had three or four at half time. 2-0 became 3-0 early in the second half as we left ourselves wide open pushing to get back into the game. We finally got a goal back seven minutes from the end and then exposed ourselves again - Andy Sinton raced on the break and his shot rebounded off the post and into the path of Bailey, who completed his hat-trick. They might have even scored again after that. It summed up a miserable second half which had been made more difficult by the windy conditions. It also suggested that in the space of two months we had come to rely on the speed of our wingers. In the first half, as we were pinned back, I remember looking up and thinking we had no outlet. It shouldn't have been that way - we had defeated Barcelona without them, after all.

Maybe New Year's Day was the first indication of our weariness. The previous season our elimination in the FA Cup had been at the 5th round stage, so when you consider that we had only played three games fewer than the maximum we could have played (excluding replays). Playing away on pitches that could not really be described as grassy at Chelsea, then the Astroturf at Oldham and muddy pitch at Leeds probably took its toll on our legs. Having said that QPR were better on the day and deserved the win. The result was embarrassing but to have only lost two league games at that point in the season was encouraging and although the manager was furious, nobody needed to let us know how badly we'd done. It's no coincidence that the result came at Christmas; the program in England is not fair to the players who are not given enough time to recover.

The best games to bounce back from those defeats are the big games but our League Cup 5th round tie at Leeds started badly when Gary Speed scored early on. When we were awarded a free kick later in the first half, fully thirty-five yards out, Neil Webb placed the ball, fancying a pop. I'd just taken one from the same spot five minutes prior and told Webby, 'I'll score'. After the early season threat to my place I had been playing regular football and I seized the opportunity to remind everyone what I was capable of. I stepped up and struck the ball well, curling it over the tall John Lukic and into the top left corner. Kanchelskis and Giggs scored in the second half – a timely reminder of their growing importance to the side. We defeated Everton in a midweek league game but the following week, when we went to Leeds for that third game, I was dropped making way for Denis to come back into the side.

The gaffer called me in to tell me I would be losing my place. 'I'm bringing Denis in because I want to attack them more,' he said. I don't know if something significant had changed in the Everton game but it must have done for it to completely overshadow my role in the 3-1 win at Leeds just a week prior! It was a tighter game in the FA Cup but we still came out on top and I was delighted when Sparky scored to give us that 1-0 win. We enjoyed the boost of defeating our nearest rivals and hoped that it would give us a psychological advantage further down the line but I think somewhere in the manager's mind he was still scarred by the capitulation against QPR. Maybe he thought that instead of it being a one-off, a bad day at the office, that kind of result could happen to us if we weren't careful. So, if he had to play Kanchelskis and Giggs, he would have to be conservative in other areas. You wouldn't expect either of those players to be shouldering the weight of defensive responsibility so early on in their careers at the club and so that came in other areas – Brian McClair would drop further back leaving Sparky sometimes as the lone forward who would hopefully do what he did best and hold the ball up so others could come into the game. I found myself in a similar situation to the one I'd been in during Ron's last few months at the club. I was technically dropped for Irwin, though the reality was that Denis and I had proven we could play down opposite flanks very successfully. Paul Parker, the new signing, wasn't going to be dropped, and I was the one who paid the price.

I was on the bench for the next game at Notts County and we fell behind to an early penalty. I came on at the start of the second half and midway through it we were awarded a penalty of our own. I stepped up to take it – I'd come on for Brucey, so our regular taker was out – but immediately was dreading the thought of missing it, because there were a lot of United fans behind that goal, and I didn't want to let them down. I scored to earn us a point but it wasn't enough to earn me a regular spot back in the team.

In my absence the lads won in the League Cup semi-final against Middlesbrough after going to extra time at Old Trafford. So, by the weekend at Bramall Lane they were understandably knackered as the game went into the last quarter of an hour at 1-1. We had been losing but McClair - stood in an offside position - received the ball from a Sheffield United player and scored. Within five minutes of coming on I found myself racing up the pitch to connect with a cross from Brian which I converted to win us the game. A lucky goal from Choccy and a late goal from the substitute - it was the sort of game where the gaffer would have hoped our luck was turning, after a run of draws which were threatening to derail our momentum. I was called back into the side but we lost at Forest and then drew at home to Wimbledon failing to score in both games. The Forest game was difficult to take as we had chances to win and the goal we conceded should maybe have been kept out by Schmeichel.

I was out again for the goalless draw at QPR but back in for our home game against Manchester City. Again, it seemed as if we were on the right track. Giggs scored a great goal in the first half but in the second we conceded a penalty when Steve Bruce - who had declared himself fit after a hernia injury - was caught out by David White and brought him down inside the box. Keith Curle scored and we were unable to get the winner. The 1-1 result meant we'd drawn eight games and lost two out of our last sixteen. It wasn't great preparation for the League Cup Final against Nottingham Forest and it wasn't form you would associate with a team who wanted to win the league, and yet, as we went to Wembley we were still top of Division One. I had played in midfield in the derby and felt I'd done enough to get the chance at Wembley.

I can't say that there were many times in my Manchester United career where I was really upset about not being selected, most of the time I could accept it and just put my head down to try and get back in to the team. Even when I was upset with Ron at the start of the 1986/87 season, I didn't question him at the time. I just got on with it. When it came to the League Cup Final, I was annoyed - Webby had been out of the side and somebody told me he went in to see the manager on the Thursday before the Cup Final and asked to be selected because we were playing Forest, his old club. So he was given a spot on the bench and I was binned. The gaffer knew I was upset and offered to try and get me a medal if we won. I said I didn't want a medal, I wanted to play. I hated missing out but I could understand it if there was a reason. I was a substitute in 1990 and Lee Martin, who was in my place, scored the winning goal. No complaint. I'm not a big fan of sentimental decisions because they aren't made on merit and that's not really fair to the other players who work their entire careers for a handful of these opportunities - if you're lucky - to come along. After the game I got drunk – I filled the Cup with champagne and drank it! We went to Mottram Hall and the gaffer asked me if I wanted to play for the reserves against Forest the next day. I insisted I did and he kept checking because he knew I was getting the worse for wear. I did play in that game and I was steaming. I didn't get a medal from the final and Webby didn't even come on. It was a low point. After losing to Wednesday the previous year I was desperate to get that medal and, even though the Wembley appearances were now starting to increase, I never took any for granted.

As I said in the introduction to this book, there is a perception that we were miles ahead in that title race only to blow a big lead. We would only have had that lead if we had won all our games in hand and, as we prepared for our run-in after Wembley, Leeds had established a decent advantage. I'm a big believer that momentum and confidence play a defining factor at important times of a season and there's just no way of knowing how we would have approached the final games if we'd had points on the board instead of games in hand. We had unwittingly given Leeds United that advantage by defeating them in the Cups. What seemed like a great boost in January was something we were counting the cost of in April. They had fixture breaks and longer rest periods but most importantly of all, they didn't have to contend with the fixture pile-up that we were presented with after beating Forest at Wembley. We had six league games to fit into sixteen days because, for some reason, the FA refused to extend the league season beyond 2nd May.

Even if we had been conservative instead of seeking to blow teams away, and even if our form had been patchy heading into that final run, in normal circumstances I'm sure we had enough to get over the finish line. The worst of it was that the organisation of those games was horrendous. We played four of the games in just seven days - Thursday, Saturday, Monday and Wednesday before playing Liverpool on the following Sunday. The manager picked the same team to play against Southampton at home on Thursday as he had done to play against Forest at Wembley the previous weekend and it was a predictably flat occasion. An Andrei Kanchelskis goal put us top of the league but we were already paying the price when Paul Ince came off in the first half with an injury. It was arguably a bigger blow than the one we'd suffered last time we played the Saints at Old Trafford - we had a perfectly good goal disallowed, and they went on to knock us out of the FA Cup on penalties. Having said that, although it was disappointing at the time, I don't know where we would have found the time to play the extra games. Maybe we would have had to play two games on the same day.

There was already talk about what would become the Premier League which was due to replace the First Division after the summer. Nobody was sure what was going to happen and nobody could predict how it would take off in the way it did but in the last weeks of the 1991/1992 season, we were all desperate to get our hands on what would be the last Division One trophy (at least in its traditional form). Likewise, the promise of more money meant that the teams near the foot of the table were just as desperate to avoid relegation and opponents fighting relegation was the last thing we needed. Unfortunately, that's what we got with trips to Luton Town and West Ham either side of a home game against Nottingham Forest. We drew at Luton - I came on at half time for Parker who picked up a knock and we suffered a further blow when Sparky had to come off with ten minutes to go. Kanchelskis came on for him - having played the full game against Southampton, it was too much to ask both him and Giggs to be at full pelt two days later. Fitness coaches have since said that players need at least 48 hours recovery time to be able to compete at anywhere near their normal levels and those estimates are made by today's fitness standards and on today's pitches, with all the modern facilities.

Hughes' injury meant he wasn't quite sharp enough to start against Forest and so we had to go with Kanchelskis and Sharpe on the wings with Giggs up front. We were already knackered but managed to hit back after conceding just after the half hour. Choccy scored within a few minutes of Ian Woan's goal but as the game entered the final stages we knew we had to go for the win - it left us exhausted and vulnerable and when Scott Gemmill scored with ten minutes to go, there was nothing left in the tank to get back into it.

Sparky was back in the team at Upton Park and came closest for us with one of his spectacular bicycle kicks. His effort was saved and from the resulting corner West Ham broke and scored. Pally had got back and done his job - or so we thought - but his clearance was met by Kenny Brown. I'm still not sure whether he shot or the ball just hit him but either way, it went into our goal, and we couldn't find an equaliser. By that point I was off the pitch having been substituted.

Our advantage had gone and we had to win at Anfield to stay in the title race after Leeds beat Sheffield United in the early kick-off. Robbo had missed a bunch of games and was rushed back for the occasion as was Incey who had been out since coming off against Southampton but we conceded early on and then Pally had to go off. You're never happy to miss a game but I was so exhausted; like I said, I'd trained so hard as well as giving everything in the games and the boys went to Anfield knackered, battered and bruised, so it was no surprise we lost 2-0, handing the league title to Leeds.

I know it sounds bitter but I just can't see how anyone could think the scheduling of those games was fair. I'm sure nowadays things would be done differently. If we'd gone all the way in Europe the second leg of the semi-final would have been played on the 15th April, one day before the Southampton game. Obviously that game would have had to have been moved, so where would it have gone? It seemed as if we had been punished for doing well in the Cups.

I've talked about competitive training and that's not something that's exclusive to Manchester United. You have to be going at it with the same intensity as you would in a match. If you let Ryan Giggs embarrass you every day in training, you won't be getting picked on Saturday because you look like a mug. At United the players are that bit better so training is that bit harder. That's not a complaint, that was something I loved about being at the club, you had to have the highest possible standards. But it's impossible to maintain those standards in a situation like the one we found ourselves in in April 1992. Our end of season win against Tottenham - little more than a glorified training match - was our 118th game in two seasons.

We lost just three league games in our first 38 games and our whole season was undermined by the fact we were forced to play four games in seven days. We suffered injuries in that run of games which hurt our chances even more, injuries that were almost certainly a direct consequence of too many games with not enough time for our bodies to recover. The scheduling was not just hurtful to our chances, it was potentially reckless to the careers of players. The gaffer was left with almost no choice but to burn out Kanchelskis and Giggs and it was to his credit that he was responsible with how he managed that situation. I believe we were the best team in the league - we'd proven that in our head to heads with Leeds - but what consolation is that? It certainly wasn't any at the time and it isn't any now.

Leeds had a good team; Gary Speed, who I knew from Wales, Strach was there, Lee Chapman, Mel Sterland, Gary McAllister, and obviously Eric Cantona. They were a very big team and very good in the air too - McAllister was great on dead balls - he was a player who'd been down at United as a kid when I was first there and he was about the same height as me and dead skinny. I think the club just binned him off because they worried he might not grow. The next time I saw him he was playing for Motherwell and was 6'1.

It was easy to see how they won a lot of games because they were so physical and tough to play against. Even their shorter players, like Speed, were great in the air. They were a footballing version of Wimbledon, without being mean to them. And still, we had seemingly got the better of them, we had the measure of Leeds. It's a strange thing to say you regret scoring a great goal, but I do slightly regret that free kick I'd scored at Elland Road. I don't say that lightly. Without being big-headed I know I scored a few good goals and that one was probably the best of my career. I might not have taken it because Webby placed the ball. I'd taken one five minutes earlier and Lukic tipped it over. Without that, maybe Leeds would hold on for the win and have to go and play the League Cup Final instead.

Despite it being a difficult year, I still managed 33 appearances, it's just that they came in a number of different positions instead of left back and I rarely got a settled run in the side. Apart from the season before, it was my best ever season for goals. It still didn't soften the pain of missing out on the league. 1992 was much worse than blowing that lead in 1986 and even though we finished second in 1988 we were never really in a 'title race' where we realistically believed we would win it. I always tried to look forward positively but there's no denying that was a miserable summer.

The Holy Grail

I DON'T KNOW IF IT WAS out of faith or blind loyalty but I had no problem believing that our team was good enough to win the league the following season. We had everything in place and we were the match of any team in the country. Liverpool were struggling through the start of their transition after a period of success, as were Arsenal and it meant the league was more open than it had been in years.

During the second half of the 1991/1992 season goals had been hard to come by and so we were heavily linked with Alan Shearer and David Hirst. People love to look back and say 'what if?' – one thing I will say is that if we had signed Alan Shearer from Southampton, I'm sure he would have been a fantastic player for us. If I had a choice of him or Sparky? Well, I'd probably go for my old mate but Shearer was probably a more natural finisher – they were both good in the air and very strong. I'd say Sparky probably had a better all around game because he was so good at bringing others into play and was probably better with the ball at his feet but the idea of the two of them together whets the appetite.

Unlike Paul Gascoigne, Alan Shearer is less forthcoming about admitting regret at not signing for United. Nobody can deny he fulfilled his potential because he became England captain and also the record goalscorer for his hometown club but when you think of all the medals he would have won at United, and how many more he might have helped us win that we missed out on, I think deep within he must have some regret. There must be a part of him that wonders.

Hirst was a different matter. In 2015 he admitted regretting not trying to force through a move to United when he learned we'd made an offer. Hirsty had scored a couple of great goals against us for Sheffield Wednesday and was always a handful for our defenders; injuries limited his potential but I still think that our first choice was Shearer and I could understand why. Hirst had a great left foot so would have added something different, although I can't say he would have necessarily improved our front line. He would have been a fine alternative to McClair and Hughes but they would still be the first choices. Choccy had gradually evolved his game from a poacher to a more industrious forward so I could see the logic in bringing in Shearer as an out-and-out goalscorer, even if I didn't think we necessarily lacked goals, we just needed to rediscover the confidence of the autumn and winter of 1991.

We did sign a centre-forward that summer; Dion Dublin came from Cambridge United after Shearer decided to go to Blackburn Rovers, who were splashing the cash under Jack Walker and the move for Hirst went nowhere. Dublin was another player who had impressed against us, scoring in the last seconds of our League Cup game with them the previous season. Cambridge had a really effective game plan that caught us out. Their warm up consisted of hitting balls the length of the pitch which gave us some indication of what they were about but they had a really clever strategy of taking free-kicks. As one of their players went to place the ball, as soon as it touched turf, another player would quickly put it behind our defence. It was a game plan they executed effectively, especially on the night as they got that late draw. Dion was tall and had a bit of a presence about him. For someone so tall he had a really clean strike on him. Again, if I'm being dead honest, he was more of a plan B than an upgrade on our plan A. Considering how exhausted we had all been at the end of the last season, even though the circumstances were pretty extreme, I think the gaffer, in his wisdom, wanted a fresh game plan. Mark Robins had gone to Norwich City, keen to become the first choice he couldn't be at Old Trafford, and we definitely needed bodies in there.

Dublin joined in early August, by which time we'd already completed our pre-season campaign. The timing of the signing was an indication of how long the Shearer saga had dragged on for and also underlined our need for squad reinforcement. Our friendly games were mostly in Norway - a nice, competitive environment with plenty of Scandinavian Reds being given the opportunity to come and watch us play a little closer to their home. I have to say that despite the terrible end to the previous season, the mood around the club was more upbeat than you'd expect. We had a good group of lads with a desire to regroup and do well and really, when you're playing for Manchester United, there is very little to grumble about. You're playing for the best club in the world and that was something I appreciated every day I was there. The supporters work hard all week to be entertained on the Saturday and they would sell out at Old Trafford or any venue we visited. They would swap places with us in an instant and I never once took that privilege for granted. To be paid to play football was a dream. Of course we were disappointed and in many ways it's more crushing to be closer to something and not win it than it is to be miles away from it, as we had been so many times in the late eighties.

The first game of the season certainly tested our resolve. Sheffield was a tough place to go to anyway, either at United or Wednesday, and our first game of the Premier League era was at Bramall Lane. The first ten minutes were a disaster, to put it lightly. Ince and Robson brought such strength and vibrancy to our midfield but Robbo was out injured and Ince had to come off after eight minutes. By that time, we were already a goal down - Brian Deane scored after five minutes to famously become the Premier League's first ever goalscorer. I headed on a throw-in, trying to divert it - unwittingly become the Premier League's first ever player to assist a goal. Five minutes into the second half Pally brought down Alan Cork in the area and Deane scored the penalty. We did get a goal, through Hughes, but two was beyond us and we ended up losing. We then lost at home to Everton - we were thumped, to put it more precisely - 3-0. Maybe there was a bit of anxiety creeping in as we were getting towards half time with no hint of a goal; we piled men forward for a free kick just before the break and were caught on the counter. A long ball forward from them found Peter Beardsley who had loads of time because Denis Irwin, who was chasing him, had been the player who took our free kick in the first place. Beardsley scored, and despite battering them in the second half, we were caught out on the counter in the 80th minute. Me and Giggsy had worked well together down the left but my cross was intercepted and hoofed upfield. To be fair Robert Warzycha turned Pally inside out to score a great goal. We were piling men forward still in the last minute and the same thing happened once again. This time Schmeichel was way out of his goal, trying to intercept their long ball but Maurice Johnston won the ball and scored to make it 3-0 and I think they must have scored from every attempt they had.

There's no defence for the results but I think we hadn't got the pre-season ring rust out of our system and when you're already playing catch up it can culminate in the sort of nightmare we experienced against Everton. Things marginally improved as we drew our next game, 1-1 at home to Ipswich, but then I was dropped for our trip to the Dell. Dublin scored in the last minute to give us our first league win of the season. I came on as a sub in the next game at Nottingham Forest as a sub just before half-time for Micky Phelan. Paul Ince was back in midfield but to be fair Mick and Darren Ferguson had been doing a good job filling in, in difficult circumstances. Neil Webb, having argued his way on to the bench for the League Cup Final, was out of favour and soon to return to Forest. At the City Ground, just after the break, I crossed for Giggsy to head in and make the result safe for us (Sparky had scored in the first half).

It seemed as if we were finally picking up momentum so it was big blow to lose Dion Dublin to injury in our next game, at home to Crystal Palace. Dion broke his leg from a challenge by Eric Young – I don't think there was any malice, even if it was clumsy. Hughes scored two minutes from time to make it three wins on the bounce and three clean sheets – we were embarking on a run that was to become a club record for wins and clean sheets and I don't think it's any coincidence that Peter Schmeichel was in goal.

Since his arrival at the club in 1991 he had already proven himself to be an outstanding goalkeeper and was regarded by most as the best in the world in that position – helped by his outstanding displays that summer for Denmark in their European Championship winning team.

Prior to Big Pete's arrival the manager hadn't made it any secret that he was after a goalkeeper. Les was a great character and a fantastic stand-in, as popular in the stands with the supporters as he was within the club, but he had been brought in as a reserve and the gaffer was after a top name to play in goal after he'd decided Jim Leighton's time in that role was up. The best around in the country was big Neville Southall and so Sparky and me made not so subtle overtures to Nev when we were on international duty.

Nev was keen so we put the word back to the manager and we were effectively just waiting for the gaffer to put in an offer. And then on the opening day of the 1990/91 season Everton were 2-0 down at half time at home to Leeds and Nev stayed on the pitch instead of going in to listen to the team talk. It was infamous and the pictures were all over the newspaper. I groaned when I saw it - there was no chance the gaffer would sign him now. I don't know if his head had already been turned so much that he was growing frustrated with events at Goodison Park but we just knew that the boss wouldn't be impressed with that show of defiance.

It was another year until we signed Schmeichel and despite his colossal frame I was a bit concerned early on. We played a friendly at Littleton Road against a team called Mazda from Japan, and they scored two screamers past him. One of the goals hit the stanchion and the referee didn't give it - the gaffer actually came on to the pitch to tell the ref they'd scored! It was good sportsmanship from the boss.

We gave Pete some stick for that but it wasn't long until he made a more positive and distinctive impression. In another session at Littleton Road we were running crossing and shooting drills and I ran to get on to the end of a cross. I collided with Pete and we both fell in a heap on the ground - he was screaming at me. I don't think he expected me to go in. He thought I'd be intimidated. I had my eyes on the ball so I didn't see him, I was running flat out to get to the ball so it was a big impact when I jumped into him. I don't think he saw me coming. He quickly became a dominating and imposing presence behind our defence; Les had been a presence in his own way, but we hadn't had a really tall goalkeeper since Gary Bailey - he was 6'3, and at 6'4, Schmeichel was even bigger than the South African. There were few holes in Peter's game. He was so agile for someone so big. He fancied himself as an outfield player and he was okay on the ball, though I would say probably a bit too wooden to really be an outfield player. That's not to say he didn't influence our attacks. When Kanchelskis and Giggs came into the side we benefited from the value of Peter's incredible throw. I lost count of how many goals we scored from an attack started by one of his throws to one of those two.

By autumn 1992 he had been our goalkeeper for a year and having him, Bruce and Pallister as our central defensive unit gave us a strong, tall, reliable and physical spine that was - usually - difficult for opposition players to crack. It was definitely helpful to us on the run that got us back on track after the early season wobble. After beating Palace we then had an early season showdown with champions Leeds. Their start had been as bad as ours - they were hardly proving to be dominant champions, perhaps they were struggling with the expectation and the increased efforts from opponents determined to claim a scalp. I can't speak for what was going on at Elland Road, whether it was a case of partying too hard in the summer or a sense of overachievement the previous season but we defeated them comfortably and despite the joy of claiming three points in a big game it was a bit frustrating that they were as poor as they were. If you lose against the better team you hold your hands up and say there's nothing you can do but our routine win against them only strengthened my belief that fixture congestion at the back end of the last season had been the decisive behind the destiny of the Championship.

We went to Goodison Park next with an early opportunity to avenge that defeat we'd suffered in the second game and succeeded with goals from McClair and Bruce. That 2-0 victory was the club-record setting game for consecutive clean sheets and victories in the league at the time. I come back to the fact that Denis and I were playing full back and that four man defensive unit had really gelled over the last two years. Of course I will be biased and say that I felt that was our strongest defence and it was only helped by Schmeichel's arrival. We had a natural understanding of our positioning and our offside trap often helped us get the ball back and after that run of games I felt that I'd finally played my way back into first choice in the position in which I'd played my best football.

Obviously, then, that's when fate decided to play its hand and I picked up a hernia injury. You can play with a hernia, so I did; it might not have been the best move but I didn't want to run the risk of losing my place.

The rules on British players playing in Europe had been relaxed so I was able to play against Torpedo Moscow in the UEFA Cup but a 0-0 draw at home meant it would be a tough ask in the second leg, even if we were still favourites. After those five wins in the league, we now drew five consecutively. I was beginning to really struggle with my hernia and was only named as a sub in our game at home to Liverpool. We were 2-0 down and I came on, playing a part in our comeback when I set up Mark Hughes with a nice ball in behind their defence and he lifted it over Grobelaar. He then scored an equaliser very late on to rescue a point.

We needed a boost but sometimes the fix isn't always obvious. I don't think anyone looking from the outside thought that Eric Cantona of Leeds United was the man to fix our problems and even when we did sign him it raised more than a few eyebrows. He had won the league with Leeds, of course, but only scored three times in fifteen games. It wasn't as if his arrival had obviously and suddenly inspired them. His start to the 1992/93 season had been eye-catching, however. He scored a hat-trick at Wembley in the Charity Shield against Liverpool which suddenly made a lot of people sit up and pay attention, and followed it up with another hat-trick against Spurs a few weeks later. He already had eleven goals for Leeds in the season and I don't think there was ever any reason to even think that him moving to Manchester was an option because he'd only been in England for a few months.

The story goes that Leeds phoned enquiring about Denis Irwin, Fergie laughed and suggested buying Cantona for £1m, almost in sarcastic response. Howard Wilkinson, then Leeds manager, agreed to the deal and, in a transfer that was as much a shock to us players as everyone else in football, we had a new centre forward.

Going back to the point I made about Shearer and Hirst and the way people say, 'if we had signed this player we wouldn't have signed that player and look how well it turned out', I'm still not sure that firstly, that's a fair statement and secondly, that it's even true in this case. You know the kind of thing – if Patrick Kluivert hadn't turned United down, they wouldn't have signed Dwight Yorke, and they might not have won the treble. Or if they signed Ronaldinho they wouldn't have got Cristiano Ronaldo. Can you imagine how good Kluivert would have been at United? Or Gabriel Batistuta or the Brazilian Ronaldo? And how good they would have made us? It's impossible to imagine that if we'd bought Ronaldinho and then if we hadn't played Sporting Lisbon we wouldn't have signed Cristiano as well.

Likewise, even if we'd signed Shearer, if the gaffer had received that call about Irwin, you can probably still imagine him making the offer for Eric because he had something in his locker that we didn't have. Just as Hirst had that left foot, Dublin had his height, so Cantona had flair and tricks as well as an obvious knack of finding the net but I don't think any of us realised how good he was until we saw him up close. When you play against someone you get a glimpse of how good they are but it's only a glimpse. I'd never seen a player his size who was as agile, not an outfield player, anyway. His touch was exceptional, he had wonderful composure and could be clinical in front of goal. People don't realise this but he's as tall as Dion Dublin so nothing was lacking in his aerial presence.

I think he made Mark Hughes a better player, too. Sparky would always hit the ball with power, be it a shot or a pass but after training and playing with Eric and observing the care with which he would pass and move the ball, he adapted his own game. Cantona would be so careful and responsible with his decision making. It rubbed off on Sparky but I think a fair few of the team benefitted from that too. Eric had a fiery streak and came with a reputation for having been badly behaved in France but most of the time he kept it under control.

I've already said that I thought the signing of Pally was the big one for me. That was the catalyst for us finally getting to grips with direct teams like Crystal Palace and Wimbledon and it was no coincidence that his arrival triggered better results in those games and, generally, better consistency overall. We'd improved year on year as the team took shape but it all stemmed from having that security in our back line. Still, nobody can deny the influence Cantona had and what followed. What he added to our team was a clinical edge that I think we had previously been missing. That composure, which gradually rubbed off on other players, helped us in situations where perhaps anxiety had got the better of one or two players, or, simply, the wrong choice had been made. With our defensive strength, it meant that we could turn the 0-0's into 1-0's - and, considering the number of times we went on to win 1-0 with Eric scoring, I'd say that point was well proven.

By now the hernia was frustrating me because I knew I'd been playing well. When I was on the ball, I felt okay, I didn't feel as if my ability had been restricted but off the ball I could feel that I wasn't able to move as quickly as I normally did!

I spoke to loads of players about it, some who'd suffered the same injury, some who knew of players who had it, and the advice was always the same. If you have an operation you have to have it on both sides, because if you don't, you're likely to need another operation a year later. The bit that is repaired becomes a lot stronger than the natural part. When it came time for my surgery I told the doctor I wanted both sides doing and he said, 'No you don't need that.' I told him that I'd looked into it and even when I explained my worries about one side being weaker than the other he told me not to worry about it. Normally the idea of going to Gran Canaria in February would seem like a great idea. That's where I spent one week in February of 1993 and 1994, recovering from my first operation and the second which I was told wouldn't be necessary! The next time the same doctor did the same operation he did both sides, that young lad was back playing within six weeks.

It wasn't just the operation they got wrong. When I was going in they gave me an epidural for the pain. That's right, the same thing pregnant women are given when they're in labour. The numbing worked for a bit but I suffered from a leakage of spinal fluid which was running up to my brain. All day I was in agony and at 5pm the doctor comes in to see me and tells me I should be lying on my back. I was taken down to theatre the next day where they took blood from my arm and made a blood clot to stop the leak. The pain up until that point was almost unbearable. I felt as if my head was going to explode. Suddenly the idea of playing football wasn't that important. I was seriously worried, I felt as if it was the end of the world.

The second time I went in to have a check up with the doctor, Jim McGregor said 'Whatever you do, tell him your groin's okay.' The same thing had happened to Sharpey. He told them it was hurting - because they didn't do the other side on him either - and they cut into his groin. He was out for about four months with it. They were poking and prodding me, opening my groin up and asking me if I could feel any pain.

'Nope.'

I was in agony.

In the early winter of 1993 I had no idea of the damage the hernia would do to my United career; that the refusal of the doctor to perform the double hernia would effectively rob me not only of one of the most important years of my career but probably also my place at Old Trafford.

Eric had taken to life at United like a duck to water and somehow the chemistry of the team seemed perfect. Observing from the sidelines and wondering about where I would fit in was nothing new for me and I was enjoying the football just as the supporters were. My run of games had mostly been at full back so I thought I could have slotted in there and done as good a job as I had done in the past. Parks was doing a good job at right back but where he was a better natural defender I think I was a better footballer. Denis was probably the best all-round full-back the club has ever had, a good defender, good attacker and a free-kick expert. Robbo was still struggling with injuries and at thirty-six he was never going to be the same player that he had been simply because of his age. He was still good enough to be first choice but I was excited about the prospect of maybe playing in the middle of the park and linking up with Eric who was like the ringleader in his slightly withdrawn forward position. He always seemed to have space and always seemed to play the right ball and that encouraged players to get forward. The balance in the team was perfect and the qualities we already had were made more prominent by the addition of Cantona. He also liked a bit of a trick and so the crowd took to him immediately.

Our form in the run-in was almost perfect – we lost only twice after Christmas, and early exits in all of our Cup competitions helped us avoid the fixture pile-up issues of the previous season. We were doing brilliantly but we'd learned not to take anything for granted. I don't know if that was the case for the players afterwards, with all the trophies they went on to win, but certainly in that first year I know our prior heartache meant there would be no resting on our laurels.

We won at Anfield to go top in March and were brought down to earth with a run of four games without a win. Then we went to Norwich and tore them apart with exactly the kind of performance where Eric made the difference. This Norwich team were no mugs, they were up there challenging for the title with a team that later went on to beat Bayern Munich in Germany, but we scored three brilliantly clinical counter attack goals in the first 21 minutes. It was a shot in the arm for the lads to remind them of their ability and then there was that very famous late win over Sheffield Wednesday where Steve Bruce scored twice and provoked a feeling that this could actually be our year. We followed that up with wins against Coventry, Chelsea and Crystal Palace to put us on the verge of winning the trophy. With two games left to play we needed to win just one, with our last home game of the season against Blackburn Rovers seeming like the opportunity to do it.

As it turned out, we didn't even need that – with Aston Villa needing to win their remaining games they played Oldham Athletic at Villa Park. I watched the game at home. Oldham scored with just under half an hour played and you just assumed that Villa would get back into it. Dean Saunders hit the bar with a free kick and then had one cleared off the line but as the game wore on their chances dried up and they didn't really look as if they would do it. I was watching by myself and for the last ten minutes of the game it felt very strange; you dream of these moments and I'd wanted it for my whole career and it just felt odd that when it came to it, I wasn't on the pitch helping to make it happen. The final whistle blew and it was official – Manchester United were Champions of England for the first time in 26 years. I don't know if I was overwhelmed or underwhelmed. I just remember thinking, 'Wow, we're Champions… what do I do now?'

There was a brief moment of quiet before the phone started ringing. Word got around that there was a party round at Brucey's so I headed right there where the celebrations continued late into the night. I had endured problems with feeling part of our successes in previous years - most notably the League Cup win in 1992 - though even with the injury forcing me to spend so much of the season on the sidelines, I felt as if I was part of the squad. After my first hernia operation I'd been trying to get my match fitness back up with a handful of reserve games but I knew it wasn't feeling right and I knew I wasn't near a first team place. I'd played enough games to win a medal and again I felt for the players who had played and didn't get one. After playing some games with Robbo for the reserves, I know there was some concern that he might not get enough appearances to qualify for a medal. Not only did that turn out alright, but he also scored our last goal of the season.

The game against Blackburn turned into a celebration for everyone at the club and the supporters. By that time it had sunk in and the overriding feeling was one of relief that it had finally happened. When I looked around Old Trafford and saw the jubilation among the fans, I realised that the triumph hadn't really been about us, it had been the fans who had waited the longest. It was a special occasion made even more so by their wait for it. The FA Cups and winning in Europe had been great but twenty-six years was such a long time for the supporters to have been following us up and down the country, up and down the divisions even, and for them to have this reward and to be able to enjoy it with them, remains one of my favourite memories.

In the dressing room before the Blackburn game the gaffer told the lads, 'It's fantastic, it's great, you've won the league title, congratulations. But make sure you win.' We did, and the feeling of going up to collect my League Champions medal with the rest of the lads was incredible.

Leaving Home Again

IN THE SUMMER OF 1993 we spent some of our pre-season in South Africa. We played the Kaizer Chiefs and they proved to be very difficult opposition. They were great on the ball and difficult to get off it but their problem was that they struggled to create chances when they got near the penalty box. It was like they'd all been coached by Louis van Gaal and told not to cross! Honestly – they were so good on the ball that I was thinking if they got their act together, it was a generation of players that had a chance of winning a World Cup. We won 1-0, purely because we had the experience of being clinical.

The trip was more memorable for the human experiences as opposed to the sporting ones. We went around the townships and played football with some of the younger children and it was a real joy. Giggsy, probably our best footballer, was doing tricks for the kids, there were seven year olds trying to imitate him and they did it! There were tricks I couldn't do! We met the recently freed Nelson Mandela and I shook his hand – it was incredible, what this man had gone through just for his beliefs. It was unbelievable and he was a remarkable man.

Once the celebrations of the 1993 title success were over, it was time for the club to look forward and build on the success we'd achieved. As with our European success you'd almost be forgiven, in a way, if, after all that time, the relief outweighed the ambition. As we all know, now, it clearly didn't. The gaffer was determined to keep winning – I'd like to think that even in the lean years we were aware of that responsibility and we certainly tried our best to win every game. The gradual changes the manager had been making; the lifestyle, the diet, the cutting out of the drinking – all of these things had slowly helped to improve us and the various personnel arriving when they did, it all helped.

Cantona had become a focal point and it was obvious that would be the case because he was the player who had added that certain something to the team that had proved the difference to previous seasons. His on-pitch contribution had been obvious and off the pitch his influence was felt around the club. He was a quiet guy; for a few months, he barely said anything, and it was sort of commonly accepted that he didn't speak a lot of English. But when he did start speaking his English was better than some of our British players! I got on fine with him. He would call me 'Blacky' in that deep accent of his. He was a bit of an eccentric and the supporters loved him even more for it; I think he had an old clapped out Beetle he used to drive around in. It seemed like an odd marriage but he fell for Manchester United and the club fell for him.

In recent years some of the younger players from that time have spoken about his attitude to training and how it rubbed off on them; the 'class of 92'. I'm not sure Ryan Giggs needed any help - he was already as good as anyone in the team and one of the first names on the team-sheet. I love that banner at Old Trafford - 'Tearing teams apart since 1991' - he really was. I said it earlier but I hated playing against him in training. I would play against Andrei any day. You might be exhausted and he might get the better of you but Giggsy would terrorise you, moving in every direction with the ball. Gary Pallister called it 'twisted blood' and he was right. Even in his post-retirement years, I spent plenty of time on the training ground with him when he was a coach at United and he still moves like he did then. I have no problem going on record as saying Ryan Giggs is the best player I ever played with, hands down, and at that time with him, Sparky, Andrei, Sharpey and Eric in attack, we had the best frontline in the country by a mile.

1993/94 was the first year squad numbers were introduced and there are two ways of looking at the fact that I was given the number 15. On the one hand, in a squad game, it was good that it was relative close to the eleven. On the other, it was an indication that I was on the way out! That's not strictly true - the decision to leave at the end of this season was ultimately mine and I take full responsibility for that. I wasn't forced out, I wasn't asked to leave. I never felt as if the club pushed me away and never felt as if I wasn't wanted. The gaffer never came to me and said, 'look, it's time to move on.' That's why, in the years which followed, I often wondered - and sometimes still do - whether or not I made the right choice.

Injury played a big part in my decision. Being injured on and off for the last year was a big reason; I also felt as if I'd been at the club for so long it was almost as if it was time for the new guard. And that was a completely personal thing, one I didn't go and discuss with anyone. I wish I had done. Instead, I looked at how the team had done and whereas at first I liked to imagine where I could play in such an exciting team, the depression of my injury started to dominate my thoughts and I began to think that the team was doing so well that there was no place I could fit in. I had 'recovered' from my first operation and was back playing football in the reserves but I knew it didn't feel right.

I was back on holiday in Gran Canaria, recovering from the second operation, as United went to Wimbledon in the FA Cup. I watched as they not only stood up to their physicality but played them off the park in a way teams never did to Wimbledon. Eric scored a brilliant goal and then Denis scored one where almost all of the team were involved. The gaffer said it was one of the best ever performances. He was right but watching from afar there was a certain level of despondency in knowing that he had a first choice team and I wasn't a part of it. Watching it on television only added to that feeling. Of course, I hoped that I would be back playing soon, but I had been told I would be back in four or five weeks a year before and I had lost all trust in the doctors. I felt as if I might always be playing with the injury.

In March, Wolverhampton Wanderers manager Graham Turner was sacked and there was a lot of speculation that Robbo would leave United to become player-manager at Molineux. However, United had got through to the League Cup Final, and throughout most of the competition the gaffer had rotated the squad. Robbo, who had been phased into second choice behind Ince and the new arrival Roy Keane, had been getting first team games in that competition and I think the idea of a last hurrah at Wembley was more tempting for him than moving to Wolves. I think that perfectly sums up what a wrench it was going to be to leave United for him; even right at the end, with a very good opportunity offered to him for his future, the prospect of one last big Cup Final at the club was too much to miss.

The gaffer went with his first choice team (with Les in goal, because Peter Schmeichel was suspended) against Aston Villa – meaning Robbo didn't even get on the bench. In the team talk before that game the manager explained that the plan was to hit them on the counter attack on the big Wembley pitch. In the end, that's what Villa did to us. What was left out of the game plan was that in order to counter attack, you need to give the opponent the ball and let them come at you. Dalian Atkinson and Dean Saunders had great games and Ron Atkinson enjoyed his second success over his old club in this competition in the space of four years.

With Robbo openly entertaining the idea of leaving, the thought started to cross my mind. My entire time at the club had been alongside him and even though my problems were caused by injury, rather than the natural passing of time I felt it might be time to call it a day. My appearances for the reserves had been sporadic due to my injury giving me such aggravation but, after I came back from holiday, I found myself gradually getting fitter and feeling more capable of doing the things I'd been able to do eighteen months before. Yet despite being in the reserves and seeing the team run away with the league in the way they were, I still felt marginalised.

In normal circumstances I should have been feeling more positive about it. The reserve team were battering everyone. It wasn't uncommon for us to hit four, five or six goals past teams. And yet, despite my age – at 29, I should have been at my peak – the length of time I'd been at the club had me feeling like it was time to move on, in much the same way as Martin Buchan and Lou Macari did when I was breaking through. You would normally think the form of the reserve team would mean we'd get a look in but the first team were so good and our reserve side also had the following players – David Beckham, Paul Scholes, Ben Thornley, Simon Davies, Keith Gillespie, Gary Neville – these youngsters were knocking on the door for an opportunity and, in keeping with the tradition of the club, they who would inevitably get their opportunity. It wasn't so obvious that some of those names would go on to become some of the most decorated ever at the club. Gary Neville always gave 100% but the talk was that Phil was better on the ball. Becks would regularly hit those cross-field balls that became his trademark but in the reserves the success rate of those kind of passes was maybe not even 50/50. It was frustrating in the reserve games because we were at him to play it simple. The difference was, when he got into the first team, that switch of play was hit to Ryan Giggs. It was mad and I felt a bit sorry for opposition defenders - imagine David Beckham being on the ball on the other side of the pitch and you're still having to worry about Ryan Giggs' pace!

The best of the bunch in that reserve team, for me, was Scholesy. At first he was playing up front but because of his size, the step up from playing youth football to reserves against fully grown men wasn't an easy one. He was moved further back into midfield where he was able to showcase the full range of his ability. He was absolutely brilliant; the range and accuracy of his passing, shooting and ability to arrive in the box unmarked as well his ability to score from outside the penalty box made him a star. To me it went to show the standard of that group that Keith Gillespie was deemed surplus to requirements and went on to be one of Newcastle's best players in the team that was challenging United for the title a few years later!

As the season came to its close there was more talk of Bryan leaving to become a manager, with Middlesbrough the team who were mentioned more often than not. Robbo made no secret of his desire to go there and he spent the last few weeks enthusiastically talking about his plans. He was talking about what players he would buy, where they would play. United had won the League, comfortably and in style, and were about to play in the FA Cup Final, where they beat Chelsea 4-0. They were doing just fine without me and without a first team appearance for a year and half I was almost questioning my own ability to play at that level, even though that wasn't the problem and hadn't been questioned by the manager. My head was turned by the idea of joining Robbo on this new adventure and the prospect of playing first team football every week.

I can't remember much of any discussions with the gaffer about leaving; Robbo was talking quite openly about the move, not only to me, but many other players in the squad, who were all sharing their opinion. I think it was just taken for granted that I was going along and pretty much agreed, and he went to the boss and spoke about the ideas and I must have been mentioned in that.

If I'd known what was going to happen in the 1994/95 season at United I think I may have made a different decision. Paul Parker played only two games and I played a full season; it's only natural to think that I might have been back in favour as he ended up playing David May (normally a centre back) and Roy Keane (a midfielder) in that position before being forced to try Gary Neville there. And Gary had played centre half in the youth team. It's logical to think Denis would have moved to the right and I would have gone in on the left, just like we had when we'd enjoyed so much success before.

Robbo was like God to all the players though and when he said he wanted me to come along, I took it as a huge compliment. This was his first job as a manager and it was a big boost to my confidence, which I suppose he could tell had been dented.

I'd had fourteen years at United – just about as many as I'd spent living at home before I moved. It did feel like I was leaving my family all over again. It didn't make it an easy decision but, at the same time, it felt like the only one at that time.

The Holy Grail (Part 2)

DESPITE PLAYING SOME reserve football and generally feeling much better in myself and my movement after the second hernia operation, the fact that I hadn't played a senior game of football for a year and a half was playing on my mind as I prepared to join Middlesbrough. Bryan Robson's opinion counted for so much, though, and his insistence that I would be the first player to join him in the North East was a boost.

Throughout my time out I'd put a bit of weight on and I was regularly down at Mulligans with Roy Keane having the odd beer. Too regular, in fact. It got to the point that I would go in and they'd put a Rolling Rock on the bar without me asking. It was fine for Roy as he was playing but for me, it wasn't my wisest move. Football had moved on and maybe I should have been more disciplined. Roy, for me, was good fun to be with and I always got on with him great. After I left United it was years until I saw him on a casual basis – Scholesy's testimonial in 2011. He came right over to talk about the good old days when we went for a few bevvies. Good old days for him, difficult ones for me.

When I first agreed to go to Middlesbrough, I was told, 'Make sure you've got a garage for the car.'

'Why?' I asked.

'Because of the acid rain.'

'What about me?! I'm going to be the one running about in it!' I laughed.

Middlesbrough were sponsored by ICI and put us up in Wilton Castle, which was an impressive setting but it wasn't long before the difference in size between Middlesbrough Football Club and Manchester United Football Club revealed itself. Boro are a big club in the North East but even so, to go from United to training on the grounds of the local prison was a bit of a leap. Under a new, young chairman, the club had big ideas - a new stadium for one which would open the following year. Saying that, one thing Ayresome Park did have going for it was the fact the pitch was better than the one I was used to at Old Trafford! Ayresome Park, like Sunderland's Roker Park, had a great atmosphere where the passionate supporters made their voices heard.

I found myself in a strange situation, much like the last 18 months, which had been unfamiliar territory for me. It's peculiar but true - I barely ever felt pressure playing for Manchester United but as soon as I arrived at Middlesbrough there it was, right from the start. Robbo had shown a great deal of faith in me even though I'd been out for a while, so long that I'm sure some neutrals forgot that I was injured and thought I just fell out of favour. I knew I'd have to prove myself on that score but also, being the proverbial big fish, I knew I'd have to hit the ground running to display my form and fitness right from the off. I was able to get a full pre-season under my belt, to make the best possible start.

The Boro fans were a sensible bunch, they didn't have unreasonable expectations. It wasn't as if I was expected to score thirty-yard blockbusters every week. Still, their hopes were high. Yes, I'd been injured but when fit, I was around that United first team squad. Robbo came to Boro disappointed that he hadn't made two Cup Final squads. Neither of us were bit part players and so our addition to their squad made the fans hope that promotion would be a realistic aim. Football doesn't always work out as people predict but thankfully for us things started swimmingly as my confidence flew back and Robbo played with the sort of dominance that a midfielder of his calibre was expected.

In our discussions prior to moving up there, Bryan had identified Nicky Summerbee as a potential right back, with me playing in front of him. He'd also spoken to Nigel Pearson who was going to come in at centre-back. I was originally flying up with Nicky to have a look around at where we would stay but he changed his mind and stayed at Manchester City, before eventually making the move North East to Sunderland. Robbo then went for Neil Cox who had bags of experience at right back in the Aston Villa side who had done so well in the first two Premier League years. These were smart, calculated signings with the division in mind.

Viv Anderson left his job as manager of Barnsley to be assistant to Robbo. He brought that same loud voice and personality to Boro as he did to United when he first arrived and, again, it was a sensible decision by Bryan, considering he'd witnessed, as I had, the positive impact Viv had on the dressing room at Old Trafford.

Ask me if I regret leaving United and I'll say yes but only in hindsight because that first year at Boro was the best I'd felt in a long time. I'd go so far as to say it was one of the most enjoyable times of my career. Everything Robbo was doing was spot on, he made clever signings and we were flying from the off, playing good football and winning our first four games. I scored in the last of those, a win at Derby's Baseball Ground, and then I scored in the following game, a 1-1 draw at Watford. The hernia was a distant memory.

In the week after our opening game of the season - a 2-0 win at home to Burnley - we played Manchester United, who had granted me a testimonial to be played up at Boro. I had been due one for some time and was talking about it in the summer of 1993 but so was Mark Hughes and I think partly because he had an agent who was more aggressive about the issue, Sparky was granted his despite the fact his service had been split over two stays.

I wasn't particularly bothered by that but then Sparky's agent said that they would prefer to move it from the start of the season to the end. Celtic would be the opponents and the capacity of Old Trafford would have increased by roughly 10,000, meaning more Celtic fans and more money. With an apparent gap in the window, I went to see Martin Edwards and asked if I could have the date Mark originally had against Celtic at the start of the season. They refused and I was a little annoyed but, as I agreed to leave for Middlesbrough, United said they'd bring a team up when I moved. We got a good crowd for that but Sparky spoiled that party too, scoring twice! It was a nice gesture by the club and one I did appreciate. It was a bit odd playing against my old team so soon; the strangest thing was that testimonials are usually there to celebrate a player towards the end of their career because it is so rare that someone stays with a club for a decade and here I was trying to prove that I was still capable of playing at the highest level and that I was still at my peak!

The Premier League was scaling back from 22 teams to 20 and that meant the promotion race in the First Division was more fierce than it normally would be, with one automatic promotion place and one play-off place. Boro had finished ninth the year before but with the calibre of player we had brought in, our ambitions matched the supporters' - I was used to competing for the top spot at United and it wasn't going to be any different here. After starting the season so well, we had a tough October, before hitting a run of three home games that we knew would test us. Swindon Town and Oldham Athletic had just come down from the top flight and Wolves were always there challenging. We won all three (despite suffering a defeat at Grimsby in the middle of those games) to send something of a statement.

Our main rivals for promotion wouldn't prove to be any of those sides but Tranmere Rovers, who had established a good reputation as a Cup team and Bolton Wanderers. Still, by Christmas we were growing increasingly confident of promotion and Robbo was already looking forward, planning for life in the Premier League and trying to assess who, from the players we had, would be good enough to compete in the top flight.

Nigel Pearson was a fantastic defender but was on his last legs - good enough for the next three years to help Boro get promoted but, if he was injured his replacements were the likes of Steve Vickers and Derek Whyte, players used to that division. They were capable of competing at that level but the difference would tell when it came to the Premier League. That's why, for a couple of years, Boro were up, then down, then up again. Curtis Fleming was a great lad and he'd throw himself in front of a runaway train trying to stop an opponent scoring but on the ball he made Paul Parker look like Ryan Giggs.

Steve Gibson was a great chairman, backing Robbo and his ambitions. John Hendrie and Paul Wilkinson were up front for us and both were good forwards for that level. Hendrie knew where the goal was and Wilks was one of the best forwards at defending corners, he was forever heading balls away. A run of two wins in eight games over the winter period threatened to derail our promotion push so Robbo went and strengthened the side with two new strikers – Uwe Fuchs on loan and Jan Aage Fjortoft on a permanent basis from Swindon. Fjortoft was the top scorer outside the top flight so that was a great move but it was arguably Fuchs who had the greater influence, with eight goals in fifteen games. It put us on the verge of promotion but three draws in a row in April meant we were stumbling towards the finish line.

It was all set up for a big occasion in our penultimate game of the season, at home to Luton. Win and our superior goal difference meant that we should be up, regardless of the result in our last game. We made hard work of it. I took a corner and from the resulting melee a penalty was awarded. Wilks and Craig Hignett had taken penalties for us earlier in the season but Neil Cox stepped up to take it - his effort was saved. We did get some luck just before half time when my corner eventually found its way to Hendrie, his shot took a heavy deflection and looped into the net. Luton equalised in the second half but Hendrie got a second to start a celebration that didn't stop – promotion was all but guaranteed and in the last game at Ayresome Park too - it was a fitting send off.

The promotion was confirmed with a 1-1 draw at Tranmere the following week and it was a moment to savour as I finally got my hands on the First Division trophy. The Premier League one was beautiful, don't get me wrong, but this was the trophy Robbo and I had coveted for so many years and it didn't even matter that it wasn't the top flight. It was a fantastic moment to cap off a great year and the opportunity to play in the top flight again made it an exciting summer.

The Mole

AMID ALL THE JUBILATION of our promotion, I'd already begun to feel uncomfortable with some of the goings on at the club. Despite Viv being the assistant, John Pickering - a coach who had been at Middlesbrough for some time - led all the training and clearly had an affinity for the players who had been there before Robbo and I arrived. It wasn't something that was obvious at first because when we were winning nobody seemed to have a problem.

At the start of the next season, however, the issues seemed to come quick and fast. One of John's favourites was Craig Hignett. Craig was a good player and had done well for Middlesbrough. When I first arrived and I was learning about my new team-mates it had been said to me that Higgy was like a bottle of champagne; he'd start seasons really well, be all over the place and scoring lots of goals and then he'd fade out. His favourite position had been right-midfield, where I had been playing so well throughout the season in the First Division.

A story made its way into the Sunday People that Robbo and I had had a falling out and I was trying to leave the club. I went into see Robbo and asked him if we'd fallen out; we laughed it off, but it pissed Robbo off that there was a mole inside the club, trying to create a problem. Neither of us knew where it had come from initially. Robbo called a meeting before training and as I walked on to the field it was odd to see Higgy sat on the floor, on his own, with a bunch of us stood around him.

'If I find out who's the mole, that's it, you're finished, you're out of the club!' Bryan shouted. I don't think he ever found out but I was told from a few of the local lads that Craig had a friend at The People. The 'story' came at the point where I'd missed a few games with injury, and Craig had come in and done well, scoring a few goals. Apparently that's what caused me to have this fictional row with one of my oldest mates.

136

I didn't know what I'd done to upset anyone. I knew Pickering had been rubbed up the wrong way but I thought it had just been a bit of fun - me, big Nige and Neil Cox would mess around with the cones as John was putting them out for training.

He only got the raving hump with me and called me in. 'Look, I know you don't like me, and I don't like you…' he starts. What?! I told him that there was nobody I'd ever come across in football that I didn't like. We said our piece and that was it; I thought that was the end of it, though I was a bit wary of his tone. I played in most of the pre-season but started in the reserves. I couldn't understand why, as I'd played well the year before but I did the same as I always did and gave my best, thinking it would be a matter of time before I'd be back in contention. I couldn't have done much more. We were winning every game and scoring three, four, five goals every week. John Pickering was at every game. There were so many Fridays when Robbo would tell me I was in the team and then come the Saturday I wasn't.

After spending all summer looking forward to playing in the top flight again it was the last game of 1995 before I was given an opportunity. The previous season Robbo had played 4-4-2 and it had brought us plenty of success but he switched to a very narrow 5-2-2-1 after signing Nick Barmby and I was one of the players to miss out. You might think that, being the first one to go to the club with Robbo, I'd be his right hand man but it didn't really work out like that. That's nothing against Bryan but he stayed in Manchester while I moved to York to be closer to the club. We weren't in each other's pockets and I let him get on with his job as manager - he had all of the club to take care of, after all.

He had big ambitions for Middlesbrough and the Barmby signing was an indication of that - Nick was a great prospect for Tottenham. Nick was a very industrious front man, a hungry young player, and very tidy and smart with his play. He scored our first goal of the season, in a 1-1 draw against Arsenal. Robbo said in his autobiography that he tried to sign Andrei Kanchelskis, who was leaving United and that would have been an unbelievable signing.

The biggest news in the first months of Boro's return to the top flight, though, was the signing of Juninho. His arrival took the club to another level – he was a truly world class player arriving at a club whose usual aspirations would have been survival in the top flight. He would have fit in at Manchester United with ease. The guy was tiny and to look at him you couldn't be sure he was able to kick a ball as far as forty yards but his dribbling ability was the best I'd seen from a player since Ryan Giggs. He settled in to the club right away and also settled into English football which said a lot about his attitude. Many South American players come to England after they've played in Italy or Spain and then they struggle with the pace of the game in the Premier League but Juninho came straight from Brazil and maybe that helped him (the same could be said for Carlos Tevez, years later, who had a similar impact).

Juninho was playing well and I was frustrated to not have the chance to play alongside him but I could barely complain at first as Boro claimed a lot of points early on, though I would say the results were a lot better than the performances. The games we would lose would tend to be against Newcastle or Man United. Even the best teams expect to hit a rough patch every season and we hit ours at Christmas. We lost to Blackburn Rovers, the Champions, the week before Christmas, and then on Boxing Day we lost 4-0 at FA Cup holders Everton. The results weren't exactly disgraceful but Robbo must have felt we needed a change, so I came in to play at our trip to the City Ground.

Nottingham Forest had finished third the previous season as a newly promoted club with Stan Collymore and Bryan Roy in their attack; Collymore had gone now but they were still formidable opposition. They won 1-0. I retained my place in the side for my first League game at the Riverside Stadium but we lost 2-0 against Aston Villa. To underline the point about how tough a run of fixtures we were facing, Villa won the League Cup again that season. We then played Arsenal – complete with Dennis Bergkamp – at home and were leading in that game but lost 3-2 and our miserable run of defeats in January wrapped up with a 2-1 loss at the Dell, again after we'd taken the lead. The narrow defeats were racking up but our trip to Stamford Bridge was the departure from that as Chelsea battered us 5-0. They were just starting their 'foreign revolution' with a team that contained Ruud Gullit and Dan Petrescu and both were in form on the day.

I can't say my form was spectacular because it clearly didn't help us get better results but, as I'd been out of the team for so long, I felt I did as well as could be expected. I didn't think I showed any signs of ring rust and I played with as much commitment as I ever had. The Chelsea defeat was very disappointing but you wouldn't say it was a completely unexpected one when you compared the recent history of both clubs. In the team talk beforehand Robbo, perhaps wary of their good performance at the Riverside despite our victory, said that we should let them have the ball in their own half but close them down once they got into ours. I thought that was a recipe for disaster as it was a small pitch so I thought it would make sense to just press them as far up the pitch as possible. Some of the lads took the instruction a little too literally and the number of goals that we conceded on the day from balls played over the top of our defence was borderline criminal.

We had a break in Tenerife the week before the game at Stamford Bridge; as soon as we landed, me and Coxy were on the golf course and the rest of the lads went to the bar. By the time Neil and I had finished our round and joined the lads, Jamie Pollock was taking on John Hendrie in an England versus Scotland drinking contest. Jamie kept cheating by throwing his sangria back into the jug so John was drinking probably four drinks to Jamie's one. They were hammered beyond belief. John got so drunk that he was throwing glasses up in the air - he walked out of the bar and collapsed on the floor.

Some of the lads went to take him back to his room to sleep it off and he was so bad that we had to take it in turns to check on him every twenty minutes or so. With a few pranksters in our side, big Nige being the chief, an opportunity like this wasn't going to go by without advantage being taken. Someone shaved the hair off on John's crown and wrote in black marker pen '666'. They shaved half of his eyebrow off too. The following day he came down for breakfast and he had shaved off both of his eyebrows. He went sunbathing and his eyes swelled up because there was no protection; on another trip, he fell asleep on his front and the lads pulled his shorts down, so he ended up with third degree burns on his arse as well.

One morning, Coxy and I got up early to go to the course and as we did, we saw John coming back from the beach. From a distance it looked like he'd been battered but as he got closer, we saw that it was sand on half of his face and realised he must have fallen asleep there. I had to catch the plane back with John which was a bit embarrassing.

We played Chelsea in our first home game earlier that season and won 2-0. Gullit was playing one of his first games for them; I think he was meant to be playing as sweeper but he was all over the pitch. It was Roy of the Rovers stuff. I couldn't believe we won that game and I remembered thinking that once they got their act together, Chelsea would be a lot better the next time we played them, and I was right. We made a lot of errors on the day – you would expect that from a newly-promoted side – but we lacked that on-pitch leadership and defensive quality at that level to be more organised. In the previous season Robbo had been playing and he would be the one sorting it out on the pitch but watching from the sidelines it was that little more difficult. We got away with it on the day but long term it felt like the gap in quality between those players we had brought in and the ones who were there when we arrived would prove to be the factor that would determine where we'd end up.

To address that defensive problem Robbo brought in Gordon McQueen to join the coaching staff. After one of the games Gordon's having a go at the defenders, explaining to them what they could have done differently. John Pickering steps in and says, 'It's not your place to say that!' I don't know what his problem was – maybe John felt he should have been the one to have identified the problems and felt embarrassed but Gordon was spot on with what he was saying and had the experience to back it up. It could be that John didn't appreciate that the players Gordon was telling off were his mates who had been at the club for a long time and was worried on their behalf but there were no ulterior motives – nobody was trying to do anything other than what was best for Middlesbrough Football Club.

I was dropped after the Chelsea game and it was massively disappointing because I thought I'd easily done enough to stay in the side and Robbo told me it'd been the best I'd played since joining. Perhaps Robbo thought that if he reverted to the team that had picked up points earlier in the season form would improve, despite the fact that those results didn't tell the whole story. I was in the reserves for the rest of the season but our results didn't pick up. We won just two games after Christmas, back to back against Leeds and Sheffield Wednesday in the early spring. Without those wins we would have been relegated - from being sixth at Christmas.

We weren't the only North East club suffering a second-half collapse. Newcastle United, with Gillespie flying down the wing, had established a twelve point lead at the top by the end of January. Manager Kevin Keegan made a big mistake for me when he brought in Faustino Asprilla; the Colombian was a tricky forward but it upset the balance of that side and slowly but surely Manchester United, inspired by the form of Eric Cantona who had returned from his suspension for kicking a Crystal Palace supporter, cut their lead down and overtook them in the finishing straight.

In the last game of the season United came to the Riverside needing a win to guarantee them the Championship. The talk before the game was that the rivalry between Middlesbrough and Newcastle, as well as Robbo's history, would mean we'd take it easy on the day. We were safe no matter what and I obviously wanted United to win the title ahead of any team that I wasn't playing for. Honestly - my loyalties were torn. But if I'd have been on the pitch, I would have been trying my best to win the game. United didn't need us to do them any favours - their form had been incredible and ours had been rotten, so it was no surprise when they defeated us 3-0. I don't think there were many disappointed Middlesbrough fans that day - probably the only people who wanted us to win were the players and the manager!

In my first season at the club, John Pickering ran all the training. I couldn't understand why but on Fridays he would have us doing a full-on session for an hour and a half. Just after Christmas, I'd been out with a little niggle and was coming back to fitness. I found myself exhausted after such an intense session the day before a tough FA Cup fixture down at Swansea's Vetch Field. In any ordinary circumstance I would have been desperate to play but this was one of the few occasions I was glad not to be selected – I travelled with the team and I was knackered just watching from the stands.

Training was like the Alamo. One of my most vivid memories from the sessions is of Curtis Fleming and Jamie Pollock constantly smashing into each other; we'd been suffering loads of injuries and Robbo found out that 65% of them were picked up in training. When you are training that hard the day before games it's only logical that people will get injured because they have worked too hard; when you take into consideration the winter conditions and the way the games come around quickly, it really was no surprise that our form in the 1995/96 season dipped drastically after Christmas.

Early in the 1996/97 campaign, Arsene Wenger joined Arsenal and it was all over the press about how he was supposedly revolutionising training and approaches to player's fitness. I didn't think there was anything particularly groundbreaking; then again, I didn't have any inside knowledge of what was going on down at Highbury, though as far as I was concerned Fergie had been leading the way on that front for years at United. However, the talk about it in the press gave me the opportunity to bring it up to Robbo on a casual basis. I told him I thought training for ninety minutes on a Friday was excessive and dangerous, causing tired muscles before a game. He agreed and cut it back to an hour.

One of the things that was obvious was that players were genuinely playing for places. There were times at United when things got heated but at Boro I quickly discovered – to my detriment – John Pickering was using his influence in those sessions to help Robbo decide on the team.

At the start of the 1996/97 season I was back in the reserves but playing well – Robbo came to watch one of the games and raved about how well I'd played but there still seemed no chance of a first team performance.

Joe Jordan was manager of Bristol City and I think he and Bryan got talking about players and, knowing I wanted first team football, Robbo suggested going there for a month's loan. It was agreed that I would do some days training up at Boro and some down in Bristol.

It wasn't brilliant to drop down two divisions but I was desperate to get a game and at least I started well, scoring a diving header at Stockport to earn us a 1-1 draw. It hit my arm as well as my head but the referee didn't see it.

The player whose place I'd taken was Martin Kuhl; we played Swansea in the FA Cup and I had a bit of an itch to play because of it being down in Wales. It was with some reluctance that I didn't, because Boro would have preferred me not to be Cup-tied when I went back (though it would later be to my benefit) and Kuhl scored a thirty yarder in a 1-1 draw. I can only imagine how pissed off he was to be out of the team the next week.

They had a really good team and were unlucky not to get promoted that year. Joe trained the team really hard and he had to because those games were very difficult. With Darren Barnard and Brian Tinnion they had two of the best left-footers in the country and they were strong up front with Shaun Goater and Paul Agostino, an Australian international who scored two goals against Brazil while Gary Owers had a great engine in midfield.

I only played a few games down there but it was brilliant to get a taste of their biggest game of the season. Football derbies are fantastic because of how certain cities treat their rivalries. Between Bristol City and Rovers there were horses on the pitch after the game and it got so aggressive that Lee Martin - playing for Rovers - got punched in the face in the tunnel! He ended up going to court over it. The atmosphere had got pretty spicy because they scored a late equaliser in a 1-1 draw. I made a hasty escape to our dressing room while our fans, annoyed that Rovers had celebrated in front of them, had run on to the pitch and chased them down the tunnel. It was chaotic.

My last game for Bristol City was supposed to be at Notts County, although Joe had asked me personally if I wanted to sign for them on a permanent basis. I wasn't sure and he said that because my initial loan was up, he played Kuhl at County as he was the player he'd be counting on. I went to watch the game but they were 2-0 down in the first half so I drove home at half time.

The next morning I got a call from Joe asking me to sign a month's loan again so I went to Boro to speak to Robbo and bumped into him in the car park. It was a bit embarrassing for both of us. Boro were struggling with another injury crisis and I think, after having known each other for so long, he was a bit embarrassed to ask me to come back. I was happy to do another month at Bristol to see how it went but Robbo eventually said, 'Yeah, I was gonna ask if you wanted to come back...'

'Oh right, fine...' I said. It was odd. It had been okay down at Bristol but I wasn't going to miss the gruelling train journeys every day.

Middlesbrough's start to the season had been horrendous. They had won only five league games in the calendar year. During that time football had exploded; the Bosman ruling was changing everything for players and clubs had more money than ever before so wages were going up at a frightening rate. When I went to Boro I was on £2,000 a week and that was basically the standard then. The Bosman ruling automatically changed everything because players were able to demand higher wages if the clubs weren't paying transfer fees. The knock-on effect of that was that the top players wanted the same wages as the ones who were on a Bosman and it skyrocketed overnight to the point where talk of £30,000 and £40,000 a week was becoming commonplace. When it was announced that Fabrizio Ravanelli was going to leave Juventus to come to Middlesbrough in the summer of 1996, these were the numbers being mentioned. It was crazy talk at the time - we were linked with Rav and Gianluca Vialli. These players had both won the Champions League with Juve the year before, as strike partners and we were in talks to get them. This was a situation where Boro were caught out by the Bosman effect - Vialli was on a free transfer, and able to name his price, but Rav knew what the club were willing to pay, and the wages for him would come on top of a £7m transfer fee. Vialli went to Chelsea and we, unbelievably, got Rav.

A little later on that season we added Gianluca Festa to our defence and the one thing I can say about the Italian lads is that despite their reputation as luxury players, they had an exceptional approach to their personal conditioning that I thought set a great example. Festa would play on the Saturday and go kick-boxing on the Sunday. He was a brilliant defender, in a period where the standard of Italian defending was arguably at its best. He was a tremendous man-marker with a history of playing against players like Diego Maradona. He was only 6 foot tall and he wasn't brilliant on the ball but his spring was tremendous which more than compensated for it. He had that fiery Latin temperament, too - in a game against Manchester City he took Steve Lomas clean out with some sort of martial arts forehand smash to his chin. It was an instant red card, I thought, but the referee missed it because it happened so quickly.

Ravanelli was a bit hot-headed too but this wasn't a case of Leeds taking a chance on Cantona, or even Liverpool taking a chance on Mario Balotelli. We were talking about a seriously world class player in his prime, with no history of any significant trouble, attracted from one of the world's top clubs. It really isn't that different to comparing them going out and signing Lionel Messi or Neymar today. It was a ridiculously huge signing and I think it said a lot about the value of having Robbo as boss. Rav was predominantly left-footed but still one of the best I ever played with because there were few weaknesses in his game. He was a very powerful player - once, we were in the gym, and he was doing extra weight training that he hadn't been asked to do. He had electrodes on his thighs pulsing away. His muscles would tense, and then the electrodes would stop, and he'd lift all the weights. He was ridiculously strong. His first touch was very good and his agility and speed reminded me of Eric. His finishing was incredible, and it was easy to see why he had achieved so much in the game, as Liverpool found out to their cost on his debut when he scored a hat-trick. He was aggressive on the ball, too - maybe not so much in the tackle - but he was similar to Sparky in that he was difficult to get the ball off.

He didn't speak much English but when he did, it generally tended to be something worth hearing, and I had a lot of time for him and what he had to say. This was a guy who'd won the European Cup, after all. He went to Italy and spoke to the press. 'If we had four defenders who could play football, we'd be a much better team,' he said, and I had to agree with him. When that came out back in England, Steve Gibson was furious and made a point of setting up a meeting down at Lilleshall for the Monday morning. 'Nine o'clock, not one minute to, not one minute past!' – he was making a point about timekeeping and really it was aimed at the foreign lads who would turn up five minutes late while we were already running and they'd just saunter on to the field. Really, though, the meeting was to address everything Rav had said and he was the only one who wasn't there!

Anyway, I had returned to the club in early December but Robbo kept faith with the team that drew at home to Leeds for next game at Anfield. Liverpool won 5-1 and I thought, well, at least I'll get my chance in the next game, as we were down to the bare bones with players dropping out all over the place. That's why I was back, after all. Thankfully our next game was against Blackburn and they were also struggling – Colin Hendry was injured, as was their goalkeeper Tim Flowers. There was talk of a flu virus down there and we were also suffering from a bug around our squad. Neil Cox and Derek Whyte were sent home and the club took the unusual step of postponing our game against Rovers due to not having enough players. The next day – still in time for the match – we had a training match where it was eight versus eight and all the top names were there; Ravanelli, Juninho, Emerson - the Brazilian midfielder – they were all fit, all available and, truth be told, they were all prepared to take advantage of an arguably worse situation down at Ewood Park. By the time we eventually did play that game, we faced a full strength Blackburn and drew 0-0. We were deducted three points by the FA and I thought that was very harsh even if, hand on heart, I thought we could have put together a squad. Those three points were to prove pivotal.

Our next game was against Everton at home on Boxing Day and I was back in the team. I was as nervous as I've ever been before a game and I think that was probably due to the fact that for the first time I was in a situation where even playing well wouldn't necessarily guarantee me a place in the next game. Once the whistle blew it was strange because those worries disappeared and I enjoyed being able to play a game of football where I had time on the ball. It certainly hadn't been like that at Bristol where I'd felt sometimes like I was doing two or three jobs instead of just my own and I definitely had never had that luxury against a team like Everton before when playing for Manchester United. We won 4-2 and I scored a good goal, curling the ball into the far corner from the edge of the area. My performance meant I was kept in the team but the confidence from our win did nothing to help us against Coventry City where we were battered 3-0 on a frozen pitch even though we made over 500 passes in the game!

Desperate times called for desperate measures and Robbo selected himself to play at Arsenal. I think it was as much a case of him wanting to get across a message about how he expected other players to compete as it was a matter that we really had few other senior options. It turned out to be his last ever game of football – and I was just as gutted as him that we lost (2-0) but I think he got his message across in terms of the level expected. The difficult thing was persisting with players who weren't good enough, players who may have given the club good service in the past but who were not of sufficient quality to move the club forward or even keep them in the division. The problem Robbo had, and I felt for him because it was a genuine dilemma, is that sometimes those players can be the heart and soul of the team and with the kind of players he'd brought in - Emerson and Juninho - he felt that he needed to complement that with the grit and commitment of players who were not as gifted. Juninho worked hard but nobody would categorise him as a grafter.

We played Southampton at home and I was on the line for a corner about an hour into the game. Ken Monkou heads it towards goal, and instinctively I and tipped it over with my hand. It was going in – I got sent off (the only red card of my domestic career), they scored the penalty, and won the game 1-0. I was worried, after the way I'd been so easily dropped in the last couple of seasons, that I would find it difficult to get back in but thankfully as soon as my suspension was up I was in contention. I did, however, have to play a couple of games in the reserves again.

After the debacle of our constant injuries, the controversy at Christmas and perhaps influenced by our Italian influx and talk around the country about better conditioning, we got fitness coaches in and it was only then that I finally discovered the truth about why I wasn't being given a chance. One of the times I was told I'd be playing and again I was left out. I asked Robbo why and he said my run in the side over Christmas had been the best I'd ever played for him. I said, 'If that's the case, why am I not playing?' Robbo told me that it was because even if I thought I'd played well in the reserves, the reports coming back was that my fitness was not right.

I went to the fitness coach and had it out with him. 'You've been watching me training, am I fit or not?'

His reply was, 'To be honest, John Pickering has been talking shit about you for ages.'

It wasn't quite a case of the penny dropping more like having my suspicions confirmed. I went right to Robbo to tell him and I was back in the team, though I never knew what - if anything - was said between Bryan and John.

We were enjoying good runs in both domestic Cup competitions and that was helping our league form. Normally, and especially with our injury problems, it would go the other way, but we benefitted from the momentum and picked up some great wins at home; destroying Derby 6-1 and beating Blackburn 2-1 either side of a 3-1 away win at Leicester. In between league fixtures we progressed to the League Cup Final despite losing our second leg at home to Stockport 1-0 - our 2-0 win in the reverse fixture had been enough. We also picked up a second win against Derby in the space of four days beating them 2-0 at their place to set up an FA Cup semi-final date with Chesterfield at Old Trafford.

We were in good form ahead of our league game against Chelsea at the Riverside and I felt even more confident of our chances when Sparky phoned me the night before to tell me he'd been dropped to

148

the bench (he had signed for them in the summer of 1995, leaving a year after me and Robbo). We had a comfortable first half and, even though Mark came on at half time, we managed to grab the lead on 53 minutes through Juninho. I've never been in a game that changed so much - when Mark came on and got into the swing of it, it was like World War 3! Strangely, though, Chelsea moved Zola and Vialli wide to accommodate Sparky in the middle. I remain certain that we wouldn't have been able to cope with Mark and Vialli up front, there was too much firepower if it had come through the middle but we scraped through for a vital three points.

I'd scored at Leicester in our league win there and thought that performance, as well as our massively improved form, would be enough to earn me a spot against the same opponents in the League Cup Final but it was a case of déjà vu as I was subjected to the Neil Webb scenario again. It was between me and Robbie Mustoe for a place and his service to Boro gave him the starting place and I was on the bench.

A few years ago I bumped into Garry Parker, who was playing for Leicester at the time, and he said that much of their preparation had involved stopping me getting on the ball because in the game at Filbert Street I'd been providing a constant supply of passes for Juninho. Stop the supply, stop the player. Having learned the disappointment of my exclusion, we spent the day before the game watching a replay of our recent victory to remind ourselves of where we'd had success in the game. As so much of it involved me, I had Viv Anderson constantly turning to me and saying, 'Wow, you're doing well there, you're looking better than Mustoe!'

'You can't fucking say that, he's playing tomorrow!' I replied.

I wasn't one to kick off, and I didn't really then, but that conversation really did annoy me, particularly when the reasons for team selection had always been 'well, so and so played better last time we played that team' - in that case it must be my turn to play because I played well against Leicester the last time we played them!

About ten minutes into the game Curtis Fleming gets a knock and I'm sent to warm up. Curtis stayed on, and I didn't get on at all; Juninho was out of the game for the entire ninety minutes because we just didn't get the ball to him. I could tell that was going to be our problem in those first few minutes and was gearing myself up to play him in to good areas as often as I could. Because he was so tightly marked by Leicester, it seemed like we were afraid to give him the ball. It was crazy, he was our best player. Their game plan worked, and the match went to extra time. We got a breakthrough when Rav scored in the first period but Leicester equalised with two minutes left. With the game so finely balanced I think Robbo was just a little cautious about making a change.

We were facing a bit of a fixture pile-up - the draw meant we faced a replay at Hillsborough ten days later and before then we had to go to Upton Park and play Chesterfield. I was back in the side for our 0-0 draw in London but back on the bench at Old Trafford.

That was a memorable fixture - the entire country seemed to be behind Chesterfield and even as a Boro player it was hard not to be captivated by the romance of their journey to this point. They had Kevin Davies in their front line, a young forward who went on to enjoy a great career at Bolton. Just before half-time Vladimir Kinder was sent off for us. I had a lot of time for Vlad, who was a talented player who didn't get as many chances as he perhaps should have. I came on for Mikkel Beck but moved to left-back which meant our 4-2-3-1 formation became more like 4-2-2-1. We struggled to get to grips with being a man down and we conceded two goals in quick succession at the start of the second half. Sean Dyche (who of course went on to be a very good manager) scored the penalty which made it two - I looked around our team to see dropped heads.

Soon after the restart I got the ball from an Emerson pass and bombed forward; I couldn't believe the lack of urgency in some of our players as I got towards the area. Luckily, Rav had made a run and he scored from my cross to get us back into the game. We now had a lifeline we barely deserved because I'd felt, in that two or three minutes since the penalty, the rest of the lads had given up. I'd seen that kind of attitude in games much too often. There were times we'd just coast through games and, more infuriating than anything, some of the lads would only turn it on when we were one or two down in the game.

Five minutes after Rav's goal came the most controversial passage of play. They had a shot which hit the crossbar and looked like it went over the line but the referee didn't give it and we played on and counter attacked while they protested. Juninho - one of the few who seemed to be showing any drive - got into the box and was fouled. Hignett scored the penalty, 2-2. That's how it finished on ninety minutes and we went to extra time - suddenly, as we talked about going back out for the game in the home dressing room I'd prepared for so many games of football in, there was a desire to win the game that befitted the venue. Festa scored to put us in front and then for the second week in a row we were left bitterly disappointed by a last-gasp equaliser. There was a great deal of professional embarrassment after that result but there could be no arguing that Chesterfield deserved the result and most neutrals would say they deserved more, with the goal that should have counted.

Both of our replays - against Leicester and Chesterfield - were scheduled to be played at Hillsborough, with Leicester first up three days after our game at Old Trafford. We were made to pay for our casual display at the weekend because as time drew on our tired legs began to tell. It finished scoreless after ninety minutes and for the second time in four days we were playing two hours of football. I was happy to have started this final but it was nothing compared to playing at Wembley and the benefit of me playing longer passes to Juninho was lost on the much tighter Hillsborough pitch. Juninho did really well in those two games not to get injured because there was so much pressure and attention on him. Up front Leicester had Emile Heskey, a real unit of a player who I thought should have made much more of his qualities. There was one game I saw him play later on in his career for Liverpool against Arsenal where he absolutely tore them apart but if anything summed up his career it was that game and then an incident from our game in Sheffield when he came out to the touchline to challenge me for a header and I won! I shouldn't have had a prayer. It was Heskey's strike partner, the experienced Steve Claridge, who ultimately made the difference, scoring in the hundredth minute. We made attacking changes but couldn't do anything, because most of us were exhausted. I came off the pitch disappointed but lamenting the fact I hadn't played at Wembley where I felt I would have made a difference.

Unsurprisingly, after two such huge occasions, we lost our next two league games 1-0, against Tottenham and relegation rivals Sunderland. At the time you're just disappointed you lost the game – the last thing you want to do is look for excuses but is it an excuse in that situation? The similarities with what was happening at Boro and what I'd experienced at United in 1992 are obvious with hindsight.

We got through the Chesterfield game with ease, helped by an early goal by Beck. It was an odd game because we were in cruise control for most of it. I don't know what this says about my concentration levels but when Ravanelli got a second for us I looked up at the scoreboard and was surprised it was only two; I could have sworn it was three. It did end up three as Emerson scored, and we were on our way back to Wembley to play Chelsea.

We had four games in the last eight days of the league season, starting on 3rd May – for some reason, our last two games had been scheduled away from home and the rearranged trip to Blackburn was also placed in this week, meaning we had three away games following our game against Villa at the Riverside. We were made to work and fight for the result late on, and enjoyed a big boost when Rav's last minute penalty gave us a 3-2 win. Next up was Manchester United at Old Trafford on May Day. With our final game away at Leeds, it meant we were facing the last three champions of the country away from home with our survival hopes resting on them. It was almost a miracle then, that we went 3-1 up against United in the first half. Juninho, Emerson and Hignett scored for us but midway through that first half we suffered a big blow when Rav decided he was unable to play on and walked off the pitch. I was stunned; I'd never seen that attitude. Emerson's strike was spectacular but Juninho's was the best of the bunch. John Motson, commentating for Match Of The Day, said that the goal was an example of the fact that on our day, we were as good a footballing side as any in the division. I remember feeling so proud at half time, the pride in our performance was matched by relief that one of the best teams in the world weren't ripping us apart. They'd pulled it back to 3-2 by that point and they were throwing everything at us, as proven by the fact

Les Sealey is prostrate as I round him to open the scoring in a 2-0 win against Luton in March 1989. I don't think Les thought then that he'd be playing for us within months.

The greatest goal I ever scored with my left foot, this time on the plastic down at Kenilworth Road in November 1989.

...ucial goal and perhaps the moment that saved Fergie's bacon, as I hit a late winner at Hereford ...the fourth round of the FA Cup to win a terrible game on an awful pitch in January 1990.

I'd experienced the walk from the Wembley tunnel as a Welsh schoolboy but doing it on Cup Final day was something else. Unfortunately, although I got on in the first game I didn't in the replay. Fortunately my replacement Lee Martin scored the winner.

I appear to be playing the 'midfield enforcer' role to a tee in the absence of the injured Bryan Robson taking on Peter Beardsley and Steve McMahon during the 1990 Charity Shield. I also netted our goal (below) and we shared the trophy following a 1-1 draw.

CLAYTON BLACKMORE

McCLAIR

INCE 1

INCE 2

BODNAR

WEBB

BLACKMORE 2

BLACKMORE 1

MANCHESTER UNITED: Sealey, Irwin, Blackmore, Bruce, Phelan, Pallister, Webb, Ince (61 Sharpe), McClair, Robins (78 Hughes), Beardsmore

PECSI MUNKAS: Bodnar, Konya, Braun, Palaczky (82 Czerna), Balogh, Berczy, Czeh, Tomka, Lovasz (74 Boyas), Megyeri, Lehota

marked the return of English clubs to Europe with probably the two greatest goals of my career.

ABOVE: *A magazine excerpt recreates in vivid detail my 20 yard curler against Pecsi Munkas that the keeper didn't even move for.*

RIGHT: *Robbo congratulates me on the 35 yard free kick which beat Montpellier's Claude Barrabe all ends up. It was a crucial goal just on half-time and deflated them hugely. I also 'won' the penalty in the second half which secured our passage to the semi-finals.*

BELOW: *My most treasured photograph, given to me by a fan a few years ago, United and Barcelona line up before the final in Rotterdam.*

Two Sparky strikes and yours truly's clearance off the line in the last minute won us the cup! Like the rest of us Gary Pallister is truly ecstatic. It was some achievement in our first season back in European club competition against a team that went on to be European Champions the following season.

Our security guard, Ned Kelly, was always telling us about his role in the Iranian Embassy seige. Naturally we thought he was fibbing, so imagine our surprise when he arranged a day down in Hereford with the SAS. It was a bit of an eye-opener, not least for the manager who nearly got his head blown off!

UNITED STARS'

SAS fired live rounds as Fergie and his lads kept their heads down

HOSTAGE TERROR

LEFT: The Premier League was a game changer for the sport, here I am battling with the league's first ever goalscorer Brian Deane during our 3-1 defeat at Bramall Lane. We started the season badly but recovered to win our first title in 26 years. Although I started the season at left-back, injury meant I didn't feature after November. I still treasure the medal though, as one of the few survivors from the mid 80s team who had failed to win the old First Division, it was great to finally get my hands on the Premier League trophy.

A moment of pride as we line up to play Kaizer Chiefs in Johannesburg on 29th July, 1993 wi[th] Nelson Mandela.

ABOVE: On the South African tour with Sparky and a stern-faced Denis Irwin in the row behind.
RIGHT: My last outing for United was against Bury in the FA Cup in January 1993. Injury frustrations and an invitation from Robbo to join Middlesbrough proved too tempting.

TOP: The highlight of my time at Boro should have been the 1997 FA Cup Final. Unfortunately Roberto di Matteo scored after 42 seconds and we never recovered.

MIDDLE: I went on loan to Bristol City, who had the maddest fans I'd ever seen and following a brief spell at Barnsley, ended up playing for Sam Allardyce at Notts County who were doing superbly until he was poached by Bolton.

BOTTOM LEFT: After professional retirement, I followed in my dad's footsteps helping Neath win the West Wales Senior Cup in 2008.

BELOW: With my twins Corey and Lulah-Beau on the Old Trafford pitch in my role as an MUTV pundit.

EXTRA SPECIAL Neath celebrate their 2-1 extra time win against Llanelli in the West Wales Senior Cup final at Stebonheath Park. *AW020408G-001*

Neath pip Reds in extra time

Rampant Ponty hit Lido for six

PONTARDAWE stormed to a 6-0 victory over relegated Pontyprldd at Afan Lido in the MacWhirter Welsh League division one.

The Swansea Valley side, who led 2-0 at the break, cruised home on the back of goals from Jonny Owen

NEATH turned the tables on Llanelli 1
Neath 2

But Pockett made no mistake with 11 minutes remaining.

TOP: *Sir Bobby and I at a golf day and (right) here I am lining up a putt on the seniors tour.*

MIDDLE: *My wedding to Tracey at Hensol Castle in the Vale of Glamorgan*

BELOW: *Our children; Rose (holding a white rose) and the twins Corey and Lulah-Beau.*

that even Gary Neville scored! Gary had established himself as the first choice right back in that team which was almost unrecognisable to the one I'd left three years earlier. Phil Neville, Beckham, Butt, and Scholes were also regulars, even though at the time I'd left, there was nothing to say that any of them were guarantees to have turned out the way they did. They had attacking options all over the pitch so were always in any game; we coped quite well in a second half that was much more nervy than the first. Then they brought on Ole Gunnar Solskjær as an extra striker; Ole was a real freak, he would come on the pitch and it would be as if he'd been playing the entire game. He was on fire straight away and got their equaliser and it ended 3-3, not the worst result to take from Old Trafford.

One player who wasn't going to be at United much longer was Eric Cantona; I'd stopped a goal-bound shot of his in the first half. Cantona retired at the end of that month and one of the most popular names being linked to replace him was Juninho. I said it earlier, he would have had no problem settling in at United, I'm sure of it. He was so good at Middlesbrough and the idea of how good he could have been if he'd gone there is scary. He went to Atletico Madrid that summer, but I have no doubt that he would have been brilliant at Old Trafford.

We drew at Ewood Park (0-0) in a game I was sure we would have won if we'd played it the first time round. It would have been a good if hadn't for the points deduction – that point would have secured our safety. As it was we had to win at Elland Road on the last day to stay up and it was always going to be a tough ask. When Brian Deane scored midway through the second half, it was even tougher. Juninho scored a couple of minutes later but even allowing for the fact that those two minutes had been the period in those decisive three games where we'd been behind, did nothing to help us. It was frustrating that it had come to this and selfishly, I did think that if I'd been in from the start of the season I could have ensured we weren't in that position. Our form over the second half of the season was good enough for mid-table. It tells you a lot about how much I gave that in the dying minutes at Elland Road, I looked up at the clock and then I waved to the bench. I had to come off, I had nothing left in the tank. I knew I had to get off the pitch to make way for someone with fresh legs – there was nothing I could do to influence the game in a positive way. I also knew that if anyone ran at me they'd tear me apart, which didn't really bother my ego that much as much as the desperation for us not to get relegated. Some players will stay on, and I have played through injury before, but there are times you just need to do what's good for the team.

Mikkel Beck had a great opportunity to win it for us and I couldn't believe it when instead of turning inside, where he'd be one on one with the goalkeeper, he turned outside, and the chance went begging. Once, I'd talked to him in training about his movement. 'When we've got the ball at the back, we need you to run,' I said. 'But when I'm up front by myself, I don't know where to run!' he replied. 'Just fucking run, anywhere you want!'

A few months later, in pre-season in Italy, Pickering was telling Mikkel to stay close to his defender with the idea we could pump balls up to him. John took training but that was the first time I ever heard him try and coach; it was no wonder Mikkel was so lost, if he was essentially being told to allow himself to be marked out of the game. Perhaps it was understandable that he was too anxious in the big moment; we drew 1-1 and were relegated. The three points we were deducted cost us our place in the top flight.

Just as missing out on silverware is more painful the closer you get to it, it was equally disappointing to be relegated when we'd come so close to staying up. I was sure that some people in the club thought we were dead and buried at Christmas; it was the same attitude I saw when I looked around my team-mates when we were 2-0 down against Chesterfield.

The mood in the camp was hardly ideal as we prepared for the FA Cup Final against Chelsea. Having missed the rest of the season after the United game to go back to Italy, Rav passed a fitness test so he would start. It was a risk you could understand Robbo taking but it didn't go down well with the rest of the lads who were pissed off that he'd up and left. One person more annoyed than most was Neil Cox; the day before, Coxy discovered he wouldn't be playing in the final and he almost came to blows with Rav over it. Neil spoke to the press and on the morning of the final Rav brings him the newspaper and asks 'What's that?'

It was nonsense; the worst sort of way to get ready for such a big day. Me and big Nige went out for the warm up and commented on how the team were coming out in dribs and drabs. It was surreal. I felt for Coxy; I'd been in his position before and thought he maybe should have been playing in Curtis Fleming's place at right back. I could also see why he'd be annoyed with Rav; not that Neil would have played up front but it maybe cost him a place on the bench. With the team in disarray it was no surprise that we conceded in the first minute. Roberto Di Matteo picked the ball up in Chelsea's half and then is allowed to run. Higgy and Emerson are half-hearted in their challenge. He has all the time in the world to hit a shot. It was pretty spectacular but it could have been avoided. Or, at least, he could have been made to work for it. Poor Ben Roberts in goal was just a little off his line and was made to pay.

Things went from bad to worse; Rav didn't even make the half hour before he had to be brought off for Beck and then minutes later Mustoe had to come off. We did have the ball in the net, when Festa headed in, but it was disallowed for offside. It was probably more than we would have deserved.

At half time me and Nigel had a bit of a go. Telling the lads we were at Wembley, that we might not get to play in an FA Cup Final ever again. These chances just don't come around too often. You have to give it everything. We played against Leicester and defeated them earlier in the season before losing to them in the Cup Final. We had beaten Chelsea too and they didn't look as good as they had been in that game. We had a chance. I'd never really stood up and spoken like that in any Cup Final before but after Chesterfield, and seeing that no-one else other than Nige who was willing to speak, I had to say something. Our response was limp; we just didn't turn up, and Chelsea got a second goal near the end to kill it off.

It was a season of fine margins. If Heskey doesn't score in the last seconds at Wembley and if we'd get a second at Leeds (or not had the points deducted) or, as I saw it, if only I'd had the chance to play earlier in the season, it could have been very different. I'm pretty sensible - I know when players are better than me but it was also easy to see, in my opinion, that I could have improved the team. Unfortunately I had people telling Robbo I wasn't fit because I'd messed around with some cones in training one time.

Two Cup successes and last day survival would have represented the best season in Middlesbrough's history. In some ways it was, in spite of the defeat, considering it was the first time the club had ever got to those finals but try telling us that when we were preparing for life in the second tier that summer.

Gazza

I HAVE A LOT OF TIME FOR Middlesbrough as a club, the people up there and the supporters are great. But when I say that 1994/95 was my favourite season there, you get the impression of how my final two years went between 1997 and 1999.

Juninho was off straight away and Ravanelli only played the first game of the 1997/98 season before he was off to Marseille. We signed Paul Merson but even that wasn't enough to make me optimistic that we could get promotion back to the Premier League. Merse turned up in Italy after signing for us and was immediately rooming with me. He was alright as a lad, despite his Arsenal background and despite giving it large because he was an England international. I remember in one training session at Rockliffe Park we were playing a game without goals. We called it line ball. Merse says halfway through, 'I'm not fucking doing that, it's boring!' He walked off the pitch. He was a good player, of course, but I did feel as though we'd downgraded a little considering the players we'd lost. One player I was very happy with us signing was Andy Townsend. He brought a combative engine in the middle of the pitch that had been sorely lacking; he did a bit of everything and gave us a presence that we needed. I can imagine other teams might have looked at us and thought we might be easy to dominate – it was a very competitive league – but Andy solved that issue for us.

If I thought my own problems were over then I was mistaken. Like Rav, I played the first game of the season but the reason for my missing most of the rest of it was because I suffered a stress fracture to my ankle. I didn't realise just how bad it was for over a month.

The Thursday before we played Charlton on the opening day we had a practice match and it was the first time in pre-season that the whole squad had got together. I scored in the practice match playing on the right hand side, so I was given a chance there on Saturday. Merse had a word with Robbo telling him he used to play as a number ten for Arsenal. I knew from our many encounters he'd played on the left hand side! He'd originally been selected on the left but Robbo said to him, 'Well, if you fancy a change in the game, just switch with Clayton.' It was a boiling hot August afternoon and the game was pretty dead, so Merse comes over for us to switch sides. I get the ball on the left and I'm about to play in Ravanelli when the Charlton defender Steve Brown goes right through my standing leg, it twisted inwards. It was a bad challenge. I was in agony.

I was out for a few weeks because the ankle was black and blue but with the international break coming up I wanted to be fit for Wales so I was willing to do whatever it took to get there. I was running around on it, hoping it was a case of breaking through the pain barrier, but I was aggravating it. I spoke to Wales manager Bobby Gould and told him of the problem and his response was, 'What's the matter, don't you want to play for your country?' I could have killed him. I'd been out of the Wales set up before and despite my good form for Boro he only called me back in when he saw me playing for Bristol – I think he was living locally so popped along to a game. But, after this ankle injury that he thought I was faking, I wasn't selected for Wales again. Pretty extreme fake, wasn't it? I missed the season with it! He never spoke to me to check on me. Game over for my international career.

I can still feel pain in my ankle. I had two MRI scans and an ultrasound but nothing was showing up and I was having arguments with the physiotherapist. 'There's nothing there!' he's saying. My breakthrough was Derek Whyte injuring his wrist – he had to go for a scan where they would inject ink or dye into you. 'Go with him,' I was told by the physio.

The bone scan showed a line right across my leg where the initial impact was, and then a white spot where the main impact had happened. The girl who did the scan wasn't allowed to say anything but did a discreet nod when I asked if it was a fracture.

I made only a couple of appearances before finally getting back to fitness in the middle of March 1998. It was too late for me to fight my way into Robbo's thoughts for our League Cup Final against Chelsea (our chance for revenge for the previous season, though we lost this game too) but I did hope to play some part in the last few games to help secure our promotion at the first time of asking.

It was a little like Jan Aage Fjortoft's signing in 1995, though it's probably the only time these players will ever get compared - Paul Gascoigne signed from Rangers to help us rubber stamp our promotion and, hopefully, prepare for life back at the top with a little extra star quality. Gazza was desperate to break into the England squad for the 1998 World Cup but his off-field controversies were undermining his chances. He had been brilliant up in Scotland but the standard of football up there was not what it had been ten years before and so there were doubts that, in a more competitive environment, he could light up the stage the way he had done for Lazio. There weren't many central midfielders like him in the world, let along England. He was able to go past two or three or four players with no problem, he had a complete range of finishing – he could score with either foot, from long range, with his head or from free kicks. In one of our first encounters against him when he was at Newcastle, Gazza had this growing reputation as the suntanned kid who tore midfields apart and I remember Robbo saying, 'We'll see how fucking good he is!' We had Bryan and Remi Moses in the middle but for once they couldn't get near their man.

It remained to be seen how Gazza could make an impact to our team but the one thing that was clear right away is that he had the talent which was worth persisting with. Robbo probably hoped that being closer to home would help him and, being as close to his roots as Gazza is, I'm sure that played a part in him coming to the club as well.

I'm not the only one who wishes he'd signed for Manchester United, I know Robbo has gone on record as saying he wanted Paul alongside him in midfield and it's scary to think of how good they could have been for United. It was difficult to tell if he was at the same level as before but only because I'd never been that close to him. And let's be fair, if anyone had anything to lose in their game, it would have been Gazza. I know some United players who played with George Best at the end of his time there who said it wasn't like playing with him at his prime. Perhaps that was the same with Gazza, who I would say was as naturally gifted as George. They were that standard of player who were a cut above, players not only good for a couple of years, or even a generation, but players who stand out on their own as the most naturally gifted of all time. I think it's fair to say that Gazza would probably be considered the best English player of all time if he'd moved to United and everything had worked out. People say that he made the wrong choice by going to Spurs because they bought his parents a house. He did it for the right reasons, for his mum and dad, and I can't be sure you can ever really regret doing something like that. He had such a big heart and wanted to give them a better life; it speaks volumes for him that he did that instead of selfishly looking to himself and thinking, I could really do a job at United. Having said that, I'm sure, if he'd have waited, we would have offered him a house!

Gazza played seven games at the end of the season; obviously he was reliable enough to be playing regularly in a very competitive league at a crucial point in the season. Of our last six games we won five and drew one; a crucial run of form at just the right time. We finished second to go up behind Nottingham Forest who were Champions. They had 94 points to our 91 and Sunderland who just missed out behind us, had 90. In almost every year since 90 would have been enough to have gone up.

Robbo seemed to have cottoned on about our defence being costly and reinforced it with the signings of Dean Gordon, the talented left back from recently relegated Crystal Palace, and our old mate Gary Pallister. Pally was 33 but only left United because they brought in Jaap Stam – he had the top level experience to take over in our back line from the retiring Nigel Pearson. Colin Cooper – another fan favourite at Middlesbrough in his first spell – was also brought back to the club.

I found myself playing most of pre-season – this always tended to be the case – and then was back in the reserves. Having done so well the previous season, even though I might be able to stake my own case for a place in the team, I now had to prove that I deserved it and I was willing to do so. My form for the reserves was okay and I was often included in the first team squad, usually as an unused substitute.

We played Villa away in our second game. I was with the team but not in the squad. Most of the lads were out warming up but there was me, Merse and a couple of others in the changing room. Doug Ellis walks past and Paul goes, 'Doug, Doug, what did you do with all that money?' He's referring to the £12m or so that the club just got for selling Dwight Yorke to Manchester United. Within the fortnight, Paul's signing for Villa, and the reason he gave was because he was coming into training and we had the racing papers open every day, as if we're leading him into temptation.

He was in the press again when Gazza had a few problems, having a go at what he said was the drinking culture at the club. Football had moved on and even if a few of us did like a drink, it was nothing worse than at other clubs. Just before Gazza went to the Priory for the first time, the lads had been over in Ireland and we'd had a few drinks. Just about all of us drunk as much, if not more, than Paul. In the airport he was getting mithered relentlessly and you could see it in his face that he just wanted to get away and be by himself where nobody could get at him.

I thought Glenn Hoddle made a massive mistake not taking Paul to the World Cup, but it really hurt Gazza. I shouldn't care, I'm Welsh after all, but I just don't see the sense in not taking one of your best footballers to the biggest tournament. Paul was absolutely devastated and I think going to the Priory in October 1998 was probably the culmination of a lot of problems that year. Typical Gazza, he came out of the Priory and returned to training bragging to the rest of us that he had got Kate Moss's number!

Paul needed a lot of help from people around him and he needed people with his best interests at heart. He's an emotional lad and mad as a hatter, but he's only like that because he wants to entertain his mates. The press quickly cottoned on to it and started making out like it was more than it was. Here's a lad having a bit of a laugh and the papers are trying to make it into something much more sinister. There was the famous time where Gazza and TV host Chris Evans got a Vauxhall Astra and drove it right into Loch Lomond. We were playing golf and suddenly this car comes right across the green. They nearly drowned because they couldn't get out. But Gazza did that just to make us all laugh. We played at a charity golf day in Portugal that was organised by

David Seaman. They did fancy dress every year and this year we were told to dress up like James Bond. Gazza went missing and nobody saw him – he suddenly turns up wearing scuba gear like Sean Connery in Thunderball! It's a good ten minutes down to the beach so that says he's walked ten minutes back wearing all this gear, flippers and all. We were watching him walk up the golf course from the club house – it was hilarious.

One time he came into training with pies he'd made for Jimmy Four Bellies – he'd been rechristened Four Bellies because he'd lost a stone – and while I can't say for sure what was in them, I'm pretty sure that brown stuff wasn't meat. We had a strong suspicion it was dog poo. Gazza told Jimmy he would give him £500 if he could hold a burning lighter upside down on his nose for five seconds. He did it, despite how hot the metal must have been. A month later he did it again. For another £500 he had a scar across his nose.

Our move to the training ground at Rockliffe was just one of Robbo's attempts to grow Boro as a club, to make things more polished and professional. The bus company that we used for games even put on a brand new coach for us. There used to be a dead narrow drive in to the complex, which must have been difficult for a driver to navigate and one day we were waiting for it and wondering what had happened. Robbo came in, fuming.

'Where's Gazza? The bus has disappeared!'

The driver had hopped out and Gazza jumped in. He wasn't insured or anything. He didn't get very far. Where the exit was narrow, he's obviously been thinking he was driving something as small as a car and didn't get the angle right and smashed the back end of the bus right into a big rock doing about £150,000 worth of damage.

I'll be honest - before I met him, over time, I had started to judge him in the same way most people would have done because of how the press portrayed him. I should have known better, after all I know as well as anyone what they can be like but it was time and time again with him. One day he rocked up at training and he's arguing with Jimmy because Jimmy had been in the press. It was a nothing story, Jimmy had maybe said one sentence and they'd made a two page spread out of it.

If anything summed Gazza up it was this – he would get something in his system, he'd get the bug about something and it could be completely random. For a short while he was mad into bingo. He was there for weeks.

'Won £200 on the bingo last night!' he boasted one morning.

'Gaz, you're getting paid thirty grand a week!' I laughed.

Then he got into fishing. He'd come into training stinking of fish. When he got into something he was at it all the time. He was the kindest, friendliest, funniest lad, who wouldn't hurt a fly. And, the thing was, he actually did make a difference for Boro at the start of that season, scoring three goals as we started life back in the Premier League pretty well. He obviously had to miss a few games with his time in rehab but still played twenty-six times in the league, which was more than his doubters expected.

Meanwhile by December I still hadn't kicked a ball in the league – I'd played just one game that season, in the League Cup down at Wycombe. Robbo came to see me play against Coventry and Bolton for the reserves. Gordon Strachan was player-manager for Coventry and was playing in this 0-0 draw; he was going mad at his own players throughout. After the Bolton game Robbo pulled me aside afterwards to tell me he thought I was the best player on the pitch. The next week he came to watch as we played Oldham and even though we lost I had a good idea I was back in his thoughts. I was back on the bench for our league win at Old Trafford, though I didn't get on – and I was an unused sub in our return there a couple of weeks later as we lost in the FA Cup. And then, a few days later, Robbo said to me, 'Mark Summerbell's in front of you now.' Instantly I knew that was it for me. It didn't matter that we were in the Premier League, it was time for me to do one. Summerbell was committed but, really, a long way away from what I thought to be of the required quality for the top league. I was 34 but still felt I was capable of contributing – in fact, the only thing that had kept me going was watching the team and thinking I would surely get a chance sooner rather than later; so, obviously I was very disappointed that Robbo had that opinion but I also knew that it was a natural time for me to leave.

About eighteen months earlier we'd been on one of our breaks where Coxy - who had since left - and I went and played golf and the other lads stayed at the bar for a drink. We came back and I saw Robbo having a good laugh with Curtis Fleming and Derek Whyte, two of Pickering's favourites. They'd obviously bonded, as you would expect they would have - after all, they'd been at the club for a while, and now Robbo had too, he'd grown to trust them as favourites of his own. It was ironic, really. I was more professional at Boro than I ever had been at United, in terms of my diet and lifestyle. Obviously I was getting older and you start thinking about your fitness more. I think I was fitter when I left Boro than I was when I joined.

It ended on a difficult note but I would never have a bad word to say about Robbo. There was a little time I admit to being unsure because it seemed as if he was saying one thing and then doing another, but I felt that our friendship was strong enough that there had to be more to it. Of course, there was, a third party and a mole, and neither of us could have done anything about that.

I thought Robbo was a brilliant manager and had done an incredible job, backed by Steve Gibson, in transforming Middlesbrough from a mid-table club in the second tier to one who were able to buy the best players in Europe. He was doing great and for me he would still be manager if he hadn't brought Terry Venables in as an adviser. El Tel came with the pedigree of having managed Barcelona and England and someone of that profile was always going to undermine him - almost the exact same thing had happened at Liverpool when Roy Evans brought in Gerard Houllier and was out soon after. Robbo's logic was sound; Terry had called him into the coaching set up for Euro '96 and they were familiar with each other and he had a wealth of experience at the highest level. Call on him for advice if need be, sure, but such a high-profile move gave the perception that Bryan needed help. If he felt like he needed guidance then fine, there's no shame in that, but people forget what an exceptional job he did in transforming that football club. He did say in that last season that because he and I had been a part of each other's life for so long - 16 years - he would look to give me a job on the staff when I retired. Retirement, though, that was not an option at that point.

For me – I was thirty-four but not finished. Feeling as fit as I did, I was only concentrating on playing football for as long as I could.

End Of An Era

CONSIDERING THAT WELL-KNOWN theory of a manager going into a new club and taking people he knows along with him, you would have presumed life for me at Middlesbrough would have been pretty comfortable. I didn't expect to be given anything, I thought that Robbo was taking me up there hopefully to use me as a standard bearer for commitment and dedication to the cause and I wasn't going to let him down on that. It's funny, because you would think that at a club like Manchester United you might get used to politics but I found that only really was the case the further down the footballing ladder I went. At Old Trafford there was always a real togetherness, and particularly in the nineties it had been the team spirit which was such a big factor in the team's success. It's no surprise that when you look at the successes of unfancied teams, the first thing they generally always say is that it is down to the unity within the team.

I think being from Manchester United counted against me when it came to certain individuals at Boro and, from the minute I knew that people had a problem with me, it made my time up there fairly difficult. I tried hard and that is probably reflected by the fact that my happiest times were when I was playing football but the eighteen months or so between the summer of 1995 to when I was recalled for a proper run during the Christmas of 1996 were some of the darkest days of my career – they were as frustrating as being injured could be, it was easier to handle than playing well and not knowing why I wasn't getting in the first team. Those last few months up at the Riverside were a bit of a blur. My last game for their first team was a League Cup game at Wycombe Wanderers in the autumn of 1998 and it had been erased from my memory completely until years later I went down there with the Wales schoolboys team I was coaching.

After getting on the bench for Boro at Old Trafford in the FA Cup, I didn't even get a reserve game for another month. In my last appearance in a Boro shirt, I scored in our 2-2 draw with West Brom reserves. I couldn't have stayed and wasted away like that and I told Robbo I'd like to leave.

In the summer of 1998 John Hendrie had taken over at Barnsley and had taken a couple of players he'd known from Boro down to Oakwell. I gather he must have contacted Robbo, or it happened the other way around, because I certainly wasn't in contact with John and I was granted a free transfer in the middle of the season. I signed a short-term deal there - after being relegated from the Premier League, they had no realistic hope of an instant return but were clearly looking towards the summer. John was reassured by the offer of a two year contract but out of nowhere John was sacked soon after and Dave Bassett was announced as his replacement.

John's assistant at the club was Eric Winstanley. Eric was Barnsley born and bred, he'd played more than four hundred league games with them and had been a coach there for about twenty years. The problem when it came to John was that even though he'd been with Barnsley since 1996 himself, Eric seemed to think he had the authority - in training, John would be saying something, and Eric would interrupt and overrule him in front of all the players. I couldn't imagine that happening with Fergie! It went on for weeks and John was so undermined that there was just no way he could continue.

I played only a few games at Barnsley; my most striking memory of it is being one of the obstacles in David Ginola's way as he scored that brilliant goal in the FA Cup for Tottenham. He'd cut inside from the wing and so I came out from midfield to try and challenge - I was nowhere near him, really - and he went past a couple of others before putting it in. We did have a good win against Sheffield United, the highlight of my time there, but shortly afterwards, my ankle started playing up and I missed the closing weeks of the season. I think going from not playing to suddenly playing every week had a big impact - especially looking at the drop in division.

The season had been a write-off for me but back at Manchester United it was anything but as they enjoyed the most successful campaign of their history. I think it's fair to say they had a little bit of luck along the way - the FA Cup semi final replay being the best example. Fergie's luck was he had Peter Schmeichel in goal. He's a big lad to try and get a penalty past. Then, there's Ryan's goal, which wasn't luck - all about skill. Two big moments. There were two big moments in the Nou Camp as well, and I was watching as a fan, just as any United supporter would have been. The only time I wasn't a fan was on the very few occasions I had to play against them. It was an amazing achievement with drama that is difficult to match. The club had been growing non-stop since I left and earlier that season there was talk of a takeover by BSkyB for £623m. That was blocked, but it gives an impression of the growth of a football club that Michael Knighton almost bought the club for £20m ten years before.

United were a commercial and sporting machine and the difference in size between them and other clubs was just ridiculous. There were no suggestions that Boro, when we went up there, were in the same league in any way but at least Boro had ambition to go places. I think that, for a while, when they moved to the Riverside, there was the idea that they were on the same road as United. You'd probably forgive the fans for hoping that would be the case when they saw us buying big name stars but the reality was that even a brand new stadium couldn't mask the truth - United were just far bigger. I'm not saying Boro had delusions, there's a big difference between that and ambition - what I mean is, even a club who had invested so much into its infrastructure still had a way to go before it could be an elite club. That was fine, and it was great to be around that ambition. Boro certainly matched most in terms of facilities in the top flight. I had been prepared that life up there wasn't going to be the same as United but the drop from Boro to Barnsley was particularly harsh.

It was a nice little club with a good recent history but it was just 'okay' and then, when I get on to the training ground and I'm seeing the assistant thinking he can undermine the manager so openly, I had severe doubts about the professional standard that was expected. I'd never witnessed anything like that - I was shocked, my reaction was to openly go, 'Woah!' and then, because I was stunned, I was cringing;

I had to walk away because I had a bit of a nervous giggle about it. It doesn't really matter what level of football you're at, you can't allow your assistant to do that. Maybe John was being respectful of Eric's history with the club but I would have sacked him on the spot. The minute you don't, you've allowed yourself to be completely undermined and those players won't take you seriously again. I knew John, so he didn't lose my respect - I was more surprised that Eric thought it was a reasonable thing to do. He should have shown John the same respect.

John was gone and Dave Bassett had his own ideas and the deal that John had suggested to me was off the table, and so, for the first time in my career, I was without a club. That news was broken to me while I was on a post-season break in Marbella. I got a telephone call telling me I'd been released. I was one of their highest earners on a couple of grand and Dave wanted to bring in Geoff Thomas, who he'd previously worked with at Crystal Palace. Ironically, Geoff was installed as a player/coach, Dave's number two and Eric was effectively demoted and in 2001 he was gone from Barnsley completely. Maybe a case of better the devil you know.

Needing a place to play, I gave Sam Allardyce - then manager of Notts County - a call and he agreed to give me a go. County, like Barnsley, aren't the biggest but they do have a very strong history in English football and at the time seemed as if they were going places under a young manager with a growing reputation. They'd redeveloped Meadow Lane in the time since I'd scored a penalty for United down there and now it was a nice little stadium. It had a capacity of over 19,000 but they would only get in four or five thousand. One of the first games I played there was a friendly against Arsenal, which had been arranged because Jermaine Pennant had left County to go to London - one of the top clubs in the country, and still, we only got about 6,000 fans turn up to the game.

Sam was a larger than life character, a bit like Big Ron. His physio was a bit mad - he was an ex-RAF fitness coach who had us running until we dropped. That was a part of Sam's philosophy. The work on defence all pre-season was apparently based on the Italian school of defending - Sam and the coaches had players in a 4-4-2 shape. Then he

RED, WHITE & BLACKMORE

would stand in different positions with the ball and ask the players what position they should be to where the ball was. Then, when it got to the games, we started playing five at the back!

I played left wing-back all that season and I enjoyed it. I was familiar with the position having played there for Wales. My attitude with that role was that I needed to be level with the ball – so, if it was up in the opposition area, I needed to be up there providing the width. It meant a lot of running. If you can read the game it's generally alright – you can conserve your energy when the ball is in other areas of the pitch but if it's coming down your side it does mean having to do a lot of work. It certainly felt like a lot of work when I'd turn on the United game and see Denis just passing the ball to Giggsy, who'd be tearing teams apart. Nice work if you can get it. I was a bit jealous, obviously!

Sam was a brilliant manipulator of using whatever advantage he could to get a result. At Notts County it was brilliant because there was barely any effort required to instil an underdog atmosphere. But he'd be doing anything he could think of – we had a defender called Matty Redmile, a big guy, almost as big as Sam himself, who was always given extra running after the end of training.

We enjoyed a very promising start to the season and there was talk of promotion – from a personal perspective it was the first time since Boro's first promotion push that I'd been part of a really positive team effort and it was a very welcome change. It compensated for the fact that I'd taken a 60% pay cut; Sam had said to me that if we were still doing well at Christmas he'd look after me with a new deal. I had all the incentive I needed and I think it was reflecting in my own form, as I settled into life down there (I say life down there, I was living in York before I moved to Cheshire and was commuting in) with a couple of goals in the early weeks. It was dark going into training and for two or three days every week, it was dark going home because we had extra training sessions and weights in the afternoon. It was knackering. We were given Creatine and I thought it was odd – I was worried, thinking it ought to be banned. I talked to Sparky about it who had moved to Southampton by then and been moved back into a midfield position. He said he'd been having Creatine because it was supposed to help your muscles with the extra running. 'I've been having trouble with my calves,' he tells me – this is Sparky, with the largest calves in the world. The day we played Bury I ruptured my calf. I start the game and five minutes in the ball is crossed from the right wing back and I hit a shot from the edge of the box. It hits both posts and comes back out for Mark Stallard to convert and give us the lead. Midway through the second half, I score a pretty sweet goal from thirty yards to help us get a 3-1 win. With a minute or two to go I come off with a tight calf. Sam said, 'You're not playing Monday! If you do, and you come back injured, you're fined!' Monday was a testimonial game for the gaffer at Old Trafford that I'd been invited to participate in.

I was still living in York at the time so I had to report down to Nottingham before I would go to the game on the Monday and I went down to Meadow Lane feeling as if there was no chance I'd be able to play. 'Go for a jog around the ground,' the physio said. I did and it didn't feel any better, so I thought I was going to have to bin it. Then one of the lads said to me, 'It's United, it's Old Trafford...'

I got in the car and headed north, knowing I was risking a fine. I was stretching my calf all day, which really was the worst thing I could have done. The United first team played the first half and then made a bunch of changes – I was in the squad to play for a 'Fergie XI' of players from earlier in his reign for the last twenty minutes or so against the current side. We were called out one by one on to the pitch from the old tunnel and I was number three (Robbo, Eric and Beckham were the three sevens). Brucey said in the old tunnel, 'Are we going to give it to them!' I laughed and knew we were going to give them a game. As soon as my foot hit the turf, bang! My calf cramped up and I was in agony. From running my socks off for the last three months for Notts County, I could barely move. I was fitter than I'd been in years, especially the last two years I'd been at United, and I'd felt worked up about the game for days as part of me felt as if I was back on trial.

I made it through but all through those minutes I'm thinking that there's no way Sam's not watching this. I was limping so much. The physio at County had said it was a strain on the lower part of my calf but I was told at United that I had a muscle spasm – I hadn't been drinking enough water with the Creatine which made much more sense, as I wasn't the biggest drinker of water. I just had to rest it and be sensible.

As soon as I got back to County, the physio disagreed and he said I had got to work through it. I've got to train on it and, sure enough, because I didn't give it rest, I didn't pass the fitness test on Friday and wasn't able to play on the Saturday. On the Wednesday, Sam told us all to meet up at the club where we had a few drinks. We went into Nottingham where the drinks continued – we said goodnight thinking we'd see him in the morning but, unbeknown to us, he'd slipped a note under the chairman's door informing him of his resignation. We were clueless! It was a great opportunity for Sam who may have thought he had taken County as far as he could. There were limited resources – the chairman, Derek Pavis, would turn the lights off in a room if nobody was in it and fair enough as it was all coming out of his pocket but from Sam's perspective, the potential to go further just didn't exist. Even if he'd taken us up, with our lack of resources we would have gone straight back down. It was a good time for Sam to go because he'd made an impact and attracted interest from a club higher up the pyramid.

Sam went to Bolton and did a brilliant job there. He then went to Newcastle, where he didn't get nearly enough time and then in 2016 he finally got the job he'd wanted, the England manager's position. He was out in months and again I have some sympathy for him – it's not been an easy situation for England in international tournaments because of how much criticism and attention is given but in recent years people haven't even waited for them to lose in a tournament before sticking the knife in. I thought that with Sam, England had their best chance of doing something positive in years, he was the best person for the job, and it was a shame it didn't work out.

As a parting shot Sam made sure to tell the chairman of his threat to fine me if I played the testimonial! Then the training started to go downhill after Sam left. Matt Redmile, who'd been doing so well under Sam's tailor-made training regime, was back to the same routine as the rest of us and his form dipped quite a bit. Many of us suffered. This was despite Sam's successor in the short-term being Gary Brazil, who had been his assistant. Gary asked if I wouldn't mind helping out; he asked if I wouldn't mind sitting in the stand for the first game and seeing how the game was going to give him feedback. Then Gary got Graham Barrow in to be his assistant in an official capacity I don't know who got the idea first but between them they seemed to be under the impression that I was a threat to them; I'm a similar age to Gary and hadn't even given a thought about management. I had no coaching badges or anything but they seemed more preoccupied with protecting their position from a political viewpoint than they were in getting results to help keep us top of the table, which would have done them the world of good. I came back fine from my calf injury but I wasn't even getting on the bench. It was ridiculous. Then they asked me to go to Rotherham - a move I politely declined - which meant I was turning up at Meadow Lane game after game watching from the stands. It's a small ground. Fans were coming up asking me when I was going to be fit. 'I am fit, they're just not playing me!' I told them. The word must have got back to the chairman because Derek went up to Gary and told him he had to play me. It was embarrassing all round. To be fair, I wouldn't have put it down to Gaz, as it only changed when Graham Barrow came in - I felt as if my curse with assistant managers had continued here too. Graham was old school and didn't seem to have his finger on the pulse when it came to identifying the problem.

We lost our way after Sam left and lost six of our last eight games to take us out of the running for even getting into the play-offs. Our last game of the season, at home to Bury, was meaningless. By this time I think Gary knew he wasn't getting the job on a permanent basis. Before the match he's got us all in the changing room and says, 'I want you all to thank Graham Barrow for all the work he's done here.' I wasn't the only one whose eyebrows rose. Graham himself looks quizzically at Gary - he's basically finding out at the same time as the rest of us that they've both been let go! I looked around and the lads were as shocked as I was. It was chaotic. I know I was used to high levels of professionalism at United but this was amateur stuff by anybody's standards. It would have been embarrassing even in the amateur leagues.

By this point I'd had enough of it. There's only so much you can take of that kind of nonsense and I feel as if injuries and political issues took away so much of what should have been the peak of my career. It shouldn't have got to the point where fans were asking me if I was fit because the psychological effect of that is next time you're playing, you're having to prove that you are, which is ridiculous, and puts you off your natural game. I knew I was in a position where I had to prove myself which I thought was unfair - arriving at a new club, of course I expect to be on trial to a certain extent. I dropped a level to go to County so maybe a few eyebrows would have been raised with some asking 'Has he still got it?' In the first five home games I was named man of the match by the supporters, so I made a promising start. When it came to the fans asking me if I was fit to play, I knew that it was as much because they wanted me back in the team but when you are playing against two opponents instead of one, it is always going to be a losing battle.

My professional career in England ended that day, too. I couldn't stay after what I'd witnessed. We drew 2-2 with Bury even though we wanted to go out with a bang and that more or less summed up a difficult couple of years for me.

From Player To Coach

I T WAS IRONIC, given the questions, that when I left Notts County I was probably the fittest I'd been in my career thanks to Sam and Roger, the RAF fitness coach. Maybe I should have joined the army! The two year spell when I was suffering with my hernia was undoubtedly the low point and I admit I put on a bit of weight. I watch the footage back of the game against Liverpool where I came off the bench to set up Sparky to lob the keeper and I could see that I had put weight on in my face.

It's too strong a word to say I regret moving to Middlesbrough because there were some good times up there but there is a part of me that wishes I'd given it one more crack at United. I played a full season in 1994/95 and again, looking at United's injury problems, it's obvious to see where I might have been able to get a few games. I'm not saying that I would have stopped Gary Neville breaking through but there are times in an injury crisis where you need the experience that I had.

But, at the time – and it sounds ridiculous to say it like this – I'd been there for fourteen years already and I almost felt as if I should give somewhere else a go. That shouldn't have mattered, it should only be whether or not you are good enough. I felt like I had enough to offer. If there's one or two things I do regret, it's making hasty decisions to drop down divisions in order to get football quicker. There's a logical reason for why I was doing it – I was desperate to play, so I took the first offer. But I should have waited, especially when I left Boro, as I might have got something in the top flight. I go back to the comment about watching Denis playing behind Giggsy and having his career extended by two or three years.

At the same time I was running the length of the pitch every week as a 35 year-old left wing back. It was a position which was a lot of fun to play but when you came up against a team playing 4-4-2 – as most teams did then - it meant playing against two players. I don't think I made too many errors which exposed myself.

All of my enthusiasm for actually playing the game had really been evaporating for sometime and I didn't look for a club for the 2000/01 season. Word got around that I wasn't playing for anybody and someone from Leigh Genesis asked me to play in their non-league version of the Charity Shield. That was my only game there, before I received a call asking me to go back to Wales.

Meirion Appleton, then manager of Bangor City, is a name I should have mentioned in my story much earlier. When I was a fifteen year-old schoolboy playing in the national under 18's, Meirion was the manager of that Welsh age bracket. We won that tournament - I scored two against Scotland, whose team included Ally Dick, the Spurs player who was rated as the next big star. I scored against England in a game at Norwich and that was the last I think I heard from Meirion until 2000, when he calls me on the telephone asking if I'd fancy a few games for Bangor. 'We've got a couple of lads coming in from England,' he said, to sell it to me. And he was true to his word. Giggs and Brown were going to be joining me, only it was Rhodri and Clive, and not their more celebrated brothers Ryan and Wes!

After leaving County I'd barely been playing any football; I'd had a few local games, and that Leigh game, but mostly I'd spent my summer playing golf and getting my handicap down to scratch. I'd been at Bangor for just a few weeks when I was offered the job of helping to coach as an assistant with the Welsh under 16's, the Victory Shield team - Sparky had been manager of the senior side for a few months. It was a bit of a tough job because results hadn't been great. They hadn't had any joy in the Victory Shield for seven years and one of our first games was at Scotland, where our age bracket hadn't won for twenty years. The last time they had, I was playing! The connection didn't stop there - Bryan Gunn, the former Norwich goalkeeper, was on the bench in that game, and his son, Angus, was starting in goal for them. Our lads were bit of a wild bunch. Rhys Carpenter, one of our forwards, had a t-shirt cut off with the words '1-0 to the sheep shaggers' written on it. He wore his football shirt over it. Ten minutes in, Rhys puts the ball in the top corner and runs around taking his shirt off. I looked over at one of the coaches and grimaced; we knew about the t-shirt, but Chris, who had been the coach since for decades, didn't realise until after the game what had happened. Rhys had to apologise on television a few weeks later. Chris was also a retired teacher who was the schools' representative on the FAW but it was meant in good fun. It ended up 3-0 to the sheep shaggers.

Then we played England at Newtown – they had Wayne Rooney on the bench. The pitch at Newtown was crap, and it had been deliberately chosen as a venue to play a part as a leveller. We went 1-0 up but they equalised when Wayne came on. We drew the game but finished the stronger side. Then, against Northern Ireland, we took the lead again. It should have been three or four but with about five minutes to go they equalised with a deflected free kick, and then took advantage of our dropped heads to get a winner too.

I loved the experience of working with the young lads because it was an opportunity to actually coach them. The wingers were helping the full backs; it was a team effort, as opposed to the eleven individuals it could often feel like at that age. Looking at it I could see they were being coached things at fifteen, that I didn't learn until I was eighteen. The drawback of that is that every single second of game-time is recorded these days. Coaches these days are on the sidelines entering data onto a laptop instead of watching the game. In my mind it's an over-complication, it's gone too far. Kids should be allowed to express themselves – one of the most thrilling sights in recent years was how Marcus Rashford broke on to the scene for Manchester United in 2016. A quick kid, eager to please, he had the knack of scoring important goals at the right time. It was so simple and yet so effective.

All in all those first months back in Wales flew by, I was enjoying it so much. I suggested that we implement the 'boxes' passing drills that we'd done at United and again, it seemed like a simple suggestion of improvement, but it helped us as a team and helped our form too. At a club like Manchester United it is good for sharpening your concentration but at Bangor, where resources are limited, the benefit of such a drill is that it helps you quickly develop an understanding of your team-mates' weaknesses and strengths; whether they are skilled at receiving the ball quickly, what side they are more comfortable, how they deal with the ball under pressure and how their attitude is when it comes to closing down and recovering the ball.

The Welsh league was really no different to any other – money talks and The New Saints had a lot of it. They normally went head to head with Barry Town, the other 'powerhouses' of the league, every season. Bangor's chairman, Ken Jones, was very good. He was an ex-rally driver who once beat Colin McRae in a race. Ken was funding the club; I'd developed a greater understanding of how difficult it was for owners when I was at Notts County. Bangor had some of the better crowds in Wales but you wouldn't normally get more than a thousand people. From the gate receipts, everybody and everything had to be paid, so it really was a good achievement that Bangor were as competitive as they were. It was also a big perk for me as I got to go to South Wales a lot to see my mum and dad and old friends.

I was back living near Manchester and Meirion said it was okay if I didn't train at the club during the week; my fitness regime consisted of a midweek run and a couple of pints of water on match day. It worked – I was injury free for six years and I was only meant to be there for a few games! The advice most professionals give is to keep playing if your body is okay, and I think that's the right thing to do as well. You're a long time finished. The most important thing was that I was enjoying playing football again. I retired after leaving Notts County and at the age of 36 I don't think anyone would have thought anything of it. That's a natural age for many players to bow out. But I was still being paid – not much, but paid nonetheless – to play a sport I still loved and that was something I considered a privilege. Cards on the table – there were times at Middlesbrough, and even Manchester United, where I didn't enjoy it. There was too much football. You work so hard that enjoyment barely comes into it. There's a fulfilment and satisfaction but enjoyment? We used to work so hard in training on shitty pitches, it was always hard work. Then there was the tiredness after games where you would feel so exhausted you were close to passing out. When I turned forty, it was obvious I was at the tail end of my career, but I was so appreciative of what I was doing that almost every game was enjoyable.

Meirion was relieved of his duties in 2001. I was playing a six-a-side competition at Stoke soon after and Peter Davenport was also playing. He asked me if I was going to take the job. I said no and suggested that Dav should apply. He came in as player-manager. In one of his first games, at Port Talbot, he was one of three of our players who got sent off – I was left in midfield by myself, on a pitch that was bigger than Old Trafford. As a player at United Dav wouldn't say boo to a goose and I think he got sent off three or four times at Bangor. The pressures of managing in the Welsh league! He was there for about four years and it was a successful time – we finished third in the league three times and qualified for Europe three times too. We played against Yugoslav team FK Sartid and beat them at home in one of our most famous victories, although home really meant Wrexham 70 miles away. We moved it there for a bigger gate, even though the better pitch would be playing into their hands instead of bringing them down to our standard. They had six internationals in their side and we won the first leg 1-0. Playing for Bangor City I knew it wasn't a record that could last but I was able to talk of the fact that I'd never yet tasted defeat in a European game. Famous last words, and yet, we were so close to qualifying for the second round. We started it well and at a corner their goalkeeper should have been sent off for throwing one of our players to the ground. The referee warned him and said that if the ball had been in play, he would have been off and it would have been a penalty. It was a vicious game. Their right back punched Paul Roberts clean in the face and took his tooth out – he was sent off. They scored the two goals they needed to go through but in the last minute of the game we had a chance – substitute Lee Hunt got the ball on the penalty spot and hit it straight at the goalkeeper. That was the difference between being eliminated and going through on away goals. The difference between a miserable flight home from Belgrade and £300,000 in the chairman's pocket and a chance to play Ipswich Town in the next round and the television receipts which would have surely come. Ken had a good time though. On the bus to the game they'd loaded our bus with beers. Despite the temptation we were good professionals and resisted. Ken didn't – he didn't need to – but he was steaming by the time we got to the game. Perhaps that's why he took defeat so well.

Peter resigned shortly after that defeat and after a couple of other managers came and went, and after years of dodging the bullet, I finally took the job as manager. I immediately thought, 'What have I done!' when I realised I'd have to turn up for training! We trained near Conwy, which was a little bit closer but still it was a long drive to do twice a week.

It was only natural that I'd have ideas and opinions of where we could improve – I'd been like that all my career – but at the end of the day I'd always been happy to just keep myself to myself and concentrate on my own performance. Now, my opinion not only mattered but I was having to make choices based on it. If someone wasn't playing well, I now had the responsibility to make that change. We had one lad who was lightning quick, so quick that in just about every game he'd go clean through two or three times and be one-on-one with the goalkeeper. He rarely scored. So I built entire sessions around him, putting him through on goal with the goalie, in order to improve his finishing. It was clearly something we could benefit from if he got it right. He didn't. We had to bin him.

We had a pretty good team and brought in some players from the English league. Simon Davies, the former Manchester United winger, was there, and we also brought in Paul O'Neill who'd played at Macclesfield. One of our best midfielders was a lad called Ricky Evans who was in the Scholesy mould. His brother Steve played for Wales but Ricky for me was the better player. Ricky played for Oldham and really could have played at a higher level but I think he didn't have the discipline required to make the difference. He enjoyed a drink and a good time. At that level of football it's not uncommon – the money funds the good time and there is rarely the kind of application and motivation which sets players apart. Still, I enjoyed playing alongside him, and he always kept himself in shape to play. He was a tough guy, would tackle anyone and scored some great goals.

Our best chance of success under my management came in a Welsh Cup final against Rhyl; we were holding our own until the referee gave a penalty for a supposed handball by Paul. It was a terrible decision but the refereeing at that level is pretty atrocious - just like players would watch European games and maybe try a trick or two they'd seen, so referees seemed keen to make odd decisions. We conceded the penalty and then, as we were trying to get back into the game, we let in another.

Things weren't easy but I felt it was going in the right direction. I brought in a lad called Carl Evans, a 16-year old who had walked out of Cardiff City when Sam Hamman had put a £200,000 price tag on him. There was no doubting Carl should have been at a top club. He played in a schoolboy game for Wales against England and gave one of the best left-wing performances I've ever seen at that age level. His close control was incredible, and I'm not overstating it to say that he's the closest Welsh player I've seen to compare to Ryan Giggs We were allowed to play him on a non-contract basis and he was tearing it up - I don't know why big clubs were put off with the price tag, maybe it was the standard of the Welsh league, but somebody should have taken a chance because that kid was quality.

A scouse lad called Steve Bleasdale - who'd been assistant coach to Mark Wright at Peterborough and then caretaker after Mark was sacked - came to watch games and he was sitting next to the chairman in the stands. I could smell what was happening a mile off; if we had a bad result, I'm sure he was there talking a good game about what he would have done to fix the problems. I resigned after we lost in the cup - a case of jumping before I was pushed - and he was appointed manager. He was gone within six months - he resigned because he didn't fancy the commute from Liverpool.

After I left Bangor I was contacted by Osian Roberts who was the manager of Porthmadog. I'd known Osian from coaching the kids at Wales and as I was still playing he asked if I fancied coming down. At the end of the season he resigned to take up a post as technical director at the Welsh FA. He was eventually named assistant manager to Chris Coleman and has done a great job.

Osh left me with the job, after he'd been there for nearly a decade. I'd just got used to the routine of coming back over for games and now I not only had to go back for training, but I faced an extra half an hour drive on top of the one I used to make to Bangor. There was a bit of a local rivalry between my old and new club so I had to win over the new fans, which was made that much more difficult by the fact I was taking over from a successful manager who spoke Welsh.

There was a bit of internal resistance, too. There were a lot of Welsh speakers at the club and so I asked the goalkeeping coach from Bangor to come with me as he spoke Welsh and I didn't. I'd told the squad of my plans, which included bringing in some players from England and gave the captaincy to one of the centre backs. He was commanding in the air and I thought giving him the armband might bring out the leader in him. After one game the goalkeeping coach came up to me and said that he'd heard the guy saying, in Welsh, that he wasn't going to pass to any of the English players I planned to bring in. I rung him right away and he denied it – I had to take the captaincy away from him. There was that sort of difficulty from day one because the club just weren't ready for the change. Osian was a great guy and I would guess that he was involved with the day-to-day running of the club – it wouldn't surprise me if he was helping them sell tickets. In the time he'd been there he'd really grown to be a part of the furniture and me? I lived in Manchester, which, I suppose, was strike one already when it came to concerns about my commitment. I brought four or five lads in and there was just no way that you can expect to see the benefit of the change overnight. It sometimes happens like that but its rare.

Nevertheless the positive signs were there. We outplayed TNS in the Cup and I was encouraged by the way we were starting to blend together but after a 7–2 Cup defeat to Port Talbot I was sacked. I don't know what kind of performance they were expecting in three months but I felt it was a little bit harsh, to say the least.

I can't say I was bitten by the management bug. Most of the benefit of playing into my forties was the routine – two or three times a month I might be playing in South Wales which gave me an opportunity to see my parents more regularly than I had done.

Then I was contacted by Neath Athletic, who had recently been promoted to the Welsh Premier Division. Technically they were founded in 2005 but the club was previously known as BP Llandarcy – the team my old man had turned out for. There's a picture of him at the club. They played at Llandarcy Park, and then at a venue called The Gnoll – the pitch was small but it was really magnificent. It gave my dad a reason to come and watch me play and it was great for him as he got to meet up with a lot of old pals he used to play with. It's a real community club and the two years playing there was a perfect way to wrap up my career. Although, even at forty-six, I wasn't officially retired!

A Proud Welshman

T HERE'S ONLY ONE PROBLEM with playing for Manchester United and that is the perception others sometimes make of it. People got the idea that because of my history, I might be better qualified for the role they wanted, regardless of whether or not I wanted it. If someone is a manager, they would prefer not to bring in someone whose CV was better than theirs.

The best option, then, was to go back to United - and that solution was presented to me when the gaffer called to say he'd had a word with the academy staff and would I like to go and help out. I was very appreciative of the invitation and I really enjoyed the experience. The memories inevitably came flooding back, even though the game had changed significantly. Attitudes towards coaching certainly have. I've rolled with it - you don't have an option - but I'm not sure the priorities are right. So much emphasis is placed upon passing the ball short and not enough on longer passing and real time situations. I say this about the game in general, not at United and it certainly wasn't the case when I returned there in 2009. There has been this clamour in recent years to try and develop a string of passing midfielders as if you'll create the next generation of Barcelona-quality superstars but people don't understand how hard those players work and how gifted they are in possession. More emphasis has to be placed on freedom of expression. I go to watch my son play football and they're always on at the kids to pass the ball short. They've barely even learned how to kick it. Let them have some fun. At the same time there's a lot of negativity about 'long ball'. David Beckham, and Paul Scholes - and Paul Pogba, now - have made it into an art form at United. If you can learn how to kick a ball with accuracy over forty or fifty yards then the odds are you'll be a tremendous passer over short distances and I think the three examples I just gave are perfect.

I was more nervous going back to United as a coach than I was when I first went as a player; you're entering a set up with established staff who have their own routine. I always think most of the training is to improve the areas of your game that need it - if it's longer passing, shorter passing, shooting, working on your weak foot. Then you need to make sure you're fit. Then it's game preparation. Some things never change - they still do the boxes that the Gaffer and Archie Knox brought in back in 1988.

At risk of sounding like an old man, the kids really don't appreciate how good they have it these days. There are so many pitches at Carrington; at the Cliff we had one pitch for the first team and reserves and then the kids. They have all these brilliant facilities and they don't play enough games - in the winter they're basically playing five-a-side tournaments for a couple of months. We'd be playing at weekends and midweek, in hail, on boggy pitches. It means that there's a lot of pressure on the fifteen and sixteen year-olds at the end of a season, gearing themselves up to try and earn a professional contract. It's easy enough to judge players and dismiss them.

There are plenty of players I saw at close quarters who I thought probably deserved more of a chance. Pogba is an obvious one because of how he went and came back but when he first arrived at the club as a sixteen year-old he had the presence of a player who wouldn't have looked out of place in the first team. I thought Josh King was perhaps unlucky to have not had more of a chance because I was always a fan of his; the same with James Wilson. He will come good if he recovers from his knee injury. More recently, there is Angel Gomes, who - if he remains fit - is as sure a guarantee to make it at the top level as anyone I've seen. That kid is frightening. He's so small, but his ability just shines through, and I actually hope it serves as a breakthrough moment for smaller players who don't always get the chances. He looked great on his debut on the final day of the 2016/17 season.

Before I rejoined the coaching I'd also been doing some hospitality work at the club and I would have to say that the 2007 title period might well have been my favourite time of watching football, with that attack of Ryan Giggs, Cristiano Ronaldo and Wayne Rooney, the three R's, and Carlos Tevez. After the 2006 World Cup all of those three players reached a level of brilliance that I haven't seen matched since. The way it all came together for that 7-1 win over Roma was just outstanding and I'm still convinced we should have won the treble that year, too. Ryan had an effort that definitely went over the line against Chelsea in the FA Cup Final, with the score at 0-0 in extra time. Against AC Milan we should have gone through and I think we would have done if we had played the same system as we did against Roma. We suffered injuries but I still felt we were by far the stronger team.

I have already mentioned about playing alongside Ryan but the way his career went from strength to strength and how he was so good he was able to play in any position, showed what a fantastic footballer he was. Over the course of his career he has been the best player to have ever played for the club in my opinion. He was in the latter end of his time at United (well, the last seven years!) and at that time I'd have to say Cristiano had grown into the role of best player in the world. He should have won the Ballon d'Or in 2007. There's a lot of talk about him and Messi and how Messi has one more than him but that shouldn't be the case. For me, Ronaldo is the better of the two. There are no weaknesses in his game and the number of goals he scores is ridiculous.

Then you add in Wayne Rooney, the all-round footballer, and we had the perfect attack. He got criticised for his goal return in seasons where he spent most of his time in midfield. For me he's the closest I've seen to Mark Hughes when it comes to powerful play and the ability to finish in a number of different ways. He has been such a hard worker that it's no wonder his team-mates have loved him. Wayne has scored so many incredible goals over his career and proved that it is possible to be a scorer of great goals and a great goalscorer, when he broke Sir Bobby Charlton's record of 249 in January 2017, the goal he scored against Stoke City was typical of him, as was his reaction at the time - let's get the ball and try and score a winner. He returned to Everton in the summer of 2017 as the all-time leading scorer for Manchester United and England, and then scored on his second debut at Goodison Park. After his famous celebration against Spurs in 2015, everyone knows Wayne has a bit of an obssession with boxing which reminds me of my ring debut.

A few years earlier, in 2010, I had a celebrity boxing match with former Liverpool striker John Aldridge. Pally was supposed to be fighting him and had been in training for ten weeks; Pally is 6 foot 4, Aldridge 6 foot 1, so it was a fair match up but on the Monday before the fight, which was due to take place on the Friday, Pally did his back in. He called me and asked if I would take his place and without really thinking what I was getting myself into, I said yes.

I called Ricky Hatton and asked for some advice so he took me down to Anthony Farnell's gym on the Wednesday and I did a bit of sparring. On the day before the fight I got a call from MUTV asking if they could come and film a segment. I agreed because it was a good opportunity for exposure for Ant's gym. Because it was on television I was leathering the gloves and then they were asking me to do it again. I worked myself out so badly that I was exhausted and on the morning of the fight I was pole-axed on the settee. Still, I made it to the MEN Arena in one piece and just about ready.

It was on a bill featuring Craig Phillips, the winner of the first ever series of Big Brother, against Terry Gibson. Philips was apparently a trained kick boxer and within thirty seconds Terry was all over the place! Then there was the 'Lotto Lout' Michael Carroll against Rhino from the Gladiators. I think it got nasty and Rhino broke his nose! Linsey Dawn McKenzie and Jodie Marsh had a fight, that was a proper scrap, they went for it.

My fight was after Terry's and as he left the ring he said, "If he hits you, just go down and stay down!" — I think he was speaking from experience — but I had good assistance from Anthony, who'd agreed to be my corner man, and he put vaseline inside the boxing helmet. Tracey and my parents were there and they thought it looked funny — though Tracey wasn't laughing as the previous evening she'd seen a segment on Granada TV showing John sparring with Craig Phillips and looking quite aggressive. "You're not doing it!" she said but there was no chance of me backing out. Although it had been nagging me why John would have said yes to fighting Pally considering the size of him but then I learned that John had been an amateur boxer when he was younger…

As we're getting ready John says to me "No low punches!" Anthony told me that when he punched me, I shouldn't go back as my instinct might tell me but instead move forward to my left and bring my arm forward to try and hit him on the outside. Good advice. Within ten seconds he'd come right out and whacked me. I rallied well and threw a few haymakers of my own; I had him on the ropes and hit some good shots to the ribs. Towards the end of the fight we were both laughing because we were so tired, even though I'd had considerably less preparation. I thought I'd done well enough to win — Anthony agreed — but the referee raises John's hand in victory. I told John I'd have a rematch with him in Liverpool.

But that's not the end of the story. In 2017 I was in Hong Kong when I was approached by a coach of West Ham's under-23 side. "You don't know who I am, do you?" he says. I admitted I didn't. "It's been nagging me for seven years. I gave the fight to John Aldridge and you won - I'm John's best mate!"

I returned to United the summer after we had matched Liverpool's eighteen title wins. Since I'd been gone the gaffer had built three or four different teams and had them all challenging for championships. Some people can't get one team together. Being there for the bookend league titles, the first two and the last two of Sir Alex's reign, well... the only word for it is disbelief. I couldn't believe he was still there, that he still had the desire and that one person had overseen so much success. For us back in 1993 it was all about that first one. There was no expectation to chase down the eighteen, only, the relief and euphoria of being able to rightly claim that we were the best team in the country again. In 2011 the gaffer surpassed eighteen and made United the most successful club in English history, and added a twentieth league title for good measure just before he retired in 2013. There's no doubt, there's no argument about it - Sir Alex Ferguson is the greatest manager the game has ever seen. The English league is so hard to win. Almost always it goes down to the last couple of games until the title or relegation is decided. Look at the Chelsea and Tottenham game from the end of the 2015/6 season. Chelsea had nothing on that game and played with such pride and determination that it turned the game into a war. It is absolutely fantastic for the integrity of the competition.

It could be argued that our 1993 team was good enough to have won the European Cup, if we hadn't been hurt by the foreigner rule. Back when we won it in 1968 we played four teams and we were in the final. In 1978 Liverpool only had to play four teams to win it, and they lost two of their six knockout games! In 2008, to win the same competition, there was a league stage, three knockout games, and then the final. Thirteen games. The expansion of the competition in 1997 – coming at a time when United were by far and away the best team in England – meant plenty of adjustments had to be made again. The gaffer was continuously trying to get a team to compete on the continent and the rules were changing every year. What he achieved has never been rivalled and never will be.

It was going to be a very difficult job for whoever came after him and as we all know it seemed like nothing went right for David Moyes. We're talking about very different levels but there is a similar theory to the one when I took over at Porthmadog if you are to look at the length of time the previous manager was in charge and how used to a certain way of working everyone was. I thought David made a mistake by letting Micky Phelan go. He had tons of experience at the club and could have helped him when it came to player's routines. The thing is, David didn't do something that most people wouldn't do – he brought in people he knew and trusted. It was a logical thing to do. I did think that he would have instilled the need for a similar work ethic with the first team players, like he did at Everton, and that seemed to be something that was obviously lacking in some of our defeats. I'm not saying the players we had were lazy – they had just won a league title – but maybe somewhere along the line it was either assumed by the manager that these players were so good they didn't have to be instructed to close down, or it was a message not delivered to the players that they needed to do it.

We lost against West Brom at home in September 2013. Ferdinand

and Carrick had played every game under Moyes; the gaffer tended to use them on a rotational basis. Against West Brom Anderson is in midfield, so Rio's not getting the defensive screen in front of him that he's used to. Moyes has a go at Rio afterwards saying that Phil Jagielka, his captain at Everton, wouldn't have defended that way, so he offered Rio a video of Phil defending. Rio played one more time until the end of February and I think he only played a handful of times under Moyes in total. They'd obviously had a falling out but United had gone from winning the league with Rio in great form to him being left out of the team completely. With all due respect to Phil, Rio didn't need to be watching any video telling him how to defend, he'd set the benchmark. I bumped into Harry Redknapp, who was manager of QPR. He asked me what was wrong with Rio because he'd been out for so long. 'He's been training really well,' I said, 'I don't know why he's not playing him.' Unwittingly I'd helped grease the wheels for that move. It's fair to say it didn't go brilliantly for Rio down at Loftus Road but I can't agree with people who are critical of him and his last couple of years. You have to understand the player and he was fantastic in his last few years under Sir Alex. Harry obviously had Rio at West Ham but he had matured so much since then - the tight little pitch at Loftus Road and the constant hard work for a team that aren't as good didn't do Rio any favours.

As we know, now, Moyes was sacked in April 2014 and Ryan took charge for a few games. I thought he should have been the gaffer's successor. People were going on about 'experience'. He'd been playing there and winning things for twenty-five years - how much more experience did he need? United is a very unique environment. David Moyes didn't have the experience and it showed. Louis van Gaal did a good job at Ajax and when he was managing Bayern Munich, Barcelona and Holland, whatever system you play with those teams they would have still won their leagues. But the fans at those clubs didn't enjoy the way they played during that time. I think, ultimately, Louis was too defensive, and supporters became frustrated with the lack of an attacking 4-4-2. They weren't attacking and they weren't creating enough chances - it's such an obvious thing to say but if you aren't having efforts on goal, you aren't going to win games, and even though we won the FA Cup in 2016, the style of football meant that there had to be a change.

Under Jose Mourinho there's almost been a different problem. We've had shot upon shot, have dominated most games and yet can't seem to find the net as much as we should. I think if we start playing 4-4-2 again we will start scoring a lot more of those chances because you have more players in the box, so those shots that are being blocked will end up in the net. Mourinho is the right profile of manager and has the experience to bring success to Old Trafford – here is a man who isn't motivated by money because he never has to work again, so he is motivated by success. He made a great start by bringing in a number of top players. The signing of Zlatan Ibrahimovic was questioned and I saw an amusing statistic that the Barcelona goalkeeper had run more than him but he was brilliant at United – he is so big, strong and powerful and proved he could score goals in the Premier League. If he had another striker alongside him I'm sure he could have scored even more.

Mourinho made the point himself after we beat Watford 2-0 in February 2017 – if there was a reservation about him, it was whether or not he could bring attacking football to United, and he appears to have answered that. I hope, as much as anyone, that the good times are coming back to Old Trafford.

As a Welshman there has been plenty to be excited about over the last few years. If there was one unfulfilled ambition from my career it was playing in a major international tournament and there were several close calls. My biggest disappointment in the national team was being sent off in 1990, against Luxembourg of all countries, who had just one professional player in their team. I was playing right back and around fifteen minutes in I slid in and fouled their left winger – it was a bit rash and probably a yellow but the referee didn't see it. I went and moved back into my position, and their centre forward – the pro, who played in Italy, pushed me, so I pushed him back and he just fell to the ground. The ref had played on and when he turned round he put two and two together and came up with five. He saw the player lying on the floor and me stood over him; he thought I'd punched him and sent me off. I wish I could have turned the clock back. I would have fallen to the ground like he did. He was rolling around holding his face and I was almost laughing, because it took me a few seconds to clock on to what he was doing. The referee came over waving the red card. After the game the Luxembourg lad came to see me and said that if I was going to appeal against the red card, he'd be happy to say I never punched him! The good thing was we won the game 1-0.

Alun Evans, the Welsh secretary, says 'We'll wait to see what they give us and then appeal.' I said, 'He sent me off for punching, what do you think they'll give us? They'll throw the book at me!' I thought we should have appealed the red card before waiting to see what the length of the ban would be. It was four matches. So we appealed afterwards, a month or so later. We had to go all the way to Geneva. John Motson is commentating on the game, 'The centre-forward's running across, I don't know what he's doing!' The referee's report says that the guy I tackled got up and I punched him in the face, when it was the centre-forward who had run about forty yards to push me. He couldn't have got it more wrong. He didn't even get the right player. I tried to be fair to the referee – I said, in his defence, he couldn't see everything, and he obviously made a guess and got it wrong. Despite everything being as obvious as it was, the four match ban stuck and, to add insult to injury, they said I was lucky I hadn't been fined! It was suggested that if we had appealed before waiting to react to the severity of the ban we would have had the right decision.

Our solicitor said if we took the case to court there was no way we could lose but the Welsh FA had already spent something like five grand taking us to Geneva, plus the money already spent on the case, and they decided it wasn't worth it. They just accepted the ban. Lovely stuff – I missed almost two years of international duty.

My next proper qualifying campaign was for the 1994 World Cup and we thought we'd cracked it. Prior to the qualifiers we played a friendly in Austria. Chris Coleman played at centre half with Eric Young and I played in an unfamiliar sweeper role. We drew 1-1 in front of 53,000 against a good Austria team - and we were missing a few names such as Mark Hughes, Kevin Ratcliffe and Ian Rush. Our next game was our first World Cup qualifier, out in Romania. Terry Yorath decides he's going to mix it up and play 4-4-2. Romania - with Dan Petrescu, Gica Popescu, and their main talisman Gheorghe Hagi, are rampant - they're five nil up at half time. Me and Giggsy were on the bench and I couldn't believe what I was seeing; of course, I thought I should have been in there, but we were so used to playing a five at the back, I don't know why we changed it for our toughest qualifier. Worst still, neither Young or Coleman were playing at the back. Instead we had Mark Aizlewood and Andy Melville - good defenders but not the quickest.

Yorath is fuming at half time - 'Well, now what are we going to fucking do?' Dean Saunders, always the funny one, quips, 'We can't fucking play five at the back can we!'

In our next game, back in our system that had worked well, we put six past Faroe Islands - I got on the scoresheet, linking well with Giggsy down the left hand side and smashing one into the top corner.

With Belgium also in the group, they and Romania were the strong favourites, but we kept ourselves in with a chance. We grabbed a great home win over Belgium - Giggsy scored a brilliant free kick - and should have beat Czechoslovakia, which would have given us a great position to be in heading into our last group game with Romania. I played when I could through the hell of my hernia injury, but I was unable to play in that last game. Our draws with Czechoslovakia (as creditable as our away point was, considering we'd never scored a goal there before that game) meant that even though we were in control of our own destiny against Romania, we had to beat them to qualify for the World Cup.

There had been the two disappointments against Scotland I mentioned earlier but in our European Championship campaign of 1988 we only needed to draw our last two games and then to qualify for Euro 1992 we only needed to avoid defeat in Germany. Having been a goal behind in the first half, Dean Saunders scored on the hour and Cardiff Arms Park was rocking five minutes later when we were awarded a penalty. It was left to Paul Bodin to take it – his effort was right down the middle but it hit the crossbar and rebounded away. Deano was the joker and he said to Paul, 'That will stick with you for the rest of your life.' I certainly didn't blame Paul. You win as a team and lose as a team. At least he was brave enough to take the penalty. It was obviously devastating to be that close to the World Cup but Paul will have felt that as much as anyone. I do wonder what might have been – my confidence was low and I was making the decision to leave United at the time. What if we'd qualified, I'd held off on my decision and then had a great World Cup? We'll never know. After the incident with Bobby Gould in 1997 I was never selected again. It took almost another twenty years for Wales to finally break that tournament bad luck when they qualified for the European Championships in 2016.

I don't think it's being biased to look back at the team I played in during the early 1990s and say that man for man we probably had a better team than the one that played in 2016. We had world class quality in Southall, Rush, Sparky, the youthful brilliance of Ryan Giggs and Gary Speed, as well as Chris Coleman and Kevin Ratcliffe, one of the best defenders I ever played with.

Having played with Chris, and being as close as I was to Osian, his assistant, it was great to see how well they did. It was nice to know they were not only going down in history but they were also having a great time while doing it. Chris and Osian did an incredible job and the players were brilliant, everyone of them. Wales had a number of standout individuals who really made a difference. Aaron Ramsey and Gareth Bale were both brilliant in Euro 2016; the squad, of course, did really well, but when Aaron was injured you could see what a huge difference he made. It might have been the difference between them going as far as they did and maybe even winning the whole thing. As the then-most expensive player in the world, Gareth was the one everyone looked to first and I admit that he is a player I'd love to see at United. He's one of the top players in the world, has done brilliantly for Real Madrid and is the kind of player who would settle right into life at Old Trafford with no problem.

From Pitch to Putt

MY FIRST MARRIAGE ENDED around the time I went to Middlesbrough; I was too young for that sort of commitment and the only surprise was that it had lasted as long as it did. It was only when I met Tracey that I think I treated marriage and commitment with the respect I should have done from the start. It was also the first time I'd really considered settling down and having children. Having made that decision, we were faced with the difficulty that it might not happen. We sought medical advice and we were told that we would never have kids; ironically, from the same place that had done my hernia operation which had a bearing on me leaving United. If we'd had listened to the doctor, we wouldn't have had children.

Tracey has a much better memory of everything that we went through; at the time, being told we couldn't have children didn't really have the impact on me that it might have simply because I didn't know what I was missing. Knowing what I do now, I feel absolutely blessed to have kids and it would have been a travesty if I hadn't experienced being a father. I've scored diving headers at the Stretford End against City but there isn't a feeling in the world that compares with being a parent. It changed me; it forced me to grow up. Maybe if I'd had kids sooner I'd have grown up a lot quicker. Everything, though, happens for a reason, and even though it took a while for it all to come together, I wouldn't change anything.

The day I became a father is vividly etched in my mind. I was playing a charity game at Old Trafford at the end of the season. The day before the game, we'd been at the hospital because the doctors had planned to induce Tracey. We'd known from pretty early on that we were expecting twins, one of each. It didn't happen on the day, so, after staying overnight in the hospital, I went to Old Trafford with my mind on other things.

I gave my phone to Alan Keegan, the stadium announcer, and asked him to let me know if any news came in. Inevitably it did and I had to leave the field rapidly; Alan's shouting in his distinctive, booming voice over the public address, 'Good luck!' as I dashed to Stepping Hill hospital still in my kit. I thought I'd arrived at a war zone; there was blood everywhere, Tracey's consultant was there, plus sixteen other doctors and nurses helping out, and a few students observing as it was a twin birth by emergency caesarean section. It seemed like chaos but it was organised chaos; the staff at the hospital did a remarkable job, and thankfully everyone was safe and healthy. We had a boy - Corey George (after George Best) who arrived first with a big flock of hair on his head, and Lulah-Beau, our daughter, arrived with none! Because of what she had gone through, Tracey was not allowed to do much in the first few days. I got very skilled in the art of double nappies.

I'd been living for myself, and my wife; sure, you have your parents and your family, but life changes in the most ultimate way when you have kids because they are always dependent on you. We are thankful for the good fortune we have had when it came to having kids because we appreciate how difficult it was to have them. They are fantastic children. The twins are quite different in their personalities; Corey is a little more outgoing, he's not afraid to put his hand up in assembly, and not afraid to speak his mind. He's very determined and inquisitive; he's always asking questions. Lulah is more laid back and observant, and Rose, our youngest daughter who arrived a few years later, is probably a mixture of the two. We think Rose has definitely benefitted from being a younger sister to a brother and sister who are a few years older than her. It really has helped to accelerate her development.

Corey plays football and enjoys it; naturally people will wonder if he will follow in my footsteps, and in my opinion he's probably better than I was at his age but as long as he enjoys himself Tracey and I are happy. We definitely won't force anything on him, although he is a Manchester United fan! All three of the kids are very clever and very academic; Corey and Lulah are doing well at school, and, as I said, Rose is so advanced for her age. We couldn't be prouder.

On that subject, having kids changes your relationship with your own parents. For me, I started to realise just what I am to my dad. We both keep our feelings to ourselves and tend to be quiet. He came up to the house in early 2017 and I think it was the first time we had a hug! I'd waited fifty-two years! Obviously he hugged me when I was a kid but you get the idea. I don't think it's to compensate for anything, and I certainly don't think I missed out on anything as far as my relationship with my Mum and Dad are concerned, I just think it was that generation. It's more common these days for parents to hug and cuddle their kids and I must admit I do enjoy that time with my children.

Dad's eighty this year and I've always been conscious of the fact that, at least since I've been a grown man, I've never told him that I love him. It's obviously something that matters to me because it's something I've kept with me. I suppose this is as good a time as any to address that – Dad, I love you. There, I said it, and it's in print!

I went from trying to get into the Middlesbrough side in the Premier League to eighteen months later, walking away from English football. That was after five months at Barnsley which were enjoyable but changed when the assistant manager started disagreeing with the manager in front of the players. One got the other the sack, the other then got sacked by the new man – better the devil you know! Then, at Notts County, we had another good start at the top of the league but Sam left and it became every man for himself. There was too much back stabbing and I had entered the political aspect of being a veteran footballer whose CV reads better than the manager at the club where you want to get a coach's job. Football in England just wasn't enjoyable.

Though I did regain some of the enthusiasm for the game playing for as long as I did in Wales, my time out in the summer of 2000 where I played a lot of golf lit the fire to take that more seriously. I got down to scratch and suddenly found people saying to me that I could be even better. I played with a pro down at Macdonald Portal in Cheshire and he said to me, 'If you could putt, you'd be on the tour.' I'm very accurate with my driving and irons; I always hit the ball straight, which has earned me a lot of compliments. I think that was something I took from football. I'd played a few events through my career where the sponsors would pair a footballer with two senior golfers; I remember doing a couple of events where I played with Christy O'Connor. You go around the green and observe the way that the pros do it and it whets the appetite. I played with the late Mike Slater – Mike was a United fan so we were talking about the club on and off – after nine holes, I was actually beating his score. He was leading the tournament! At the end, all the pros would play against each other for £100,000. I thought 'I hope I'm not putting him off by talking about United!'

I played with Maurice Bembridge, who broke the course record, 64, at Augusta – he said that if I kept myself fit, when I was forty-nine or fifty, I could get into the seniors. I thought it was a long way off but the closer it got, the more seriously I took the idea and I turned professional in 2015.

I took the advice on putting and it has improved; I have four or five putters now and I enjoy playing with them all. There are so many variables that affect a golfer's game; the quality of the green, the length of the grass and the weather – I suppose it's similar to football but even more technical. You can hit a ball in the UK with an 8 iron and the ball will travel 140 yards. You can hit the same exact strike in South Africa and because the air is thinner and the weather is twenty-five degrees, the ball will travel 180 yards. And, like every sport, technological advances have had an impact. I'm a quite conservative player and I have my own style – I only had one lesson, some time after I started playing, where I got advice about taking the putter back low, not too far back and hit through the ball. The strongest part of my game is driving but I don't understand that when a new driver comes out and the advertisement for it says it can add ten yards to your drive. That's been going on for fifteen years, if that was the case, I should be able to hit the ball five hundred yards! I realised that it really comes down to your own ability and I just went back to using my own clubs, which were reliable. I've got a lot to learn, I know that, but I'm enjoying it. I'm under no illusions about my own ability, I don't go out thinking I'm Rory McIlroy – in the first tournament I played, I found myself learning a lot from the younger players. I'd like to take the time to thank Ged Mason at Morson who has really helped me with sponsorship; you need big backing to succeed and Ged has been great with me.

I've tried to qualify for a couple of senior Opens and I hope that either that happens or I get an invitation. I played at Camberley Heath a couple of years ago trying to qualify for the Senior Open and I was two under after five holes - level par got in. I learned so much about myself as a player on that round because silly little things cost me. The most important golf club in your bag is your head and you have to always remember that it's about the next shot. No matter how bad your last one was, there is absolutely no point dwelling or thinking about how you can improve. You have to leave it behind and move on. I made a number of bad decisions which distracted me from my natural game and ended up two over.

I know I can be a lot better. The funny thing is, for one reason or another, I played more golf when I was an amateur than I have done since turning professional. I was playing at Portal three times a week and could get seven or eight birdies in a round but now - since having children - I don't get to play more than once a week.

I'm a realist, though. I love playing golf and I do have ambitions - I'd love to play in a senior's Open and see if I could compete but I can put things into perspective and acknowledge how lucky I've been. Loads of people dream of playing for Manchester United, of scoring a goal for them, of winning a trophy for them. There's the other side of it where even those who did manage to do those things look at different eras and say they wish they could have played with other players or in another time. I've kept myself fit and so I've been able to play alongside a lot of players who I just missed out playing with at United. Andy Cole, for example, who arrived the year after I left, Ronny Johnsen, Louis Saha, players like that. Because of all of the money in the game, the question I get asked most of all is, would I like to play in today's game. I would but purely because of the pitches. I went to see a FC United game and their pitch was perfect. For the last five years Old Trafford has had the best pitch in the country.

Overall, though, how can I not be happy with my lot? I feel fortunate that I was one of the few players from the 80's team that won a Championship medal; a team I feel deserved one, and would have got one if the pitches had been better or Paul McGrath had been fit for a full season. I'm proud to be part of a very select group of players, alongside Steve Bruce, Gary Pallister, Denis Irwin, Paul Ince, Brian McClair and Mark Hughes who can say they won an FA Cup, European Cup Winners' Cup, Super Cup and League Championship medal playing for Manchester United. I played 245 times for United and scored 26 goals - many of those goals, people still remember and talk to me about. Just as many people talk to me about that goal-line clearance in Rotterdam. I made my own name and have my own place in the history of the biggest football club in the world; and, as a proud Welshman, I played for my country alongside some of the greatest players to pull on a Wales shirt. I can't complain - it was a fantastic career.

Question Time

We decided to start ask Clayton ten questions based on Bernard Pivot's French series 'Boullion de Culture', later popularised by James Lipton at the end of every episode of 'Inside the Actor's Studio'.

What is your favourite word?
Manchester! I don't know, is that too... you're supposed to answer them instinctively aren't you? Manchester was the first word that came into my head.

What is your least favourite word?
City.

What turns you on creatively, spiritually or emotionally?
Stepping onto a football pitch. The whole thing about it, the idea that for the next ninety minutes anything could happen, you don't know how it will pan out... the adrenalin and the potential of the unknown.

What turns you off?
Nothing really annoys me... I'm pretty laid back. If I have to say anything I'd say obnoxious people.

What is your favourite curse word?
Puta que pariu... I'm not sure exactly what it means, I got it from Ravanelli and Juninho and so I used to say it to referees because I knew I'd get away with it!

What sound or noise do you love?
Obviously the roar of Old Trafford after we scored a goal. There's nothing better. Or when you're chasing a goal and you pick the ball up and the crowd gets behind you. They really are like a twelfth man, and even if you feel you've given one hundred percent, that support inspires you to give more than you thought you had in you.

What sound or noise do you hate?
The sound of a baby crying or in distress.

What profession other than your own would you like to attempt?
Well, I'm a golfer now, or, trying to be... so I can't say that... I suppose a racing driver.

What profession would you not like to do?
I'd hate to have an indoor nine to five job. I wouldn't mind it outdoors but not inside.

If Heaven exists, what would you like to hear God say when you arrive at the Pearly Gates?
"It's not your time, get back down there!"

Some supporters over social media to put some questions to Clayton.

David Coverdale asks what is your favourite TV show and favourite movie?
My favourite TV show is probably the X Factor, I just like that so many people have that opportunity for their dream to come true. My favourite film, I would say Kelly's Heroes with Clint Eastwood.

Favourite place to visit on holiday?
Dubai. The weather is always great and there's plenty of activities to do, you can do anything you want out there.

And favourite type of music?
Rock - I'm a fan of the Foo Fighters and Stereophonics.

Favourite food?
Steak and chips. I'm partial to a Chinese but I'll go with steak.

Dan Burdett asks if you and your team-mates used to read Red Issue and what did you think of it if so?
I know that it came out when I was there at the club but I have to admit I never really read it.

Tony Park asks what do you think stopped United winning the title in the 1980s (if you had to choose one reason above all others)?
The pitch!

John McNicol asks, did the youth players really have to pretend to

chat up the Clayton Blackmore cut out?

Yep, so I've heard! I was a bit surprised when I heard, and it was Becks and Ryan, although Ryan kept it quiet! The worst thing that happened when we were kids was singing at Christmas to put a show on for the first team. Can you imagine having to kiss Joe Jordan? He'd probably have knocked me out!

Andy Howatson asked: Did the nickname "Sunbed" bother you at all?

Honestly, it did a little bit, but only because I rarely went on it. At the club I never went on it for superficial reasons; I was told that it was good for healing injuries and scars so I would go on now and again. I tan very easily so whenever I'd go away in the summer I'd come back very dark.

Darren Whalley asked: Who is the player you would liked to have played with in any era, and who was the player you didn't like playing against…?

Cristiano Ronaldo to play with, I wouldn't have to do anything, just get out a deck chair, sit in midfield and watch the game… Ryan was someone I didn't enjoy playing against in training but I never had to play against him directly in a game. I suppose the best answer I can give is Dejan Savicevic for Red Star but we won that game!

Paul Jarvis asked: Which United team would you liked to have played in the most – 98/99 or 07/08?

I'd probably go 99 because they won the treble and I'd played with a few of those lads. I never got to play with Yorke and Cole and they were one of the best combinations I've ever seen.

Tim Starbuck asked : If you could change one thing about your career what would it be?

Again, the pitches. This question gets asked a lot and people expect you to say the money but I would have loved to have played on the pitches. My love for playing football was greater than anything else that came with it.

CLAYTON'S ALL TIME XI

Selected from former team-mates

Schmeichel

Irwin   Pallister   McGrath   Blackmore

Kanchelskis Keane   Robson   Giggs

Cantona   Hughes

Subs: Juninho, Ravanelli

CAREER STATISTICS

HONOURS

WALES

1985-97 39 Caps, 1 Goal

MANCHESTER UNITED

Premier League: 1992–93
FA Cup: 1989–90
FA Charity Shield: 1990 (shared)
UEFA Cup Winners' Cup: 1990–91
UEFA Super Cup: 1991

MIDDLESBROUGH

Football League First Division: 1994–95

SUMMARY

SEASONS	CLUB	APP	GLS
1982–1994	MANCHESTER UNITED	186	19
1994–1999	MIDDLESBROUGH	53	4
1996	BRISTOL CITY (LOAN)	5	1
1999	BARNSLEY	7	0
1999–2000	NOTTS COUNTY	21	2
2000	LEIGH RMI	1	0
2000–2006	BANGOR CITY	176	11
2006–2007	PORTHMADOG	18	4
2007–2010	NEATH ATHLETIC	22	0
	Total	489	41

MANCHESTER UNITED FIRST TEAM APPEARANCES

Date	Opponent	Venue	Score	Goals	Competition
16/05/1984	Nottingham Forest	A	0-2		Div 1
09/10/1984	Burnley	A	3-0		League Cup
08/12/1984	Nottingham Forest	A	2-3		Div 1
21/09/1985	WBA	A	5-1	1	Div 1
24/09/1985	Crystal Palace	A	1-0		League Cup
26/11/1985	Liverpool	A	1-2		League Cup
14/12/1985	Aston Villa	A	3-1	1	Div 1
21/12/1985	Arsenal	H	0-1		Div 1
26/12/1985	Everton	A	1-3		Div 1
01/01/1986	Birmingham City	H	1-0		Div 1
09/01/1986	Rochdale	H	2-0		FA Cup
11/01/1986	Oxford United	A	3-1		Div 1
25/01/1986	Sunderland	A	0-0		FA Cup
29/01/1986	Sunderland	H	3-0		FA Cup
22/02/1986	WBA	A	3-0		Div 1
09/03/1986	West Ham United	A	0-2		FA Cup
15/03/1986	Queens Park Rangers	A	0-1		Div 1
16/04/1986	Newcastle United	A	4-2		Div 1
19/04/1986	Tottenham Hotspur	A	0-0		Div 1
26/04/1986	Leicester City	H	4-0	1	Div 1
03/05/1986	Watford	A	1-1		Div 1
23/08/1986	Arsenal	A	0-1		Div 1
25/08/1986	West Ham United	H	2-3		Div 1
30/08/1986	Charlton Athletic	H	0-1		Div 1
16/09/1986	Watford	A	0-1		Div 1
08/11/1986	Oxford United	A	0-2		Div 1
15/11/1986	Norwich City	A	0-0		Div 1
22/11/1986	Qpr	H	1-0		Div 1
29/11/1986	Wimbledon	A	0-1		Div 1
24/01/1987	Arsenal	H	2-0		Div 1
31/01/1987	Coventry City	H	0-1		FA Cup
04/05/1987	Tottenham Hotspur	A	0-4		Div 1
06/05/1987	Coventry City	A	1-1		Div 1
09/05/1987	Aston Villa	H	3-1	1	Div 1
26/09/1987	Tottenham Hotspur	H	1-0		Div 1
03/10/1987	Luton Town	A	1-1		Div 1
07/10/1987	Hull City	A	1-0		League Cup
10/10/1987	Sheffield Wednesday	A	4-2	1	Div 1
17/10/1987	Norwich City	H	2-1		Div 1
25/10/1987	West Ham United	A	1-1		Div 1
28/10/1987	Crystal Palace	H	2-1		League Cup
15/11/1987	Liverpool	H	1-1		Div 1
18/11/1987	Bury	H	2-1		League Cup
21/11/1987	Wimbledon	H	1-2	1	Div 1
01/01/1988	Charlton Athletic	H	0-0		Div 1
20/01/1988	Oxford United	A	0-2		League Cup
24/01/1988	Arsenal	A	2-1		Div 1
30/01/1988	Chelsea	H	2-0		FA Cup
13/02/1988	Chelsea	A	2-1		Div 1
20/02/1988	Arsenal	A	1-2		FA Cup
23/02/1988	Tottenham Hotspur	A	1-1		Div 1
05/03/1988	Norwich City	A	0-1		Div 1
12/03/1988	Sheffield Wednesday	H	4-1	1	Div 1
19/03/1988	Nottingham Forest	A	0-0		Div 1
26/03/1988	West Ham United	A	3-1		Div 1
02/04/1988	Derby County	H	4-1		Div 1
04/04/1988	Liverpool	A	3-3		Div 1
12/04/1988	Luton Town	A	3-0		Div 1
30/04/1988	Qpr	H	2-1		Div 1
02/05/1988	Oxford United	A	2-0		Div 1
07/05/1988	Portsmouth	H	4-1		Div 1
09/05/1988	Wimbledon	H	2-1		Div 1
27/08/1988	Qpr	H	0-0		Div 1
03/09/1988	Liverpool	A	0-1		Div 1
10/09/1988	Middlesbrough	H	1-0		Div 1
17/09/1988	Luton Town	A	2-0		Div 1
24/09/1988	West Ham United	H	2-0		Div 1
28/09/1988	Rotherham United	A	1-0		League Cup
12/10/1988	Rotherham Utd	H	5-0		League Cup
22/10/1988	Wimbledon	A	1-1		Div 1
26/10/1988	Norwich City	H	1-2		Div 1
30/10/1988	Everton	A	1-1		Div 1
02/11/1988	Wimbledon	A	1-2		League Cup
05/11/1988	Aston Villa	H	1-1		Div 1
12/11/1988	Derby County	A	2-2		Div 1
19/11/1988	Southampton	H	2-2		Div 1
23/11/1988	Sheffield Wednesday	H	1-1		Div 1
27/11/1988	Newcastle United	A	0-0		Div 1
03/12/1988	Charlton Athletic	H	3-0		Div 1
10/12/1988	Coventry City	A	0-1		Div 1
17/12/1988	Arsenal	A	1-2		Div 1
11/01/1989	Queens Park Rangers	A	2-2		FA Cup
14/01/1989	Millwall	H	3-0	1	Div 1
21/01/1989	West Ham United	A	3-1		Div 1
23/01/1989	Qpr	H	3-0		FA Cup
28/01/1989	Oxford United	H	4-0		FA Cup
05/02/1989	Tottenham Hotspur	H	1-0		Div 1
11/02/1989	Sheffield Wednesday	A	2-0		Div 1
18/02/1989	Bournemouth	A	1-1		FA Cup
22/02/1989	Bournemouth	H	1-0		FA Cup
25/02/1989	Norwich City	A	1-2		Div 1
12/03/1989	Aston Villa	A	0-0		Div 1
18/03/1989	Nottingham Forest	H	0-1		FA Cup
25/03/1989	Luton Town	H	2-0	1	Div 1
27/03/1989	Nottingham Forest	A	0-2		Div 1
02/04/1989	Arsenal	H	1-1		Div 1
08/05/1989	Queens Park Rangers	A	2-3	1	Div 1
10/05/1989	Everton	A	1-2		Div 1
13/05/1989	Newcastle Utd	A	2-0		Div 1
19/08/1989	Arsenal	H	4-1		Div 1
22/08/1989	Crystal Palace	A	1-1		Div 1
26/08/1989	Derby County	A	0-2		Div 1
30/08/1989	Norwich City	H	0-2		Div 1
09/09/1989	Everton	A	2-3		Div 1
28/10/1989	Southampton	H	2-1		Div 1
04/11/1989	Charlton Athletic	A	0-2		Div 1
12/11/1989	Nottingham Forest	H	1-0		Div 1
18/11/1989	Luton Town	A	3-1	1	Div 1
25/11/1989	Chelsea	H	0-0		Div 1
03/12/1989	Arsenal	A	0-1		Div 1
09/12/1989	Crystal Palace	H	1-2		Div 1
16/12/1989	Tottenham Hotspur	H	0-1		Div 1
23/12/1989	Liverpool	A	0-0		Div 1
26/12/1989	Aston Villa	A	0-3		Div 1
30/12/1989	Wimbledon	A	2-2		Div 1
01/01/1990	Qpr	H	0-0		Div 1
07/01/1990	Nottingham Forest	A	1-0		FA Cup
13/01/1990	Derby County	H	1-2		Div 1
21/01/1990	Norwich City	A	0-2		Div 1
28/01/1990	Hereford United	A	1-0	1	FA Cup
03/02/1990	Manchester City	H	1-1	1	Div 1
10/02/1990	Millwall	A	2-1		Div 1
14/03/1990	Everton	H	0-0		Div 1
18/03/1990	Liverpool	H	1-2		Div 1

Date	Opponent	Venue	Score		Competition
3/1990	Sheffield Wednesday	A	0-1		Div 1
4/1990	Aston Villa	H	2-0		Div 1
4/1990	Tottenham Hotspur	A	1-2		Div 1
04/1990	Wimbledon	H	0-0		Div 1
05/1990	Nottingham Forest	A	0-4		Div 1
5/1990	Crystal Palace	N	3-3		FA Cup
8/1990	Liverpool	N	1-1	1	C Shield
08/1990	Coventry City	H	2-0		Div 1
08/1990	Leeds United	A	0-0		Div 1
9/1990	Sunderland	A	1-2		Div 1
9/1990	Luton Town	A	1-0		Div 1
9/1990	Qpr	H	3-1		Div 1
9/1990	Liverpool	A	0-4		Div 1
9/1990	Pecsi Munkas	H	2-0	1	ECWC
9/1990	Southampton	H	3-2	1	Div 1
9/1990	Halifax Town	A	3-1	1	League Cup
9/1990	Nottingham Forest	H	0-1		Div 1
0/1990	Pecsi Munkas	A	1-0		ECWC
/1990	Hailfax Town	H	2-1		League Cup
0/1990	Arsenal	H	0-1		Div 1
0/1990	Wrexham	H	3-0		ECWC
0/1990	Manchester City	A	3-3		Div 1
/1990	Liverpool	H	3-1		League Cup
/1990	Crystal Palace	H	2-0		Div 1
/1990	Wrexham	A	2-0		ECWC
1990	Derby County	A	0-0		Div 1
1990	Sheffield United	H	2-0		Div 1
1990	Chelsea	H	2-3		Div 1
1990	Arsenal	A	6-2	1	League Cup
1990	Everton	A	1-0		Div 1
2/1990	Leeds United	H	1-1		Div 1
1990	Coventry City	A	2-2		Div 1
2/1990	Wimbledon	A	3-1		Div 1
2/1990	Norwich City	H	3-0		Div 1
2/1990	Aston Villa	H	1-1		Div 1
1991	Tottenham Hotspur	A	2-1		Div 1
1991	Qpr	H	2-1		FA Cup
1991	Sunderland	H	3-0		Div 1
1991	Southampton	A	1-1		League Cup
1991	Queens Park Rangers	A	1-1		Div 1
/1991	Southampton	H	3-2		League Cup
/1991	Bolton W	H	1-0		FA Cup
2/1991	Liverpool	H	1-1		Div 1
/1991	Leeds Utd	H	2-1		League Cup
/1991	Norwich City	A	1-2		FA Cup
2/1991	Leeds United	A	1-0		League Cup
2/1991	Sheffield United	A	1-2	1	Div 1
3/1991	Everton	H	0-2		Div 1
3/1991	Montpellier	H	1-1		ECWC
3/1991	Chelsea	A	2-3		Div 1
/1991	Nottingham Forest	A	1-1	1	Div 1
/1991	Montpellier Herault	A	2-0	1	ECWC
3/1991	Luton Town	H	4-1		Div 1
2/1991	Norwich City	A	3-0		Div 1
4/1991	Wimbledon	H	2-1		Div 1
/1991	Legia Warsaw	A	3-1		ECWC
1991	Derby County	H	3-1	1	Div 1
/1991	Sheffield Wednesday	N	0-1		League Cup
/1991	Legia Warsaw	H	1-1		ECWC
/1991	Manchester City	H	1-0		Div 1
/1991	Arsenal	A	1-3		Div 1
1991	Barcelona	N	2-1		ECWC
20/05/1991	Tottenham Hotspur	H	1-1		Div 1
17/08/1991	Notts County	H	2-0		Div 1
21/08/1991	Aston Villa	A	1-0		Div 1
24/08/1991	Everton	A	0-0		Div 1
28/08/1991	Oldham Ath	H	1-0		Div 1
31/08/1991	Leeds Utd	H	1-1		Div 1
03/09/1991	Wimbledon	A	2-1	1	Div 1
07/09/1991	Norwich City	H	3-0		Div 1
21/09/1991	Luton Town	H	5-0		Div 1
25/09/1991	Cambridge Utd	H	3-0		League Cup
28/09/1991	Tottenham Hotspur	A	2-1		Div 1
06/10/1991	Liverpool	A	0-0		Div 1
09/10/1991	Cambridge United	A	1-1		League Cup
19/10/1991	Arsenal	H	1-1		Div 1
26/10/1991	Sheffield Wednesday	A	2-3		Div 1
30/10/1991	Portsmouth	H	3-1		League Cup
02/11/1991	Sheffield Utd	H	2-0		Div 1
06/11/1991	Atletico Madrid	H	1-1		Cup Winners
16/11/1991	Manchester City	A	0-0		Div 1
19/11/1991	Red Star Belgrade	H	1-0		Super Cup
23/11/1991	West Ham Utd	H	2-1		Div 1
30/11/1991	Crystal Palace	A	3-1		Div 1
04/12/1991	Oldham Ath	H	2-0		League Cup
07/12/1991	Coventry City	H	4-0		Div 1
15/12/1991	Chelsea	A	3-1		Div 1
26/12/1991	Oldham Athletic	A	6-3		Div 1
29/12/1991	Leeds United	A	1-1		Div 1
01/01/1992	Qpr	H	1-4		Div 1
08/01/1992	Leeds United	A	3-1	1	League Cup
11/01/1992	Everton	H	1-0		Div 1
18/01/1992	Notts County	A	1-1	1	Div 1
27/01/1992	Southampton	A	0-0		FA Cup
26/02/1992	Chelsea	H	1-1		Div 1
29/02/1992	Coventry City	A	0-0		Div 1
14/03/1992	Sheffield United	A	2-1	1	Div 1
18/03/1992	Nottingham Forest	A	0-1		Div 1
21/03/1992	Wimbledon	H	0-0		Div 1
31/03/1992	Norwich City	A	3-1		Div 1
07/04/1992	Manchester City	H	1-1		Div 1
18/04/1992	Luton Town	A	1-1		Div 1
20/04/1992	Nottingham Forest	H	1-2		Div 1
22/04/1992	West Ham United	A	0-1		Div 1
15/08/1992	Sheffield United	A	1-2		Premiership
19/08/1992	Everton	H	0-3		Premiership
22/08/1992	Ipswich Town	H	1-1		Premiership
29/08/1992	Nottingham Forest	A	2-0		Premiership
02/09/1992	Crystal Palace	H	1-0		Premiership
06/09/1992	Leeds Utd	A	2-0		Premiership
12/09/1992	Everton	A	2-0		Premiership
16/09/1992	Torpedo Moscow	H	0-0		UEFA Cup
19/09/1992	Tottenham Hotspur	A	1-1		Premiership
26/09/1992	Qpr	H	0-0		Premiership
03/10/1992	Middlesbrough	A	1-1		Premiership
18/10/1992	Liverpool	H	2-2		Premiership
24/10/1992	Blackburn Rovers	A	0-0		Premiership
28/10/1992	Aston Villa	A	0-1		League Cup
31/10/1992	Wimbledon	H	0-1		Premiership
07/11/1992	Aston Villa	A	0-1		Premiership
05/01/1993	Bury	H	2-0		FA Cup

MIDDLESBROUGH FIRST TEAM APPEARANCES

Date	Opponent	H/A	Score		Competition
13/08/1994	Burnley	H	2-0		Championship
20/08/1994	Southend Utd	A	2-0		Championship
27/08/1994	Bolton Wanderers	H	1-0		Championship
31/08/1994	Derby County	A	1-0	1	Championship
03/09/1994	Watford	A	1-1	1	Championship
11/09/1994	Sunderland	H	2-2		Championship
14/09/1994	West Brom	H	2-1		Championship
01/10/1994	Millwall	H	3-0		Championship
05/10/1994	Cesena	H	1-1		Anglo Italian Cup
08/10/1994	Tranmere Rovers	H	0-1		Championship
15/10/1994	Luton Town	A	1-5		Championship
18/10/1994	Udinese	A	0-0		Anglo Italian Cup
23/10/1994	Portsmouth	A	0-0		Championship
26/10/1994	Aston Villa	A	0-1		League Cup
29/10/1994	Swindon Town	H	3-1		Championship
01/11/1994	Oldham Athletic	H	2-1		Championship
05/11/1994	Grimsby Town	A	1-2		Championship
20/11/1994	Wolves	H	1-0		Championship
03/12/1994	Portsmouth	H	4-0		Championship
18/12/1994	Burnley	A	3-0		Championship
26/12/1994	Sheffield Utd	A	1-1		Championship
15/01/1995	Swindon Town	A	1-2		Championship
21/01/1995	Grimsby Town	H	1-1		Championship
18/02/1995	Charlton Athletic	H	1-0		Championship
21/02/1995	Wolves	A	2-0		Championship
26/02/1995	Millwall	A	0-0		Championship
04/03/1995	Bristol City	H	3-0		Championship
07/03/1995	Watford	H	2-0		Championship
11/03/1995	Bolton Wanderers	A	0-1		Championship
21/03/1995	Sunderland	A	1-0		Championship
26/03/1995	Port Vale	H	3-0		Championship
01/04/1995	West Brom	A	3-1		Championship
05/04/1995	Oldham Athletic	A	0-1		Championship
08/04/1995	Stoke City	H	2-1		Championship
17/04/1995	Sheffield Utd	H	1-1		Championship
22/04/1995	Barnsley	A	1-1		Championship
30/04/1995	Luton Town	H	2-1		Championship
20/09/1995	Rotherham Utd	H	2-1		League Cup
04/11/1995	Leeds Utd	H	1-1		Prem
08/11/1995	Crystal Palace	H	2-0		League Cup
02/12/1995	QPR	A	1-1		Prem
30/12/1995	Nottingham Forest	A	0-1		Prem
01/01/1996	Aston Villa	H	0-2		Prem
13/01/1996	Arsenal	H	2-3		Prem
20/01/1996	Southampton	A	1-2		Prem
04/02/1996	Chelsea	A	0-5		Prem
02/03/1996	Everton	H	0-2		Prem
24/09/1996	Hereford Utd	A	3-0		League Cup
26/12/1996	Everton	H	4-2	1	Prem
28/12/1996	Coventry City	A	0-3		Prem
01/01/1997	Arsenal	A	0-2		Prem
04/01/1997	Chester City	H	6-0		FA Cup
08/01/1997	Liverpool	H	2-1		League Cup

Date	Opponent	H/A	Score		Competition
11/01/1997	Southampton	H	0-1		Prem
18/01/1997	Sheffield Wednesday	H	4-2		Prem
01/02/1997	Wimbledon	A	1-1		Prem
15/02/1997	Manchester City	A	1-0		FA Cup
22/02/1997	Newcastle Utd	H	0-1		Prem
26/02/1997	Stockport County	A	2-0		League Cup
05/03/1997	Derby County	H	6-1		Prem
08/03/1997	Derby County	A	2-0		FA Cup
12/03/1997	Stockport County	H	0-1		League Cup
15/03/1997	Leicester City	A	3-1	1	Prem
19/03/1997	Blackburn Rovers	H	2-1		Prem
22/03/1997	Chelsea	H	1-0		Prem
24/03/1997	Nottingham Forest	H	1-1		Prem
06/04/1997	Leicester City	N	1-1		League Cup
09/04/1997	West Ham	A	0-0		Prem
13/04/1997	Chesterfield	N	3-3		FA Cup
16/04/1997	Leicester City	N	0-1		League Cup
19/04/1997	Sunderland	H	0-1		Prem
22/04/1997	Chesterfield	N	3-0		FA Cup
24/04/1997	Tottenham Hotspur	A	0-1		Prem
03/05/1997	Aston Villa	H	3-2		Prem
05/05/1997	Manchester Utd	A	3-3		Prem
08/05/1997	Blackburn Rovers	A	0-0		Prem
11/05/1997	Leeds Utd	A	1-1		Prem
17/05/1997	Chelsea	N	0-2		FA Cup
09/08/1997	Charlton Athletic	H	2-1		Championship
10/01/1998	Charlton Athletic	A	0-3		Championship
17/04/1998	Manchester City	H	1-0		Championship
24/04/1998	Port Vale	A	1-0		Championship
29/04/1998	Wolves	H	1-1		Championship
16/09/1998	Wycombe Wanderers	H	2-0		League Cup
19/09/1998	Everton	H	2-2		Prem
23/09/1998	Wycombe Wanderers	A	1-1		League Cup
26/09/1998	Chelsea	A	0-2		Prem
03/10/1998	Sheffield Wednesday	H	4-0		Prem
24/10/1998	Wimbledon	A	2-2		Prem
28/10/1998	Everton	H	2-3		League Cup
01/11/1998	Nottingham Forest	H	1-1		Prem
07/11/1998	Southampton	A	3-3		Prem
14/11/1998	Charlton Athletic	A	1-1		Prem
21/11/1998	Coventry City	H	2-0		Prem
19/12/1998	Manchester Utd	A	3-2		Prem
03/01/1999	Manchester Utd	A	1-3		FA Cup

INTERNATIONAL CAREER

DATE	OPPOSITION				COMPETITION	GOALS
05 Jun 1985	NORWAY	A	L	4-2	International Friendly	
10 Sep 1985	SCOTLAND	H	D	1-1	WCQ	
16 Oct 1985	HUNGARY	H	L	0-3	International Friendly	
25 Feb 1986	SAUDI ARABIA	A	W	1-2	International Friendly	
26 Mar 1986	REPUBLIC OF IRELAND	A	W	0-1	International Friendly	
21 Apr 1986	URUGUAY	H	D	0-0	International Friendly	
10 Sep 1986	FINLAND	A	D	1-1	EURO Qualifier	
18 Feb 1987	USSR	H	D	0-0	International Friendly	
01 Apr 1987	FINLAND	H	W	4-0	EURO Qualifier	
29 Apr 1987	CZECHOSLOVAKIA	H	D	1-1	EURO Qualifier	
09 Sep 1987	DENMARK	H	W	1-0	EURO Qualifier	
14 Oct 1987	DENMARK	A	L	1-0	EURO Qualifier	
11 Nov 1987	CZECHOSLOVAKIA	A	L	2-0	EURO Qualifier	
23 Mar 1988	YUGOSLAVIA	H	L	1-2	International Friendly	
27 Apr 1988	SWEDEN	A	L	4-1	International Friendly	
01 Jun 1988	MALTA	A	W	2-3	International Friendly	
04 Jun 1988	ITALY	A	W	0-1	International Friendly	
14 Sep 1988	NETHERLANDS	A	L	1-0	WCQ	
19 Oct 1988	FINLAND	H	D	2-2	WCQ	
08 Feb 1989	ISRAEL	A	D	3-3	International Friendly	
31 May 1989	WEST GERMANY	H	D	0-0	WCQ	
06 Sep 1989	FINLAND	A	L	1-0	WCQ	
11 Oct 1989	NETHERLANDS	H	L	1-2	WCQ	
15 Nov 1989	WEST GERMANY	A	L	2-1	WCQ	
20 May 1990	COSTA RICA	H	W	1-0	International Friendly	
17 Oct 1990	BELGIUM	H	W	3-1	EURO Qualifier	
14 Nov 1990	LUXEMBOURG	A	W	0-1	EURO Qualifier	
19 Feb 1992	REPUBLIC OF IRELAND	A	W	0-1	International Friendly	
29 Apr 1992	AUSTRIA	A	D	1-1	International Friendly	
20 May 1992	ROMANIA	A	L	5-1	WCQ	
30 May 1992	NETHERLANDS	A	L	4-0	International Friendly	
03 Jun 1992	ARGENTINA	N	L	1-0	KIRIN JAPAN CUP	
07 Jun 1992	JAPAN	A	W	0-1	KIRIN JAPAN CUP	
09 Sep 1992	FAROE ISLANDS	H	W	6-0	WCQ	1
14 Oct 1992	CYPRUS	A	W	0-1	WCQ	
18 Nov 1992	BELGIUM	A	L	2-0	WCQ	
28 Apr 1993	CZECHOSLOVAKIA (RCS)	A	D	1-1	WCQ	
20 Apr 1994	SWEDEN	H	L	0-2	International Friendly	
29 Mar 1997	BELGIUM	H	L	1-2	WCQ	

Index